Wellness and Writing Connections

Writing for Better Physical, Mental, and Spiritual Health

WELLNESS & WRITING

CONNECTIONS

SM

Writing for Better Physical,
Mental, and Spiritual Health

Edited by John Frank Evans, EdD

Idyll Arbor, Inc.

39129 264th Ave SE, Enumclaw, WA 98022 (360) 825-7797

ISBN: 9781882883790

Printed in the United States of America

Library of Congress Cataloging-in-Publication Data

Evans, John Frank.

  Wellness & writing connections : writing for better physical, mental, and spiritual health / John Frank Evans.

    p. cm.

  Includes bibliographical references.

  ISBN 978-1-882883-79-0 (alk. paper)

  1. Graphotherapy. I. Title. II. Title: Wellness and writing connections.

  RC489.W75E93 2010

  615.8'515--dc22

2009033702

To Angela Jane Bailey with special thanks for her tireless efforts to make the Wellness & Writing Connections Conference possible and for her generous collaborations with me to make our story over the last sixteen years truly one for the books.

— John Frank Evans, Atlanta, GA, August 2009

Contents

Part One:
Overview of Wellness and Writing Connections:
Theory, Research, and Practice

1

Introducing Wellness & Writing Connections Conference Papers

John F. Evans

Writing about stressful situations is one of the easiest ways for people to take control of their problems and release negative effects of stress from their bodies and their lives. This conference is a call for writers and other professionals to collaborate and to help people find ways to help themselves and their students, clients, and patients.

— James Pennebaker, PhD

Wellness and writing are connected in ways yet to be fully researched and exploited, but the literature of several disciplines declares that for many people wellness and writing are connected in ways useful for emotional, physical, and spiritual health. A growing body of research shows that the heart rate lowers and people are more equipped to fight off infections when they release their worries in writing. In addition to coping better with stressful situations, writing can have a positive impact on self-esteem and result in works that can help others overcome their own obstacles. Much of the research about writing and healing was pioneered and sustained by James Pennebaker and others who work in

3

the disciplines of writing, psychology, medicine, counseling, and education.

To reach professionals in these disciplines, my passion for and my personal experience with writing and healing convinced me to establish a conference that would attract people who see therapeutic value in writing memoirs, essays, fiction, poetry, and drama. I wished to provide a lively resource for these like-minded people who write and for those working in the healthcare and counseling professions who wish to include writing as part of their practice. The culmination of my conviction that writing can be good for those who write is the Wellness & Writing Connections Conference series and the book you are holding.

Within these pages is a collection of essays offered by a representative sampling of keynote address speakers, presenters, and workshop leaders from the 2007 and 2008 conferences. The essay writers come from many parts of the United States and from many professions, including therapists, psychologists, counselors, nurses, poets, novelists, teachers, and researchers. Some of the essays are formal, but most of the essays are informal. Some of the essays follow a documentation style required by the writer's discipline in the humanities (MLA) or the sciences (APA). But no matter what area of the country the writers come from or what discipline they represent, all of the contributors write from the personal conviction that writing has served them and others in healthful ways they wish to share with you.

You do not have to follow a linear path to benefit from reading this book. Please indulge your curiosity if a perusal of the contents compels you to dip into this essay or that because the title intrigues you. You will notice that the essays are divided into four parts. The first part of the collection includes Pennebaker's and L'Abate's keynote addresses. The second part of the collection includes essays about the uses of specific writing genres, from poetry to the braided essay, from workshop writing to writing in an academic setting. The third part of the collection includes essays that describe writing-to-heal workshops and programs. Cheryl

Stiles concludes this collection with a bibliography that I hope you will find useful in your further study.

If you wish to learn about the theoretical and research underpinnings for writing to heal, I recommend that you begin with the Pennebaker and Chung essay, "Expressive Writing, Emotional Upheavals, and Health." If you wish to learn how a cancer survivor became a writing-to-heal advocate, read Leatha Kendrick's essay "Writing Illness — Writing Healing." To further guide your reading, I offer these brief introductions to the book's contents.

The first essay in this collection, "Expressive Writing, Emotional Upheavals, and Health" by James Pennebaker and Cindy Chung represents Pennebaker's keynote address at the 2007 Wellness & Writing Connections Conference. In this essay you will find a description of the early experiments testing the theory that expressive writing could have physical health benefits. The authors also provide a wonderful overview of writing-to-heal studies from the last twenty-five years. "Writing forces people to stop and re-evaluate their life circumstance. ... [The writing] process demands a different representation in the brain, in memory, and in the ways people think on a daily basis. The cognitive changes themselves now allow the individuals to begin to think about and use their social worlds differently." While the authors are enthusiastic about the promises of writing-to-heal, they strongly encourage more studies under rigorous research design protocols

In his 2008 keynote address, Luciano L'Abate, professor emeritus in psychology at Georgia State University, echoes Pennebaker's call for more rigorous research studies to document the effects of writing-to-heal strategies. The perspective of his essay is to proffer a historical and systematic background about technology in mental health especially related to experimental and clinical applications of distance writing in the field of self-help. This perspective is presented in two parts. The first, historical part deals with past and present applications of writing and wellness. The second, systematic part deals with theoretical and applicative implications of writing and wellness.

Debbie McCulliss starts the second part of the essay collection, "Writing in the Genres," with her description of an interactive workshop based on poetry that exposes participants to the bibliotherapeutic multi-stage process of recognition (the material engages the participant), examination (questions are asked), juxtaposition (putting side by side, for purposes of comparison and contrast, two impressions of an object or experience), and application to self (integration). Her goal is to increase self-understanding by helping participants value their own personhood through awareness and insight.

According to Leatha Kendrick, "When we write, we can learn (again) to trust the voice that is great within us — our true speaking voice, not that voice that seems small, fearful, judgmental, smothered. In creating concrete, coherent narratives of what has befallen us, we can recover — recover from illness, from crisis and trauma, from the years of living in fear and with self-condemnation." Kendrick's workshop allows participants to write together and experience what constitutes a healing narrative. Her theoretical underpinnings arise from writings by James Pennebaker, Arthur Frank, and Louise DeSalvo.

In Gail Radley's workshop, participants experience writing exercises, prompts, and strategies designed to help writers move from despair to transcendence. Radley stresses that as important as self-expression is, writing that only expresses angst may deepen a feeling of victimization. Meaning and control, for Radley, are key elements in moving away from a victim mentality, as is writing toward satisfying resolutions. Readers will gain a variety of ideas to help patients both express their feelings and gain insights through creative journaling.

Fran Dorf divides her essay into two parts. In the first part she integrates theory, the work of other fiction writers and memoirists, her own bereavement, and her writing/publishing experience. Dorf reflects on the process and consequences of turning her grief into *Saving Elijah*, an unconventional novel that is part ghost story, part thriller, and part family drama. The novel is an extended metaphor for the psychological process of grief. Dorf also focuses on writing as "reinvestment," the choice to write a novel instead of a memoir, re-traumatization, Dorf's decision to publicly reveal the inspiration for her third novel, and other issues that are instructive to an interdisciplinary group. In part two, Dorf describes a "Write-To-Heal" Workshop, which she has conducted with bereaved parents, cancer patients, homeless, and addiction support groups, using fictional techniques to help people identify, claim, give voice to, and integrate the complex, difficult emotions surrounding grief, loss, and/or trauma.

Emily Simerly claims there is something about a person's spirit that wants expression, wants to tell the world its story. Simerly offers readings and examples of personal essay that mark primary passages through life. The unique structure of Simerly's essay offers readers a chance to generate six "starter" chapters of a personal narrative to use as a memoir in the continuing adaptation to life. Whether you are 90 or 20, your spirit and truth will find welcome and healing here.

"Self-exploratory writing," says Brenda Shoemaker, "need not be bereft of the elements of craft and style associated with literary writing." Shoemaker's essay begins with a brief discussion about integrating writing as a means of self-expression and writing as a creative discipline. Shoemaker shares excerpts from her essay, "Jacqueline's Swing." This is an essay written about the death of an eight-year-old girl who lived with the author. The girl was killed in an accident by her drunken-driving father. Shoemaker looks at the context of loss, the grieving process, and the multi-cultural aspects of this tragedy, dealing with the conflicts and emotional responses she experienced because of this death.

Noreen Groover Lape and Kristin N. Taylor offer a unique collaboration. Taylor, as a student in one of Lape's college creative writing classes, submitted an essay that described how she became a victim of a predatory high school teacher. Lape and Taylor describe their very different viewpoints on the process they went through to both revise the essay and revise the thinking surrounding victim-predator roles. They argue that the process of improving the way a story is written can greatly improve the way the author thinks about the situation she is describing.

The focus of Diana Raab's essay is on the benefits of keeping a notebook as a place to capture feelings, musings, and sentiments before they vanish. The essay will be useful for the beginning writer, therapist, or patient. Journal keeping, as a healing art, is described, as well as the different types of journals that may be kept. Raab shares writing exercises and journaling tips. Readers will benefit from learning how to use journaling to heal and also as a medium in overcoming writer's blocks.

Leading the third part of this collection, Workshops and Programs, Julie Davey writes about her Writing for Wellness program, which was born of personal experience, engendered in the crucible of cancer. Davey tells how she first came to make wellness and writing connections, first as a patient, then as a volunteer workshop leader, and finally, as an author of *Writing for Wellness: A Prescription for Healing*. Describing her workshops, she shares the joys and tears, the delights and dissonance of her student wellness writers, but most importantly, she shows through her work that the City of Hope National Cancer Center is not just a place but also a community.

Sara Baker raises the possibility that sometimes writing may re-traumatize the writer. This essay explores why this can be so, and is written from the point of view of practice seeking theory, rather than practice implementing theory. It includes both praxis and theoretical explorations, and explores issues of memoir and fiction writing as avenues to healing. Baker points out that despite the literature supporting the healing efficacy of writing directly about trauma — of naming, containing, and re-externalizing the traumatic event in order to integrate it — she often finds in her workshops that having patients write explicitly about a trauma can inhibit their writing. Baker encourages her readers to "tell it slant."

Through various forms of writing, including different creative journal writing techniques, memoir writing, third person writing, poetry, and art, Angela Buttimer discusses her work at Cancer Wellness at Piedmont Hospital. Her essay is specific about how writing aids in a cancer patient's journey through recovery. She discusses the structure of her groups, explores the processes she employs, gives some sample writing exercises, and shares some anecdotal outcomes.

Describing a developing writing-to-heal program, Austin Bunn provides a brief presentation about the work of the Patient Voice Project, created in 2005 by the University of Iowa graduate writing program, to teach expressive writing to the chronically ill. With multi-year grants from Johnson & Johnson and the Society for Arts in Healthcare, the project aims to expand to other MFA programs across the nation.

Championing an important and unique program, Voices of the Innocent, Laura Naughton highlights the healing work of a group of Angola prison and death row exonerees who are writing and presenting their personal experiences with the goal of helping to transform the criminal justice system. Using specific examples from the group, Naughton suggests larger "hows": how to lead a writing group for non-writers; how to develop trust within a group that has been traumatized and betrayed; how to document complex stories for public audiences; how to use writing to change dysfunctional social systems; how writing can assist the spiritual acts of healing and forgiveness; and how the healing and revealing aspect of the group's work is transferable to other populations of writers who are seeking to use memoir to bring about social change.

Whatever your current wellness and writing practice, the essays in this book offer illustrations of the current state of research, theory, and practice. Much remains to be done. I agree with Pennebaker and L'Abate that writing-to-heal research needs more rigorous science, what Pennebaker calls the "big science, big medicine" approach applied to large samples of people with differing diagnoses. But I would like to emphasize that a significant contribution to the science of writing-to-heal can come from individuals and professionals in settings large and small if they engage in reflective practices, carefully documenting their processes and results. From these reflective practitioners, a richer description and deeper understanding of writing-to-heal theory will emerge providing models of practice.

My vision for future practice in wellness and writing connections is a braided column. One braid suggests that writing is one of the most effective self-help methods for individuals. Another braid suggests a curriculum for training professionals who will include writing as a significant treatment modality. Joining the first two braids is one that suggests program guidelines for individuals who work in institutional settings like hospital wellness programs, cancer treatment clinics, trauma centers, prisons, counseling offices, schools, and universities. If you share this vision and desire to learn more, please come to the next Wellness & Writing Connections Conference. Visit us on the Writing & Wellness Connections website and sign up to receive our monthly newsletter <http://www.wellnessandwritingconnections.com/>.

2

Expressive Writing, Emotional Upheavals, and Health

James W. Pennebaker and Cindy K. Chung

There is a long history in psychology and medicine linking the occurrence of traumatic experiences with subsequent physical and mental health problems. What is it about a trauma that influences health? Several candidates immediately come to mind. Psychologically, personal upheavals provoke intense and long-lasting emotional changes. The unexpected events are generally associated with cognitive disruption including rumination and attempts to understand what happened and why. Socially, traumas are known to cause wholesale disruptions in people's social networks. Behaviorally, and perhaps because of the social and psychological changes, traumas are often associated with lifestyle changes such as unhealthy smoking, drinking, exercise, sleeping, and eating patterns. Each of these psychological, social, and behavioral effects is associated with a host of biological changes including elevations in cortisol, immune disruption, cardiovascular changes, and a cascade of neurotransmitter changes.

Individuals who are highly reactive to novel stimuli (Vaidya & Garfield, 2003), are highly anxious (Miller, 2003), avoidant and self-blaming (Sutker, Davis, Uddo, & Ditta, 1995), and high in hypnotic ability (Bower & Sivers, 1998) may be particularly susceptible to traumatic experiences. Similarly, the more extreme the trauma and the longer time over which it lasts are predictors of Post-Traumatic Stress Disorder (PTSD) incidence (e.g., Breslau, Chilcoat, Kessler, & Davis, 1999). It is also generally agreed that people most prone to PTSD have had a history of depression, trauma, and other PTSD episodes in the past, even prior to their most recent traumatic experience (cf., Miller, 2003).

Perhaps more surprising than the discovery of the trauma-illness link is in realizing that most people don't become sick after a trauma. There is another group of perhaps 30% who do not evidence PTSD symptoms but are still upset by the experience several weeks and months after. In a classic article, Wortman and Silver (1989) summarized several studies showing that at least half of people who have faced the death of a spouse or child did not experience intense anxiety, depression, or grief. Numerous studies report that at least 65 percent of male and female soldiers who have lived through horrific battles or war-zone stress never show any evidence of PTSD (Keane, 1998; Murray, 1992). Multiple studies with individuals who have survived major motor vehicle accidents (Brom, Kleber, & Hofman, 1993) or witnessed tragic airplane accidents (Carlier & Gersons, 1997) find that the majority of research participants did not experience depression or PTSD in the weeks or months after their experiences. Across studies, 40-80 percent of rape survivors did not evidence symptoms of PTSD (Kilpatrick, Resnick, Saunders, & Best, 1998; Resnick, Kilpatrick, & Lipovsky, 1991).

Why is it that some people seem to deal with major upheavals better than others? What is the profile of healthy coping? This, of course, is a central question among trauma researchers. We know, for example, that people with an intact social support group weather upheavals better than others (e.g., Murray, 1992). Beyond basic genetic predispositions, do some people adopt certain coping strategies that allow them to move past an upheaval more efficiently? If such coping strategies exist, can they be trained? If such techniques are available, how do they work?

Given that as many as 30% of people who face massive traumatic experiences will experience PTSD, what can we, as researchers and clinicians, do to reduce this rate? It is likely that many (perhaps most) PTSD-prone individuals will not benefit from any simple interventions. The nature of their trauma, their genetic, biological, and/or personality predispositions, or pre-trauma life experiences will override social or psychological therapies. Nevertheless, some PTSD-prone individuals as well as the majority of distressed but sub-clinical cases may benefit by focusing on their psychological and social worlds in the wake of their traumatic experiences.

As we lay out in this chapter, there is reason to believe that when people transform their feelings and thoughts about personally upsetting experiences into language, their physical and mental health often improve. The links to PTSD are still tenuous. However, an increasing number of studies indicate that having people write about traumas can result in healthy improvements in social, psychological, behavioral, and biological measures. As with the trauma-illness link, however, there is probably not a single mediator that can explain the power of writing. One promising candidate that is proposed concerns the effects of translating emotions into language format, or, as we suggest, a metaphorical translation of an analog experience into a digital one.

Emotional Upheavals, Disclosure, and Health

Not all traumatic events are equally toxic. By the 1960s, Holmes and Rahe (1967) suggested that the health impact of a trauma varied with the degree that the trauma disrupted a person's life. Interestingly, the original scales tapping the health risks of traumas generally measured socially acceptable traumas — death of spouse, loss of job. No items asked if the participant had been raped, had a sexual affair, or had caused the death of another. By the mid-1980s, investigators started to notice that upheavals that were kept secret were more likely to result in health problems than those that could be spoken about more openly. For example, individuals who were victims of violence and who had kept this experience silent were significantly more likely to have adverse health effects than those who openly talked with others (Pennebaker & Susman, 1988). In short, having any type of traumatic experience is associated with elevated illness rates; having any trauma and not talking about it further elevates the risk.

These effects actually are stronger when controlling for age, sex, and social support. Apparently, keeping a trauma secret from an intact social network is more unhealthy than not having a social network to begin with (cf., Cole, Kemeny, Taylor, & Visscher, 1996).

If keeping a powerful secret about an upsetting experience is unhealthy, can talking about it — or in some way putting it into words — be beneficial? This is a question we asked two decades ago. Going on the untested assumption that most people would have had at least one emotional upheaval that they had not disclosed in great detail, we began a series of studies that involved people writing and, in some cases, talking about these events.

In the first study, people were asked to write about a trauma or about superficial topics for four days, 15 minutes per day. We found that confronting the emotions and thoughts surrounding deeply personal issues promoted physical health, as measured by reductions in physician visits in the months following the study, fewer reports of aspirin usage, and overall more positive long-term evaluations of the effect of the experiment (Pennebaker & Beall, 1986). The results of that initial study have led to a number of similar disclosure studies, in our laboratory and by others, with a wide array of intriguing results. Next we briefly review the paradigm and basic findings.

The basic writing paradigm. The standard laboratory writing technique has involved randomly assigning participants to one of two or more groups. All writing groups are asked to write about assigned topics for one to five consecutive days, for 15 to 30 minutes each day. Writing is generally done in the laboratory with no feedback given. Those assigned to the control conditions are typically asked to write about superficial topics, such as how they use their time. The standard instructions for those assigned to the experimental group are a variation on the following:

> For the next three days, I would like for you to write about your very deepest thoughts and feeling about the most traumatic experience of your entire life. In your writing, I'd like you to really let go and explore your very deepest emotions and thoughts. You might tie this trauma to your childhood, your relationships with others, including parents, lovers, friends, or relatives. You may also link this event to your past, your present, or your future, or to who you have been, who you would like to be, or who you are now. You may write about the same general issues or experiences on all days of writing or on different topics each day. Not everyone has had a single trauma but all of us have had major conflicts or stressors — and you can write about these as well. All of your writing will be completely confidential. Don't worry about spelling, sentence structure, or grammar. The only rule is that once you begin writing, continue to do so until your time is up.

Whereas the original writing studies asked people to write about traumatic experiences, later studies expanded the scope of writing topics to general emotional events or to specific experiences shared by other participants (e.g., diagnosis of cancer, losing a job, coming to college). The amount of time people have been asked to write has also varied tremendously from 10 minutes to 30 minutes for three, four, or five days — sometimes within the same day to once per week for up to four weeks.

The writing paradigm is exceptionally powerful. Participants — from children to the elderly, from honor students to maximum-security prisoners — disclose a remarkable range and depth of human experiences. Lost loves, deaths, sexual and physical abuse incidents, and tragic failures are common themes in all of our studies. If nothing else, the paradigm demonstrates that when individuals are given the opportunity to disclose deeply personal aspects of their lives, they readily do so. Even though a large number of participants report crying or being deeply upset by the experience, the overwhelming majority report that the writing experience was valuable and meaningful in their lives.

The interest in the expressive writing method has grown over the years. The first study was published in 1986. By 1996, approximately 20 studies had been published. By 2006, well over 150 have been published in English language journals. Although many studies have examined physical health and biological outcomes, an increasing number have explored writing's effects on attitude change, stereotyping, creativity, working memory, motivation, life satisfaction, school performance, and a variety of health-related behaviors. It is beyond the scope of this chapter to provide a detailed review of the findings of the writing paradigm. Rather, we briefly summarize some of the more promising findings before focusing on the underlying mechanisms that may be at work.

Effects of disclosure on health-related outcomes. Researchers have relied on a variety of physical and mental health measures to evaluate the effect of writing. Writing or talking about emotional experiences relative to writing about superficial control topics has been found to be associated with significant drops in physician visits from before to after writing among relatively healthy samples. Over the last decade, as the number of expressive writing studies has increased, several meta-analyses either have been conducted or are being conducted as of this writing.

The original expressive writing meta-analysis was published by Joshua Smyth (1998) and was based on 14 studies using healthy participants. His primary conclusions were that the writing paradigm is associated with positive outcomes with a weighted mean effect size of $d=.47$ ($r=.23$, $p<.0001$), noting that this effect size is similar to or larger than those produced by other psychological interventions. The highest significant effect sizes ($p<.0001$) were for psychological ($d=.66$) and physiological outcomes ($d=.68$), which were greater than those for health ($d=.42$) and general functioning outcomes ($d=.33$). A non-significant effect size was found for health behaviors. He also found that longer intervals between writing sessions produced larger overall effect sizes, and that males benefited more from writing than did females.

Almost seven years after the Smyth article was published, another meta-analysis by Meads (2003) was released by the Cochran Commission. In an analysis of dozens of studies, the author concluded that there was not sufficient evidence to warrant adopting the writing method as part of clinical practice. One problem that the report underscored was the lack of any large randomized clinical trials (RCTs) that were based on large, clearly identified samples. Coming from a medical background, the Meads article was befuddled by the fact that most of the experimental studies of expressive writing were more theory-oriented and not aimed at clinical application. Since the release of the Meads paper, a new wave of RCTs is now being conducted with a diverse group of patient populations.

Most recently, Frisina, Borod, and Lepore (2004) performed a similar meta-analysis on nine writings studies using clinical populations. They found that expressive writing significantly improved health outcomes (d=.19, p<.05). However, the effect was stronger for physical (d=.21, p=.01) than for psychological (d=.07, p=.17) health outcomes. The authors suggested that a possible reason for these small effect sizes was due to the heterogeneity of the samples. Writing was less effective for psychiatric than physical illness populations.

Researchers have relied on a variety of physical and mental health measures to evaluate the effect of writing. Across multiple studies in laboratories around the world, writing or talking about emotional experiences, relative to writing about superficial control topics, has been found to be associated with significant drops in physician visits from before to after writing among relatively healthy samples. Writing and/or talking about emotional topics has also been found to influence immune function in beneficial ways, including t-helper cell growth (using a blastogenesis procedure with the mitogen PHA), antibody response to Epstein-Barr virus, and antibody response to hepatitis B vaccinations (for reviews, see Lepore & Smyth, 2002; Pennebaker & Graybeal, 2001; Sloan & Marx, 2004a).

Activity of the autonomic nervous system is also influenced by the disclosure paradigm. Among those participants who disclose their thoughts and emotions to a particularly high degree, skin conductance levels are significantly lower during the trauma disclosures than when describing superficial topics. Systolic blood pressure and heart rate drop to levels below baseline following the disclosure of traumatic topics but not superficial ones (Pennebaker, Hughes, & O'Heeron, 1987). In short, when individuals talk or write about deeply personal topics, their immediate biological responses are congruent with those seen among people attempting to relax. McGuire, Greenberg, and Gevirtz (2005) have shown that these effects can carry over to the long term in participants with elevated blood pressure. One month after writing, those who participated in the emotional disclosure condition exhibited lower systolic and diastolic blood pressure than before writing. Four months after writing, diastolic blood pressure remained lower than baseline levels.

Similarly, Sloan and Marx (2004b) found that participants in a disclosure condition exhibited greater physiological activation, as indexed by elevated cortisol levels, during their first writing session, relative to controls. Physiological activation then decreased, and was similar to that of controls in subsequent writing sessions. The initial elevation in cortisol from the first writing session predicted improved psychological but not physical health at one-month follow-up. It is possible that confronting a traumatic or distressing experience led to reactions aimed for in exposure-based treatments (e.g. Foa & Rothbaum, 1988).

Behavioral changes have also been found. Students who write about emotional topics evidence improvements in grades in the months following the study (e.g., Lumley & Provenzano, 2003). Senior professionals who have been laid off from their jobs get new jobs more quickly after writing (Spera, Buhrfeind, & Pennebaker, 1994). Consistent with the direct health measures, university staff members who write about emotional topics are subsequently absent from their work at lower rates than controls. Interestingly, relatively few reliable changes emerge using self-reports of health-related behaviors. That is, in the weeks after writing, experimental participants do not exercise more or smoke less. The one exception is that the study with laid off professionals found that writing reduced self-reported alcohol intake.

Self-reports also suggest that writing about upsetting experiences, although painful in the days of writing, produces long-term improvements in mood and indicators of well-being compared to controls. Although some studies have failed to find clear mood or self-reported distress effects, Smyth's (1998) meta-analysis on written disclosure studies indicates that, in general, writing about emotional topics is associated with significant reductions in distress.

Procedural differences that affect the expressive writing. Writing about emotional experiences clearly influences measures of physical and mental health. In recent years, several investigators have attempted to define the boundary conditions of the disclosure effect. Some of the most important findings are as follows:

Topic of disclosure. Although two studies have found that health effects occur only among individuals who write about particularly traumatic experiences (Greenberg & Stone, 1992; Lutgendorf et al., 1994), most studies have found that disclosure is more broadly beneficial. Choice of topic, however, may selectively influence outcomes. Although virtually all studies find that writing about emotional topics has positive effects on physical health, only certain assigned topics appear to be related to changes in grades. For beginning college students, for example, when asked to write specifically about emotional issues related to coming to college, both health and college grades improve. However, when other students are asked to write about emotional issues related to traumatic experiences in general, only health improvements — and not academic performance — are found (see Pennebaker, 1995; Pennebaker & Keough, 1999).

Over the last decade, an increasing number of studies have experimented with more focused writing topics. Individuals diagnosed with breast cancer, lung cancer, or HIV have been asked to write specifically about their living with the particular disease (e.g., de Moor, et al, 2002; Mann, 2002; Petrie, et al., 2004; Stanton & Danoff-Burg, 2002). Similarly, people who have lost their job have been asked to write about that experience (Spera et al., 1994). In each case, however, participants are asked to write about this topic in a very broad way and are encouraged to write about other topics that may be only remotely related. For example, in the job layoff project, participants in the experimental conditions were asked to explore their thoughts and feeling about losing their jobs. Fewer than half of the essays dealt directly with the layoff. Others dealt with marital problems, issues with children, money, and health.

It has been our experience that traumatic experiences often bring to the fore other important issues in people's lives. As researchers, we assume that, say, the diagnosis of a life-threatening disease is the most important issue for a person to write about in a cancer-related study. However, for many, this can be secondary to a cheating husband, an abusive parent, or some other trauma that may have occurred years earlier. We recommend that writing researchers and practitioners provide sufficiently open instructions to allow people to deal with whatever important topics they want to write about. As described in greater detail below, the more that the topic or writing assignment is constrained, the less successful it usually is.

Topic orientation: focusing on the good, the bad, or the benefits. There are a number of theoretical and practical reasons to assume that some strategies for approaching emotional upheavals might be better than others. With the growth of the field of Positive Psychology, several researchers have reported on the benefits of having a positive or optimistic approach to life (Carver & Scheier, 2002; Diener, Lucas, & Oishi, 2002; Seligman, 2000). Particularly persuasive have been a series of correlational studies on benefit finding — that is, people who are able to find benefits to negative experiences generally report less negative affect, milder distress, fewer disruptive thoughts, and greater meaningfulness in life. People who engage in benefit-finding fare better on objective physical and mental health outcomes (e.g. children's developmental test scores, recurrence of heart attacks) even after controlling for a host of possible confounding factors (for a review, see Affleck and Tennen, 1996). Being able to see things in a positive light, then, might be a critical component to successful adjustment.

In one study examining adjustment to college, Cameron and Nicholls (1998) had participants previously classified as dispositional optimists or pessimists write in one of three conditions: a self-regulation condition (writing about thoughts and feelings towards coming to college and then formulating coping strategies), a disclosure condition (writing about thoughts and feelings only), or a control task (writing about trivial topics). Overall, participants in the disclosure task had higher GPA scores at follow-up, but only those in the self-regulation task experienced less negative affect and better adjustment to college over the control participants. Optimists visited their doctors less in the following month if they had participated in either of the experimental writing conditions. On the other hand, only pessimists in the self-regulation condition had significantly fewer visits to the doctor after the study. With the added encouragement of formulating coping strategies, pessimists may be able to reap the same health benefits from writing about their thoughts and feelings as optimists naturally might do.

When confronting traumatic experiences, is it best to ask people to simply write about them or to write about the positive sides of the experiences? Several studies have addressed this question. Particularly interesting has been a series of studies by Laura King and her colleagues. When asked to write about intensely positive experiences (IPE) or control topics, participants who wrote about IPEs reported significantly better mood, and fewer illness-related health center visits than did those who wrote about trivial topics (Burton & King, 2004). In another study, students were asked to write about traumas in the standard way (King &

Miner, 2000). In the benefit-finding condition, participants were encouraged to focus on the benefits that have come from the trauma. Finally, in the mixed condition, participants were first asked to write about the trauma, and then to switch to the perceived benefits arising from the trauma experience. Counter to predictions, the trauma only and benefits only participants evidenced health improvements whereas the mixed group did not. It could be that writing about the perceived benefits is enough to organize thoughts and feelings about a trauma, and to cope effectively. However, as evidenced from the mixed condition, if people aren't able to integrate their perceived benefits into their trauma story in their own way, writing may be ineffective.

Several unpublished studies from our own lab paint a similar picture about the problems of constraining participants' orientations. For her dissertation, Cheryl Hughes (1994) asked students to write either about the positive or the negative aspects of their coming to college for three days. Neither group evidenced any benefits of writing compared to a non-emotional control condition. Indeed, both groups complained that there were some real negative (in the positive condition) and positive (in the negative condition) aspects of coming to college that they also wanted to write about. Similarly, in an unpublished project by Lori Stone (2002), students were asked to write about their thoughts and feelings about the September 11 attacks. In one condition, they received the standard unconstrained instructions. In a second condition, participants were asked to focus on their own feelings on one day and on other perspectives on alternating days. The perspective-switching instructions proved to be less beneficial than the unconstrained methods.

Although several variations on the expressive writing method have been tested, none have been found to be consistently superior to the original trauma writing or other methods that encourage the participants' freely choosing their writing topic. Forcing individuals to write about a particular topic or in a particular way may cause them to focus on the writing itself rather than the topic and the role of their emotions in the overall story.

Writing versus talking alone versus talking to others. Most studies comparing writing alone to talking either into a tape recorder (Esterling, et al., 1994) or to a therapist in a one-way interaction (Murray, Lamnin, & Carver, 1989; Donnelly & Murray, 1991) find comparable biological, mood, and cognitive effects. Talking and writing about emotional experiences are both superior to writing about superficial topics.

A striking exception to this was a study by Gidron, Peri, Connolly, and Shalev (1996) where a group of 14 Israeli PTSD patients were randomly assigned to either write about traumas (N = 8) or about superficial topics (N = 6) on three occasions. After writing, experimental participants were asked to discuss their most traumatic events to a group whereas controls were asked to describe a daily routine. Unlike all other published writing studies, this one found that experimental participants were significantly more distressed with poorer health at five-week follow-up. Because other studies have been conducted with participants coping with PTSD, the findings are not solely due to the nature of the participants or disorder. Rather, reading or discussing one's traumas in a group format after writing may pose unexpected problems. Clearly, additional research is needed to help understand this process.

Actual or implied social factors. Unlike psychotherapy and everyday discussions about traumas, the writing paradigm does not employ feedback to the participant. Rather, after individuals write about their own experiences, they are asked to place their essays into an anonymous-looking box with the promise that their writing will not be linked to their name. In one study comparing the effects of having students either write on paper that would be handed in to the experimenter or on a magic pad (wherein the writing disappears when the person lifts the plastic writing cover), no autonomic or self-report differences were found (Czajka, 1987). The benefits of writing, then, occur without explicit social feedback. Nevertheless, the degree to which people write holding the belief that some symbolic other person may "magically" read their essays can never be easily determined.

Typing, handwriting, and finger-writing. Although no studies have compared ways of writing on health outcomes, a few have explored if mode of writing can influence people's ratings of the expressive writing procedure itself. Brewin and Lennard (1999), for example, reported that writing by hand produced more negative affect, and led to more self-rated disclosure than did typing. One possibility is that writing by hand is slower and encourages individuals to process their thoughts and feelings more deeply. Recently, the first author has tested the idea of finger writing. In finger writing exercises, people are asked to use their finger and to "write" about a trauma as if they were holding a pen. Over the last two years, six expressive writing workshops have been given in Wisconsin, Sweden, Australia, The Netherlands, Norway, and Canada that involved a total of 271 participants (mean age = 46.0, SD =12.3; 76% female) in groups ranging from 28 to 71 people.

In each workshop, participants have been asked to write for five to ten minutes about an emotional topic on at least two occasions. Typically, people are asked to write using a pen; however, one time they are asked to write only with their finger. At the conclusion of the four to six hour workshop, individuals are asked to rate "how valuable and meaningful" each of the writing exercises had been. Along a seven-point unipolar scale, where 7 = a great deal, the mean rating for the finger writing has been 4.50 (SD=1.7) and the mean for the pen-writing occasions has also been 4.5 but with a lower standard deviation (SD=1.3). Interestingly, women prefer the finger writing significantly more than men. When queried about their preference for finger writing, many women reported that finger writing allowed them to freely express some of their most secret thoughts. Indeed, in every workshop, several people reported that they used more swear words when finger writing compared to writing with a pen.

Timing: How long after a trauma. In the last 30 years, advances in emergency medicine have been astounding. Although we know how to treat people medically in the first hours and days after a trauma, our knowledge about psychological interventions during the same time period has grown very little. Without the guidance of any research, several groups have created immediate crisis intervention businesses. Perhaps the most successful, now called Critical Incident Stress Management (CISM, e.g., Mitchell & Everly, 1996), argues that people victimized by trauma should be attended to within the first 72 hours after a trauma. Although the CISM system has many components, the most interesting and controversial encourages individuals to openly acknowledge their emotions and thoughts within a group concerning the trauma. The CISM system has now been adopted by thousands of businesses, governmental organizations, and other groups around the world. Despite the intuitive appeal of CISM, there is very little evidence that it works. Indeed, most studies suggest that it is more likely to cause harm than benefits (McNally, Byrant, & Ehlers, 2003; Wessley, Rose, & Bison, 1999).

The CISM findings as well as other projects interested in self-disclosure immediately after an upheaval have relevance for the timing for an expressive writing intervention. For example, one study asked women who had recently given birth to talk about their deepest thoughts, feelings, and fears to their midwives. These women were actually more likely to subsequently experience depression than women not asked to talk about these topics (Small, Lumley, Donohue, Potter, & Walden-strom, 2000). Women who were asked to write about the treatment they were undergoing for breast cancer during the last week of radiation treatment evidenced no benefits for any measures compared to controls (Walker, Nail, & Croyle, 1999).

Is there an optimal time after a trauma that expressive writing would most likely work? Unfortunately, no parametric studies have been conducted on this. Over the years, we have been involved in several projects that have attempted to tap people's natural disclosure patterns in the days and weeks after upheavals. For example, using a random digit dialing in the weeks and months after the 1989 Loma Prieta Earthquake in the San Francisco Bay area, we asked different groups of people the number of times that they had thought about and talked about the earthquake in the previous 24 hours. We used a similar method a year later to tap people's responses to the declaration of war with Iraq during the first Persian Gulf War. In both cases, we found that people talked with one another at very high rates in the first two to three weeks. By the fourth week, however, talking rates were extremely low. Rates of thinking about the earthquake and war showed a different pattern: it took considerably longer (about eight weeks) before people reported thinking about them at low rates (from Pennebaker & Harber, 1993).

More recently, we have analyzed the blogs of almost 1100 frequent users of an internet site in the two months before and two months after the September 11 attacks. Rates of writing increased dramatically for about two weeks after the attacks. More striking was the analysis of word usage. Use of first person singular (I, me, and my), dropped almost 15% within 24 hours of the attacks and remained low for about a week. However, over the next two months, I-word usage remained below baseline (Cohn, Mehl, & Pennebaker, 2004). Usage of first person singular is significant because it correlates with depression (Rude, Gortner, & Pennebaker, 2004). What was striking was that these bloggers — who expressed an elevated rate of negative moods in the days after 9/11 — were generally quite healthy. They were psychologically distancing themselves from the emotional turmoil of the event.

Considering the current evidence, it is likely that defenses such as denial, detachment, distraction, and distancing may, in fact, be quite healthy in the hours and days after an upheaval. A technique such as expressive writing may be inappropriate until several weeks or months later. Indeed, we now encourage clinicians to delay their use of expressive writing until at least one to two months after an upheaval or until they think their patient is thinking "too much" about the event. Obsessing and ruminating about a trauma a few weeks after it has occurred is probably not too much. Thinking about it at the same high rate six months later might in fact signal that expressive writing might be beneficial.

Timing between writing sessions. Different experiments have variously asked participants to write for one to five days, ranging from consecutive days to sessions separated by a week, ranging from 10 to 45 minutes for each writing session, for anywhere from one to seven sessions. In Smyth's (1998) meta-analysis, he found a trend suggesting that the more days over which the experiment takes place, the stronger the impact on outcomes. Two subsequent studies that actually manipulated the times between writing failed to support Smyth's findings.

The first, by Sheese, Brown, and Graziano (2004), asked students to write either once per week for three weeks or for three continuous days about traumatic experiences or superficial topics. Although the experimental-control difference was significant for health center differences, no trend emerged concerning the relative benefits of once a week versus daily writing. More recently, the authors randomly assigned 100 students to write either about major life transitions or about superficial topics. Participants wrote three times, 15 minutes each time, either once a day for three days, once an hour for three hours, or three times in a little more than an hour (Pennebaker & Chung, 2005). Immediately after the last writing session and again at one-month follow-up, no differences were found between the daily versus three-times-in-one-hour condition. Indeed, at follow-up, the three experimental groups evidenced lower symptom reports (p = .05, one-tailed test) than the controls after controlling for the pre-writing symptom levels.

Time until follow-up. Another suspect for inconsistent or null results across writing studies is the varied duration between the final writing session and the follow-up assessment. Expressive writing outcomes have been measured up to about six months after the writing sessions are completed. While some psychological and physical health changes may be immediately apparent, they may be fleeting. On the other hand, some effects may take days, weeks, months, or even years to emerge as significant changes on various health measures, if at all. The timing of improvements may also vary as a function of sampling characteristics. In an expressive writing study examining those suffering from asthma or rheumatoid arthritis (RA), health benefits were seen in people with asthma in the experimental writing condition as early as two weeks after writing. However, the health profile of people with RA in the experimental writing condition did not differ from those in the control condition until the four-month assessment period (Smyth, Stone, Hurewitz, & Kaell, 1999).

Considering all the other variants on the writing method already mentioned, it would be difficult to come up with some standard time for follow-up. Instead, knowing the general time-course of proposed underlying mechanisms, and providing multiple convergent measures to validate specific outcomes may be a more practical approach in thinking about follow-up assessments.

Individual differences. No consistent personality measures have distinguished who does from who does not benefit from writing. A number of variables have been unrelated to outcomes, including age, anxiety (or Negative Affectivity), and inhibition or constraint. A small number of studies that have either preselected participants or performed a median split on a particular variable have reported some effects. However, given the large number of studies, these effects should probably be viewed as promising rather than definitive.

Christensen et al. (1996) preselected students on hostility and found that those high in hostility benefited more from writing than those low in hostility. A couple of studies have found that individuals high on alexithymia (a trait that taps the inability of people to label or feel particular negative emotions) tended to benefit from writing more than those low on alexithymia (Paez, Velasco, & Gonzalez, 1999; Solano et al., 2003). However, later research by Lumley (2004) suggests that unlike the participants in the aforementioned studies, alexithymics suffering from chronic illnesses or elevated stress may not reap the same benefits after writing.

Finally, there has been a great deal of interest in knowing if sex differences exist in the potential benefits of expressive writing. Smyth's

(1998) meta-analysis revealed that males tend to benefit more from the writing paradigm than females. Several studies have explored this with reasonably large samples — usually with college students — and have not replicated the meta-analytic results. Clearly, more studies are needed with more diverse samples.

Educational, linguistic, or cultural effects. Within the United States, the disclosure paradigm has benefited senior professionals with advanced degrees at rates comparable to rates of benefit in maximum-security prisoners with sixth grade educations (Spera, Buhrfeind, & Pennebaker, 1994; Richards, Beal, Segal, & Pennebaker, 2000). Among college students, we have not found differences as a function of the students' ethnicity or native language. The disclosure paradigm has produced positive results among French-speaking Belgians (Rimé, 1995), Spanish-speaking residents of Mexico City (Dominguez, et al., 1995), multiple samples of adults and students in The Netherlands (Schoutrop, Lange, Brosschot, & Everaerd, 1997), and English-speaking New Zealand medical students (Petrie, et al., 1995).

Summary. When individuals write or talk about personally upsetting experiences in the laboratory, consistent and significant health improvements are found. The effects include both subjective and objective markers of health and well-being. The disclosure phenomenon appears to generalize across settings, many individual difference factors, and several Western cultures, and is independent of social feedback.

Why Does Expressive Writing Work?

Psychology, like most sciences, is dedicated to understanding how things work. We are also driven by the law of parsimony and assume that, ideally, a single explanatory mechanism for a phenomenon should exist. If you are expecting a clean and simple explanatory world, we have some very bad news: There is no single reason that explains the effectiveness of writing. Over the last two decades, a daunting number of explanations have been put forward and many have been found to be partially correct. Ultimately, there is no such thing as a single cause for a complex phenomenon. The reason is two-fold. First, any causal explanation can be dissected at multiple levels of analysis ranging from social explanations to changes in neurotransmitter levels. Second, an event that takes weeks or even months to unfold will necessarily have multiple determinants that can inhibit or facilitate the process over time.

In this section, we briefly summarize some of the more compelling explanations for the expressive writing-health relationship. Keep in mind that many of these processes occur simultaneously or may influence one another.

Individual and social inhibition. The first expressive writing projects were guided by a general theory of inhibition (cf., Pennebaker & Beall, 1986; Pennebaker, 1989). Earlier studies had discovered that people who had experienced one or more traumas in their lives were more likely to report health problems if they did not confide in others about their traumas than if they had done so (e.g., Pennebaker & Susman, 1988). The inhibition idea was that the act of inhibiting or in some way holding back thoughts, emotions, or behaviors is associated with low-level physiological work — much the way that Sapolsky (2004) or Selye (1978) thought about stress. Further, people were especially likely to inhibit their thoughts and feelings about traumatic experiences that were socially threatening. Hence, individuals who had experienced a sexual trauma would be far less likely to talk about it with others than if they had experienced the death of a grandparent.

Following the logic of inhibition, it was assumed that if people were encouraged to talk or write about a previously inhibited event, health improvements would be seen. Perhaps, we reasoned, once people put the experience into words, they would no longer have the need to inhibit. Despite the helpfulness of the theory in generating interesting and testable hypotheses, the supporting evidence has been decidedly mixed. Several studies attempted to evaluate the degree to which people wrote about secret versus more public traumas and previously disclosed versus not previously disclosed events. In no case did these factors differentially predict improvements in health (e.g., Greenberg & Stone, 1992; Pennebaker, Kiecolt-Glaser, & Glaser, 1988).

Promising research in this vein has been conducted by Steve Lepore and his colleagues (e.g., Lepore, Fernandez-Berrocal, Ragan, & Ramos, 2004; Lepore & Ragan, 2000). Across several studies, they find that people who are encouraged to talk about an emotional experience — such as a movie — are less reactive to the movie if what they say is validated. That is, if their comments about seeing the movie on the first occasion are supported by another person, they find the movie less aversive on a second screening on another day. However, if another person disagrees with their thoughts and feelings about the movie, the participants are more biologically aroused on a second screening — even though they are watching the movie alone.

Ultimately, real-world inhibitory processes are almost impossible to measure. For example, people have great difficulty in evaluating the degree to which they have been actively holding back in telling others about an emotional experience. Some people who don't tell others about an upsetting experience may never think about the event and others do. Of those who think about it, some may want to tell others; others may not. Of these various cases, it is not clear which people are inhibiting or even who might benefit most from writing. Although experimental studies may be effective in demonstrating the potential dangers of inhibition, the task of isolating these psychological processes in the real world will be a far more difficult enterprise. As described in a later section on the social dynamics of expressive writing, one potential strategy is to simply track changes in people's social behaviors after expressive writing in order to infer the possibility of inhibition.

Emotions and emotional expression. Emotional reactions are part of all important psychological experiences. From the time of Breuer and Freud (1957/1895), most therapists have explicitly or tacitly believed that the activation of emotion is necessary for therapeutic change. The very first expressive writing study found that if people just wrote about the facts of a trauma, they did not evidence any improvement (Pennebaker &

Beall, 1986). Consistent with an experiential approach to psycho-therapeutic change, emotional acknowledgement ultimately fosters important cognitive changes (Ullrich & Lutgendorf, 2002).

Although experiencing emotions while writing is clearly a necessary component of the expressive writing effects, cognitive work is required as well. As an example, students were randomly assigned either to express a traumatic experience using bodily movement, or to express an experience using movement and then write about it, or to exercise in a prescribed manner for three days, 10 minutes per day (Krantz & Pennebaker, 1995). Whereas the two movement expression groups reported that they felt happier and mentally healthier in the months after the study, only the movement plus write group evidenced significant improvements in physical health and grade point average. The mere emotional expression of a trauma is not sufficient. Health gains appear to require translating experiences into language.

Habituation to emotional stimuli. A variation on the emotional expression idea is that the benefits of writing accrue because individuals habituate to the aversive emotions associated with the trauma they are confronting. The role of habituation to emotional stimuli has a long and rich history in classical conditioning and a variety of behavioral therapies (e.g., Wolpe, 1968). More nuanced approaches have been proposed by Edna Foa and her colleagues (e.g., Foa & Kozak, 1986; Meadows & Foa, 1999). Repeated exposure to emotional stimuli can help to extinguish the classically conditioned link between an event and people's reactions to it. At the same time, these authors note, people change in their understanding and/or representation of it.

Another test of a habituation model would be to see if people who wrote about the same topic in the same general way from essay to essay would benefit more than people who changed topics. In earlier studies (e.g., Pennebaker & Francis, 1996), judges evaluated the number of different topics people wrote about across a three-day writing study. Number of topics was unrelated to health improvements. A more elegant strategy involved the use of Latent Semantic Analysis (LSA, Landauer,

Foltz, & Laham, 1998). LSA, a technique developed by experts in Artificial Intelligence, is able to mathematically evaluate the similarity of content of any sets of text, such as essays. Using LSA, we attempted to learn if the content similarity of essays written by people in the experimental conditions in three previous writing studies was related to health improvements. The answer is no. If anything, the more similar the writing content was from day to day, the less likely people's health was to improve (Campbell & Pennebaker, 2002).

A pure habituation argument is probably insufficient in explaining the expressive writing effects. The findings from the emotion-only condition in the Pennobaker and Deall (1986) study together with the expressive movement-only condition in the Krantz and Pennebaker (1995) experiment both suggest that the mere activation of emotions associated with a trauma can provide only limited benefits. Beyond any habituation processes, some form of cognitive change is also important.

Language and emotions: Towards an A-to-D (analog to digital) theory of emotional processing. What happens when emotions or emotional experiences are put into words? Research has shown that verbally labeling an emotion may itself influence the emotional experience. Keltner, Locke, and Audrain (1993) found that after reading a depressing story, participants who were given the opportunity to label their emotions subsequently reported higher life satisfaction than those who did not label them. Berkowitz and Troccoli (1990) found that after labeling their own emotions, participants were more magnanimous in evaluating others than if not given the emotion labeling opportunity. These approaches are consistent with Schwarz (1990) who has demonstrated that defining and making attributions for internal feelings can affect the feelings themselves. Similarly, Wilson (2002) summarized several studies indicating that when individuals focus on their feelings, the correspondence between attitudes and behaviors increases, whereas attending to the reasons for one's attitudes reduces attitude-behavior consistency.

Indeed, changing any sensory experience into language affects the experience. In an important study on language's effects on sensory experience, Schooler and Engstler-Schooler (1990) suggested that once an individual attempts to translate a picture into words, it changes the memory of the picture. Most experiences are like pictures. Sights, sounds, smells, and feelings are often vague, complicated, and dynamic. To provide a detailed image of any experience would require more than the presumed one thousand word limit. However, because language is flexible, relatively few words or even several thousand words can be used to describe a single experience.

The problem of capturing an experience with language is comparable to the engineering difficulty of defining an analog signal using digital technology. In the world of measuring skin conductance, for example, a person's fingers will change in their sweatiness almost continuously. As can be seen in Figure 1a, skin conductance level (SCL), as measured by an old-fashioned polygraph, initially increases after the person hears a loud tone and then gradually returns to normal. For this signal to be computer analyzed, the analog line must be converted into numbers using an analog-to-digital (A-to-D) converter. To convert the line to numbers, however, one needs to decide how frequently the numbers should be sampled.

Assume the tick marks on the x-axis refer to seconds, meaning that the entire graph encompasses 15 seconds. Should one sample SCL 200 times per second, once per second, once every five seconds? Obviously, the more times one samples, the truer the representation of the line will be (see Figure 1b). However, sampling at such a high frequency can be a tremendous waste of time and computer space since most of the adjacent readings will be redundant. Similarly, if the sampling rate is once every five seconds, most of the information of the change in SCL will be lost (see Figure 1c).

Verbally labeling an emotion is much like applying a digital technology (language) to an analog signal (emotion and the emotional experience). Assume that novel or emotion-provoking experiences tend

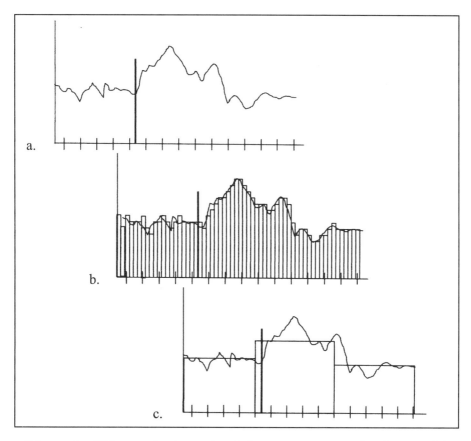

Figure 1: Skin conductance level in response to a loud tone (a) measured with a polygraph, and digitally sampled (b) at a high frequency and (c) at a low frequency.

to remain in awareness until they are either cognitively understood or they extinguish with time.

It is hypothesized that if an emotion or experience remains in analog form, it cannot be understood or conceptually tied to the meaning of an event. The only way by which an emotion or experience in non-linguistic form can leave awareness is through habituation, extinction, or the introduction of a new or competing emotion. Once an experience is translated into language, however, it can be processed in a conceptual manner. In language format, the individual can assign meaning, coherence, and structure. This would allow for the event to be assimilated and, ultimately, resolved and/or forgotten, thereby alleviating the maladaptive effects of incomplete emotional processing on health.

Following from the above reasoning, if an experience and its emotions are described too briefly, the experience will not adequately capture or represent the event (hereafter referred to as verbal underrepresentation). In this case, it would be predicted that the many parts of the experience that were not represented in the brief linguistic description would continue to be processed until they gradually extinguished over time. If a moderate number of words are used to describe the experience (moderate representation), its representation should adequately mirror the event. This should reduce the degree to which the event takes up cognitive capacity, and, at the same time, enhance self-regulation, coping, and health. On the other hand, if the emotional event is described in exhaustive detail (overrepresentation), the experience is essentially reconfigured in its entirety, but in a new format.

The argument, based on the A-to-D Emotion Theory, is that once an event is adequately represented in language format, the verbal/conceptual processing takes over. In theory, one could argue that the ideal way to talk about an emotional event is to employ language in the form of moderate representation. The moderate representation view is that the most efficient way to process an event is to use as few words as possible that adequately capture the entire emotional experience. The event, then, would be summarized in a relatively tight way that would allow for later leveling and sharpening. Alternatively, the overrepresentation view would argue that representing the event in detailed linguistic form would lessen the possibility for reappraisal or assimilation into broader knowledge structures and identity.

In recent years, Lisa Feldman Barrett has distinguished between individuals who describe their emotion experience using highly differentiated emotion terms, and those who more or less categorize their emotion experience using like-valenced terms interchangeably (Feldman, 1995; Feldman Barrett, 1998). In her studies, participants are asked to keep a daily diary for two weeks to rate their most intense emotional experience each day on several affect terms using a Likert scale. Emotional differentiation is reflected by a small correlation between positive emotions words (e.g. happiness, joy, enthusiasm, and amusement), and a small correlation between negative emotions words (e.g. nervous, angry, sad, ashamed, guilty). Feldman Barrett, Gross, Conner, Christensen, and Benvenuto (2001) showed that the more individuals differentiated their negative emotions, the more they endorsed engaging in various emotion regulation strategies (situation selection, situation modification, attentional deployment, cognitive change, and response modulation) over the course of the study, especially for more intense negative emotion experiences. These findings provide support for the A-to-D theory. That is, individuals who more precisely identify a verbal label representing their actual emotion experience are more likely to make attributions and effectively plan for future actions.

Use of emotion words in writing. The A-to-D approach is a valuable working model by which to understand the connection between emotional experience and its translation into words. A complementary approach to the understanding of emotional processes in the expressive writing paradigm is to look at the words people use while describing traumatic experience. If we merely counted the ways people use emotion words in natural text, could we begin to capture the underlying emotional processes that occur during writing?

Although a number of computerized text analysis programs have been developed (for a review, see Pennebaker, Mehl, & Niederhoffer, 2003), we are most familiar with Linguistic Inquiry and Word Count (LIWC), which was initially created to analyze essays from emotional writing studies. LIWC was developed by having groups of judges evaluate the degree to which about 2,000 words or word stems were related to each of several dozen categories (for a full description, see Pennebaker, Francis, & Booth, 2001). The categories include negative emotion words (sad, angry), positive emotion words (happy, laugh), causal words (because, reason), and insight words (understand, realize). For each essay, LIWC computes the percentage of total words that these and other linguistic categories represent.

The LIWC program enabled language explorations into previous writing studies, linking word usage among individuals in the experimental conditions with various health and behavioral outcomes (Pennebaker, Mayne, & Francis, 1997). One re-analysis of data was based on six writing studies: two studies involving college students writing about traumas where blood immune measures were collected (Pennebaker, Kiecolt-Glaser, & Glaser, 1988; Petrie, Booth, Pennebaker, Davison, & Thomas, 1995), two studies including first year college students who wrote about their deepest thoughts and feelings about coming to college (Pennebaker, Colder, & Sharp, 1990; Pennebaker & Francis, 1996), one study by maximum security prisoners in a state penitentiary (Richards, Beal, Seagal, & Pennebaker, 2000), and one study using professional men who had unexpectedly been laid off from their jobs after over 20 years of employment (Spera et al., 1994).

Analyzing the use of negative and positive emotion words yielded two important findings. First, the more that people used positive emotion words, the more their health improved. Negative emotion word use, however, was curvilinearly and not linearly related to health change after writing. Individuals who used a moderate number of negative emotions in their writing about upsetting topics evidenced the greatest drops in physician visits in the months after writing. The curvilinear emotion indices were computed using the absolute value of the difference between each person's emotion word use and the means of the sample. The simple correlations between change in physician visits with the curvilinear negative emotion index was r (152) = .27, $p < .05$ whereas the positive words were unrelated, r = -.14, *ns*. Individuals who use very few negative emotion words or who use a very high rate of them are the ones most likely to remain sick after writing, compared with those who use a moderate number of negative emotion words. The findings support the

A-to-D theory, and in many ways also square with other literatures. Individuals who maintain verbal underrepresentation and tend to use very few negative emotion words are most likely to be characterized as repressive copers (cf., Schwartz & Kline, 1995) or alexithymics (Lumley, Tojek, & Macklem, 2002). Those who overuse negative emotion words may well be the classic high Negative Affect individuals described by Watson and Clark (1984). That is, those individuals who describe their negative conditions in such detail may simply be in a recursive loop of complaining without attaining closure (overrepresentation). Indeed, as discussed below, this may be exacerbated by the inability of these individuals to develop a story or narrative (Nolen-Hoeksema, 2000).

Beyond emotions: The construction of a story. One of the basic functions of language and conversation is to communicate coherently and understandably. By extension, writing about an emotional experience in an organized way is healthier than in a chaotic way. Indeed, growing evidence from several labs suggest that people are most likely to benefit if they can write a coherent story (e.g., Smyth, True, & Sotto, 2001). Any technique that disrupts the telling of the story or the organization of the story is undoubtedly detrimental.

Unfortunately, we are not yet at the point of being able to precisely define what is meant by coherent, understandable, or meaningful when it comes to writing about emotional upheavals (cf., Graybeal, Segal, & Pennebaker, 2002). One person's meaning may be another's rumination. Many times in our own research we have been struck how a person appears to be writing in a way that avoids dealing with what we see as a central issue. Nevertheless, the person's health improves and he or she exclaims how beneficial the study was. Meaning, then, may ultimately be in the eye of the writer.

Although talking about the upsetting experience will help to organize and give it structure, talking about such a monumental experience may not always be possible. Others may not want to or even be able to hear about it. Within the discourse literature, particular attention has been paid to the role of written language in demanding more integration and structure than spoken language (Redeker, 1984; see also Brewin & Lennard, 1999). It would follow that writing — and to a lesser degree talking — about traumatic experiences would require a structure that would become apparent in the ways people wrote or talked about the events.

The components of a story: The analysis of cognitive words. It is beyond the bounds of this chapter to explore the philosophical definitions of knowledge, narrative, or meaning. For current purposes, knowledge of an event can encompass a causal explanation of it or the ability to understand the event within a broader context. The degree to which individuals are able to cognitively organize the event into a coherent narrative is a marker that the event has achieved knowledge status. In many ways, it is possible to determine the degree to which people have come to know their emotions and experiences by the language they use. Words or phrases such as, "I now realize that..." or "I understand why..." suggest that people are able to identify when they have achieved a knowing state about an event.

The LIWC analyses find promising effects for changes in insight and causal words over the course of emotional writing (see also Klein & Boals, 2001; Petrie et al., 1998). Specifically, people whose health improves, who get higher grades, and who find jobs after writing go from using relatively few causal and insight words to using a high rate of them by the last day of writing. In reading the essays of people who show this pattern of language use, judges often perceive the construction of a story over time (Graybeal, Sexton, & Pennebaker, 2002). Building a narrative, then, may be critical in reaching understanding or knowledge. Interestingly, those people who start the study with a coherent story that explained some past experience generally do not benefit from writing.

Those who use more insight and causal words in their emotional writing tend to gain the most improvements in working memory, and, at the same time, report drops in intrusive thinking about negative events (Klein & Boals, 2001). Consistent with the A-to-D Emotion Theory, for those in the experimental condition, the writing experience packages the event in a way that frees their minds for other cognitive tasks. Another way to interpret the salutary effects of using insight and causal words is that, together with the use of positive emotion words, this type of language reflects a positive reappraisal of events, which fuels cognitive broadening (Fredrickson, 1998; 2001). Narrating an emotional event into the bigger picture might help to integrate the experience into one's greater knowledge structures and personal identity.

Either way, the findings are consistent with current views on narrative and psychotherapy (e.g., Mahoney, 1995) in suggesting that it is critical for the client to create and come to terms with a story to explain and understand behavioral or mental problems and their history. Merely having a story may not be sufficient since the quality of stories as well as the people themselves change over time. A story, then, is a type of knowledge. Further, a narrative that provides knowledge must label and organize the emotional effects of an experience as well as the experience itself.

Writing as a way to change perspective. A central tenet of all insight-oriented therapies is that through psychotherapy people are able to develop a better understanding of their problems and reactions to them (e.g., Rogers, 1980). Inherent in this understanding is the ability to stand back and look at oneself from different perspectives. Although most therapists would agree with the importance of shifting perspectives, the difficulty for a researcher is in devising a way to track this shift. Some recent linguistic analyses offer some promising new strategies.

As described earlier, latent semantic analysis or LSA is a powerful mathematical tool that allows investigators to determine the similarity of any sets of essays. LSA was originally designed to look at the linguistic content of text samples. Consequently, most LSA applications routinely delete all non-content words. These non-content or "junk" words include pronouns, prepositions, conjunctions, articles, and auxiliary verbs. A more formal designation of junk words would be function words or particles. Function words can be thought of as the glue that holds content words together. Rather than reflecting what people are saying, these function words connote how they are speaking. In short, function words reflect linguistic style (cf., Pennebaker & King, 1999; Pennebaker, Mehl, & Niederhoffer, 2003).

Is it possible that peoples' linguistic styles can predict who benefits from writing? Using LSA, we discovered that the answer is yes. Analyzing three previous expressive writing studies, we discovered that the more that people change in their use of function words from day to day in their writing, the more their health improved (Campbell & Pennebaker, 2003). Closer analyses revealed that these effects were entirely due to changes in pronoun use. Specifically, the more that people oscillated in their use of first person singular pronouns (I, me, my) and all other personal pronouns (e.g., we, you, she, they), the more people's health improved. If individuals wrote about emotional upheavals across the three to four days of writing but they approached the topic in a consistent way — as measured by pronoun use, they were least likely to show health improvements. The findings suggest that the switching of pronouns reflect a change in perspective from one writing day to the next. Interestingly, it doesn't matter if people oscillate between an I-focus to a we-or-them-focus or vice versa. Rather, health improvements merely reflect a change in the orientation and personal attention of the writer.

A note on causality is in order. The various studies that have examined the relationship between word use and health outcomes in the emotional writing conditions imply a causal arrow: people who change perspectives, use positive emotion words, and people who construct a story ultimately evidence better health. Be cautious in interpreting these findings. The use of these word patterns may simply be reflecting some underlying cognitive and emotional changes occurring in the person. As noted earlier, some studies have attempted to get people to write with more positive emotion words, changing perspectives, and even constructing a story. These manipulations have not been particularly successful. The issues of mediation, moderation, and emergent properties of word use, cognitive and emotional activity, and long-term health will provide fertile grounds for research in the years to come.

Expressive writing and social dynamics. One of the popular appeals of the expressive writing paradigm is that it sounds almost magical. Write for 15 minutes a day for three days (a total of 45 minutes) and your health will improve for months. You may also get a job, fall in love, and make better grades. This is a bit of an overstatement. When people write about emotional upheavals for three or four days, they report thinking about the topics quite frequently. Many spontaneously tell us that they have been dreaming about the topics. Expressive writing's effects exist beyond the walls of the experiment.

Even more striking have been some of the social changes that occur as a result of expressive writing. Across multiple studies, individuals report that they talk to others about their writing topics. Many years ago, we conducted a study with Holocaust survivors and asked them to tell their stories orally. Prior to the study, approximately 70% reported that they had not talked about their experiences during World War II in any detail to anyone. After the interview, all participants were given a copy of their videotaped testimony. A month later, the average person reported watching the videotape 2.3 times and showing it to 2.5 other people (Pennebaker, Barger, & Tiebout, 1989). Disclosure begets disclosure.

Recently, we have developed a digital recording device called the Electronically Activated Recorder, or the EAR (Mehl & Pennebaker, 2003). The EAR has been engineered to record for 30 seconds every 12-13 minutes. The recordings are then transcribed and rated by judges concerning where the participant is and what he or she is doing. Recently, Youngsuk Kim (2005) had 95 bilingual students either write about traumatic experiences or participate in control tasks for four days, 15 minutes each day. Prior to writing and assignment to condition, individuals wore the EAR for two days. Approximately one month after writing, they wore the EAR again for two days. Overall, those who wrote about emotional upheavals talked more with others after writing than before writing. An earlier pilot study of approximately 50 students had found a similar effect (Pennebaker & Graybeal, 2001).

Across the various studies, we are now becoming convinced that one of the powers of expressive writing is that it brings about changes in people's social lives. Consider that writing has been shown to increase working memory and that these effects apparently last several weeks (Klein & Boals, 2001). After people write about troubling events, they devote less cognitive effort on them. This allows them to be better listeners, better friends. They writing may also encourage people to talk more openly with others about the secrets that they have been keeping.

The big picture: Life course correction. Part of the human experience is that we all deal with a variety of major and minor life issues. Often, we are taken off guard by an upheaval and don't have sufficient time to think about it or to explore the broader implications the event might have on us and those around us. One reason that we believe that expressive writing has been effective is that it serves as a life course correction. Occasionally, most of us benefit from standing back and examining our lives. This requires a perspective shift and the ability to detach ourselves from our surroundings. If we are still in the midst of a massive upheaval, it is virtually impossible to make these corrections.

The idea of expressive writing as a life course correction has not been tested empirically. The idea is certainly consistent with McAdam's (2001) life story approach. It is also relevant to work in autobiographical memory (e.g., Neisser & Fivush, 1994; Conway, 1990). There are times when we are forced to stop and look back at our lives and evaluate what issues and events have shaped who we are, what we are doing, and why.

Summary and Conclusions

The purpose of this chapter has been to provide a broad overview of the expressive writing paradigm. Since its first use in the 1980s, dozens of studies have been exploring the parameters and boundary conditions of its effectiveness. Perhaps most interesting has been the growing awareness that its value cannot be explained by a single cause or theory.

Expressive writing ultimately sets off a cascade of effects. For this chapter and certainly for this book, one of the more important effects is an improvement in physical health.

There is a certain irony that the original explanation for the writing phenomenon was inhibition. In the 1980s, our belief was that when people didn't talk about emotional upheavals, the work of inhibition ultimately led to stress and illness. The explanation was partially correct. Now, however, we are all beginning to appreciate the nuances of the problem. Not talking about a traumatic experience is also associated with a breakdown of one's social network, a decrease in working memory, sleep disruptions, alcohol and drug abuse, and an increased risk for additional traumatic experiences. Expressive writing or the unfettered talking about a trauma can often short-circuit this process.

Writing forces people to stop and reevaluate their life circumstance. The mere act of writing also demands a certain degree of structure as well as the basic labeling or acknowledging of their emotions. A particularly rich feature of the process is that these inchoate emotions and emotional experiences are translated into words. This analog-to-digital process demands a different representation of the events in the brain, in memory, and in the ways people think on a daily basis.

All of these cognitive changes have the potential for people to come to a different understanding of their circumstances. The cognitive changes themselves now allow the individuals to begin to think about and use their social worlds differently. They talk more; they connect with others differently. They are now better able to take advantage of social support. And with these cognitive and social changes, many of their unhealthy behaviors abate. As recent data suggest, expressive writing promotes sleep, enhanced immune function, reduced alcohol consumption, etc.

Despite the large number of promising studies, expressive writing is not a panacea. The overall effect size of writing is modest at best. We still don't know for whom it works best, when it should be used, or when other techniques should be used in its place. One of the difficulties of studying expressive writing is that the best studies have found that writing influences slow-moving but important outcome measures such as physician visits, illness episodes, and other real world behaviors that may take months to see. Self-report outcomes, although common and easy to use, generally do not bring about extremely strong findings. Future researchers would be wise to try to agree on one or more outcome measures that are sufficiently robust and also easy to measure.

After two decades of research on expressive writing, two strategies must continue to grow. The first is applying the method to large samples of people with differing diagnoses using rigorous RCT designs. This "big science, big medicine" approach is essential. At the same time, we should continue to nurture innovative smaller science. It will be the individual labs around the world that will ultimately tell us the boundary conditions of the phenomenon and the underlying mechanisms that explain its effectiveness.

This chapter, used with permission of James Pennebaker, first appeared in H. Friedman and R. Silver (Eds.), (2007) **Handbook of health psychology** *(pp. 263-284). New York: Oxford University Press.*

Correspondence should be addressed to James W. Pennebaker, Department of Psychology A8000, University of Texas, Austin, TX 78712 (e-mail: Pennebaker@mail.utexas.edu). Preparation of this paper was aided by a grant from the National Institutes of Health (MH52391).

References

Affleck, G., & Tennen, H. (1996). Construing benefits from adversity: Adaptational significance and dispositional underpinnings. *Journal of Personality, 64,* 899-922.

Berkowitz, L. & Troccoli, B.T. (1990). Feelings, direction of attention, and expressed evaluations of others. *Cognition and Emotion, 4,* 305-325.

Bower, G. H., & Sivers, H. (1998). Cognitive impact of traumatic events. *Developmental & Psychopathology, 10,* 625-653.

Breuer, J., & Freud, S. (1957). *Studies on hysteria* (J. Strachey, Trans.). New York: Basic Books. (Original work published 1895).

Breslau, N., Chilcoat, H. D., Kessler, R. C., & Davis, G. C. (1999). Previous exposure to trauma and PTSD effects of subsequent trauma: Results from the Detroit Area Survey of Trauma. *American Journal of Psychiatry, 156,* 902-907.

Brewin, C.R. & Lennard, H. (1999). Effects of mode of writing on emotional narratives. *Journal of Traumatic Stress, 12*, 355-361.

Brom, D., Kleber, R. J., & Hofman, M. C. (1993). Victims of traffic accidents: Incidence and prevention of post-traumatic stress disorder. *Journal of Clinical Psychology, 49*, 131-140.

Burton, C. M., & King, L. A. (2004). The health benefits of writing about intensely positive experiences. *Journal of Research in Personality, 38*, 150-163.

Campbell, R.S., & Pennebaker, J.W. (2003). The secret life of pronouns: Flexibility in writing style and physical health. *Psychological Science, 14*, 60-65.

Cameron, L D., & Nicholls, G. (1998). Expression of stressful experiences through writing: Effects of a self-regulation manipulation for pessimists and optimists. *Health Psychology, 17*, 84-92.

Carlier, I. V. E., & Gersons, B, P. R. (1997). Stress reactions in disaster victims following the Bijlmermeer plane crash. *Journal of Traumatic Stress, 10*, 329-335.

Carver, C. S., & Scheier, M. F. (2000). Optimism. In C. R. Snyder and S. J. Lopez (Eds.), *Handbook of Positive Psychology*, pp. 231-243. London: Oxford University Press.

Christensen A.J., Edwards D.L., Wiebe J.S., Benotsch E.G., McKelvey L., Andrews M., Lubaroff D.M. (1996). Effect of verbal self-disclosure on natural killer cell activity: Moderating influence of cynical hostility. *Psychosomatic Medicine, 58*, 150-155.

Clark, L.F. (1993). Stress and the cognitive-conversational benefits of social interaction. *Journal of Social and Clinical Psychology, 12*, 25-55.

Cole, S. W., Kemeny, M. E., Taylor, S. E., & Visscher, B. R. (1996). Elevated physical health risk among gay men who conceal their homosexual identity. *Health Psychology, 15*, 243-251.

Conway, M. A. (1990). *Autobiographical memory: An introduction.* Buckingham, England: Open University Press.

Conners, C.K. (1985). The Conners Rating Scales: Instruments for the assessment of childhood psychopathology. In J. Sattler (Ed.), *Assessment of academic achievement and special abilities* (pp 328-399). San Diego, CA: Jerome Sattler Publisher.

Czajka, J. A. (1987). *Behavioral inhibition and short term physiological responses.* Unpublished Masters Thesis. Dallas, TX: Southern Methodist University.

Damasio, A. R. (1998). Emotion in the perspective of an integrated nervous system. *Brain Research Reviews, 26*, 83-86.

De Moor, C., Sterner, J., Hall, M., Warneke, C., Gilani, Z., Amato, R., et al. (2002). A pilot study of the effects of expressive writing on psychological and behavioral adjustment in patients enrolled in a phase II trial of vaccine therapy for metastatic renal cell carcinoma. *Health Psychology, 21*, 615-619.

Diener, E., Lucas, R., & Oishi, S. E. (2002). Subjective well-being: The science of happiness and well-being. In C. R. Snyder and S. J. Lopez (Eds.), *Handbook of Positive Psychology*, pp. 463-473. London: Oxford University Press.

Donnelly, D. A., & Murray, E. J. (1991). Cognitive and emotional changes in written essays and therapy interviews. *Journal of Social & Clinical Psychology, 10*, 334-350.

Esterling, B. A., Antoni, M. H., Fletcher, M. A., Margulies, S. et al., (1994). Emotional disclosure through writing or speaking modulates latent Epstein-Barr virus antibody titers. *Journal of Consulting & Clinical Psychology, 62*, 130-140.

Feldman, L. (1995). Valence focus and arousal focus: Individual differences in the structure of affective experience. *Journal of Personality and Social Psychology, 69*, 153-166.

Feldman Barrett, L. (1998). Discrete emotions or dimensions? The role of valence focus and arousal focus. *Cognition and Emotion, 12(4)*, 579-599.

Feldman Barrett, L., Gross, J., Conner Christensen, T., & Benvenuto, M. (2001). Knowing what you're feeling and knowing what to do about it: Mapping the relation between emotion differentiation and emotion regulation. *Cognition & Emotion, 15(6)*, 713-724.

Feldman Barrett, L., & Salovey, P. (2002). The wisdom in feeling: Psychological processes in emotional intelligence. New York, NY: Guilford Press.

Foa, E. B., & Kozak, M. J. (1986). Emotional processing of fear: Exposure to corrective information. *Psychological Bulletin, 99,* 20-35.

Francis, M.E. & Pennebaker, J.W. (1992). Putting stress into words: Writing about personal upheavals and health. *American Journal of Health Promotion, 6,* 280-287.

Fredrickson, B. L. (1998). What good are positive emotions? *Review of General Psychology: Special Issue: New Directions in Research on Emotion, 2,* 300-319.

Fredrickson, B. L. (2001). The role of positive emotions in positive psychology: The broaden-and-build theory of positive emotions. *American Psychologist, 56,* 218-226.

Frisina, P. G., Borod, J. C., & Lepore, S. J. (2004). A meta-analysis of the effects of written emotional disclosure on the health outcomes of clinical populations. *The Journal of Nervous and Mental Disease, 192,* 629-634.

Gidron, Y., Peri, T., Connolly, J. F., & Shalev, A. Y. (1996). Written disclosure in posttraumatic stress disorder: Is it beneficial for the patient? *Journal of Nervous & Mental Disease, 184,* 505-507.

Graybeal, A., Sexton, J. D., & Pennebaker, J. W. (2002). The role of story-making in disclosure writing: The psychometrics of narrative. *Psychology and Health, 17,* 571-581.

Greenberg, M. A., & Stone, A. A. (1992). Emotional disclosure about traumas and its relation to health: Effects of previous disclosure and trauma severity. *Journal of Personality and Social Psychology, 63,* 75-84.

Greenberg, M. A., Wortman, C. B., & Stone, A. A. (1996). Emotional expression and physical health: Revising traumatic memories fostering self-regulation? *Journal of Personality & Social Psychology, 71,* 588-602.

Hughes, C. F. (1994). Effects of expressing negative and positive emotions and insight on health and adjustment to college. *Dissertation Abstracts International: Section B: The Sciences & Engineering, 54,* 3899.

Heberlein, A.S., Adolphs, R., Pennebaker, J.W., & Tranel, D. (2003). Effects of damage to right-hemisphere brain structures on spontaneous emotional and social judgments. *Political Psychology, 24,* 705-726.

Holmes, T. H., & Rahe, R. H. (1967). The Social Readjustment Rating Scale. *Journal of Psychosomatic Research, 11,* 213-218.

Keane, T. M. (1998). Psychological effects of military combat. In B. P. Dohrenwend (Ed.), *Adversity, stress, and psychopathology,* pp. 52-65. London: Oxford University Press.

Keltner, D., Locke, K.D., & Audrain, P.C. (1993). The influence of attributions on the relevance of negative feelings to personal satisfaction. *Personality and Social Psychology Bulletin, 19,* 21-29.

Kilpatrick, D. G., Resnick, H. S., Saunders, B. E., & Best, C. L. (1998). Rape, other violence against women, and posttraumatic stress disorder. In B. P. Dohrenwend (Ed.), *Adversity, stress, and psychopathology,* pp. 161-176. London: Oxford University Press.

King, L. A., & Miner, K. N. (2000). Writing about the perceived benefits of traumatic events: Implications for physical health. *Personality & Social Psychology Bulletin, 26,* 220-230.

Klein, K., & Boals, A. (2001). Expressive writing can increase working memory capacity. *Journal of Experimental Psychology: General, 130(3),* 520-533.

Krantz, A. & Pennebaker, J.W. (1995). Bodily versus written expression of traumatic experience. Unpublished manuscript.

Labov, W. & Fanshel, D. (1977). *Therapeutic discourse.* New York: Academic Press.

Landauer, T. K., Foltz, P. W., & Laham, D. (1998). An introduction to Latent Semantic Analysis. *Discourse Processes, 25,* 259-284.

Ledoux, J. (1999). Can neurobiology tell us anything about human feelings? In D. Kahneman, and E. Diener (Eds.), *The foundations of hedonic psychology.* (pp. 489-499). New York, NY: Russell Sage Foundation.

Lepore, S. J., Fernanadez-Berrocal, P., Ragan, J., & Ramos, N. (2004). It's not that bad: Social challenges to emotional disclosure enhance adjustment to stress. *Anxiety, Stress & Coping: An International Journal, 17,* 341-361.

Lepore, S. J., Ragan, J., & Jones, S. (2000). Talking facilitates cognitive-emotional processes of adaptation to an acute stressor. *Journal of Personality & Social Psychology, 78,* 499-508.

Lepore, S. J., & Smyth, J. M. (2002). *Writing cure: How expressive writing promotes health and emotional well-being.* Washington, DC: American Psychological Association.

Lumley, M. A. (2004). Alexithymia, emotional disclosure, and health: A program of research. *Journal of Personality, 72,* 1271-1300.

Lumley, M. A., & Provenzano, K. M. (2003). Stress management through written emotional disclosure improves academic performance among college students with physical symptoms. *Journal of Educational Psychology, 95(3),* 641-649.

Lumley, A., Tojek, T. M., & Macklein, D. J. (2002). Effects of written emotional disclosure among repressive and alexithymic people. In, S. J. Lepore, and J. M. Smyth (Eds.). *The writing cure: How expressive writing promotes health and emotional well-being,* (pp. 75-95). Washington, DC: American Psychological Association.

Lutgendorf, S., Antoni, M. H., Schneiderman, N., Ironson, G., & Fletcher, M. A. (1995). Psychosocial interventions and quality of life changes in the HIV spectrum. In J. E. Dimsdale and A. Baum (Eds.), *Quality of life in behavioral medicine research,* pp. 205-239. Hillsdale, NJ, England: Lawrence Erlbaum Associates, Inc.

Mahoney, M.J. (1995). *Cognitive and constructive psychotherapies: Theory, research, and practice.* New York: Springer.

Mann, T. (2001). Effects of future writing and optimism on health behaviors in HIV-infected women. *Annals of Behavioral Medicine, 23,* 26-33.

McAdams, D. P. (2001). The psychology of life stories. *Review of General Psychology, 5,* 100-122.

McGuire, K. M. B., Greenberg, M. A., & Gevirtz, R. (2005). Autonomic effects of expressive writing in individuals with elevated blood pressure. *Journal of Health Psychology, 10,* 197-207.

McNally, R.J., Bryant, R.A., & Ehlers, A. (2003). Does early psychological intervention promote recovery from posttraumatic stress? *Psychological Science in the Public Interest, 4,* 45-79.

Meadows, E. A., & Foa, E. B. (1999). Cognitive-behavioral treatment of traumatized adults. In P. A. Saigh and J. D. Bremmer (Eds.), *Posttraumatic stress disorder: A comprehensive text,* pp. 376-390. Needham Heights, MA, US: Allyn & Bacon.

Meads, C. (2003, October). *How effective are emotional disclosure interventions? A systematic review with meta-analyses.* Paper given at the 3rd International Conference on The (Non)Expression of Emotions in Health and Disease. Tilburg, NL.

Miller, M. W. (2003). Personality and the etiology and expression of PTSD: A three-factor model perspective. *Clinical Psychology: Science & Practice, 10,* 373-393.

Mitchell, J. T., & Everly, G. S. *Critical Incident Stress Debriefing (CISD): An operations manual.* Ellicot City; Chevron: 1996.

Mumford, E., Schlesinger, H.J., & Glass, G.V. (1983). Reducing medical costs through mental health treatment: Research problems and recommendations. In A. Broskowski, E. Marks, & S.H. Budman (Eds.), *Linking health and mental health* (pp 257-273). Beverly Hills, CA: Sage.

Murphy, F. C., Nimmo-Smith, I., & Lawrence, A. D. (2003). Functional neuroanatomy of emotions: A meta-analysis. *Cognitive, Affective, & Behavioral Neuroscience, 3(3),* 207-233.

Murray, J. B. (1992). Posttraumatic stress disorder: A review. *Genetic, Social, & General Psychology Monographs, 118,* 313-338.

Murray, E. J., Lamnin, A. D., & Carver, C. S. (1989). Emotional expression in written essays and psychotherapy. *Journal of Social & Clinical Psychology, 8,* 414-429.

Neisser, U., & Fivush, R. (1994). *The remembering self: Construction and accuracy in the self-narrative.* New York, NY: Cambridge University Press.

Nolen-Hoeksema, S. (2000). The role of rumination in depressive disorders and mixed anxiety/depressive symptoms. *Journal of Abnormal Psychology, 109,* 504-511.

Paez, D., Velasco, C., & Gonzalez, J. L. (1999). Expressive writing and the role of alexithymia as a dispositional deficit in self-disclosure and psychological health. *Journal of Personality and Social Psychology, 77,* 630-641.

Pennebaker, J.W. (1993). Putting stress into words: Health, linguistic, and therapeutic implications. *Behaviour Research and Therapy, 31,* 539-548.

Pennebaker, J.W. (1995). *Emotion, disclosure, & health.* Washington, DC: American Psychological Association.

Pennebaker, J. W. (1997). Writing about emotional experiences as a therapeutic process. *Psychological Science, 8,* 162-166.

Pennebaker, J.W., Barger, S.D., & Tiebout, J. (1989). Disclosure of traumas and health among Holocaust survivors. *Psychosomatic Medicine, 51,* 577-589.

Pennebaker, J. W., & Beall, S. (1986). Confronting a traumatic event: Toward an understanding of inhibition and disease. *Journal of Abnormal Psychology, 95,* 274-281.

Pennebaker, J. W., & Chung, C. K. (2005). Variations in expressive writing formats. Unpublished technical report. Austin, TX: The University of Texas at Austin.

Pennebaker, J. W., Colder, M., & Sharp, L. K. (1990). Accelerating the coping process. *Journal of Personality & Social Psychology, 58(3),* 528-537.

Pennebaker, J. W., & Francis, M. E. (1996). Cognitive, emotional, and language processes in disclosure. *Cognition & Emotion, 10(6),* 601-626.

Pennebaker, J. W., Francis, M. E., & Booth, R. J. (2001). *Linguistic Inquiry and Word Count (LIWC): LIWC2001.* Mahwah, NJ: Erlbaum Publishers.

Pennebaker, J. W., & Graybeal, A. (2001). Patterns of natural language use: Disclosure, personality, and social integration. *Current Directions, 10,* 90-93.

Pennebaker, J. W., Hughes, C. F., & O'Heeron, R. C. (1987). The psychophysiology of confession: Linking inhibitory and psychosomatic processes. *Journal of Personality & Social Psychology, 52,* 781-793.

Pennebaker, J.W., & Keough, K.A. (1999). Revealing, organizing, and reorganizing the self in response to stress and emotion. In R. Ashmore and L. Jussim (Eds.), *Self and Social Identity: Vol. II* (pp 101-121). New York: Oxford.

Pennebaker, J.W., Kiecolt-Glaser, J., & Glaser, R. (1988). Disclosure of traumas and immune function: Health implications for psychotherapy. *Journal of Consulting and Clinical Psychology, 56,* 239-245.

Pennebaker, J.W. & King, L.A. (1999). Linguistic styles: Language use as an individual difference. *Journal of Personality and Social Psychology, 77,* 1296-1312.

Pennebaker, J.W., Mayne, T.J., & Francis, M.E. (1997). Linguistic predictors of adaptive bereavement. *Journal of Personality and Social Psychology, 72,* 166-183.

Pennebaker, J. W., Mehl, M. R., & Niederhoffer, K. G. (2003). Psychological aspects of natural language use: Our words, our selves. *Annual Review of Psychology, 54,* 547-577.

Pennebaker, J. W., & Susman, J. R. (1988). Disclosure of traumas and psychosomatic processes. *Social Science & Medicine, 26,* 327-332.

Petrie, K.P., Booth, R.J., & Pennebaker, J.W. (1998). The immunological effects of thought suppression. *Journal of Personality and Social Psychology, 75,* 1264-1272.

Petrie, K.J., Booth, R., Pennebaker, J.W., Davison, K.P., & Thomas, M. (1995). Disclosure of trauma and immune response to Hepatitis B vaccination program. *Journal of Consulting and Clinical Psychology, 63,* 787-792.

Petrie, K. J., Fontanilla, I., Thomas, M. G., Booth, R. J., & Pennebaker, J. W. (2004). Effect of written emotional expression on immune function in patients with Human Immunodeficiency Virus infection: A randomized trial. *Psychosomatic Medicine, 66,* 272-275.

Redeker, G. (1984). On differences between spoken and written language. *Discourse Processes, 7,* 43-55.

Resnick, H. S., Kilpatrick, D. G., & Lipovsky, J. A. (1991). Assessment of rape-related posttraumatic stress disorder: Stressor and symptom dimensions. *Psychological Assessment, 3,* 561-572.

Richards, J. M., Beal, W. E., Seagal, J. D., & Pennebaker, J. W. (2000). Effects of disclosure of traumatic events on illness behavior among psychiatric prison inmates. *Journal of Abnormal Psychology, 109(1),* 156-160.

Rime, B. (1995). Mental rumination, social sharing, and the recovery from emotional experience. In J. W. Pennebaker (Ed.), *Emotion, disclosure, & health,* pp. 271-291. Washington, DC: American Psychological Association.

Salovey, P., & Mayer, J. D. (1989-90). Emotional Intelligence. *Imagination, Cognition & Personality, 9(3),* 185-211.

Sapolsky, R. M. (2004). *Why zebras don't get ulcers.* New York, NY: Henry Holt and Company.

Schooler, J.W., & Engstler-Schooler, T.Y. (1990). Verbal overshadowing of visual memories: Some things are better left unsaid. *Cognitive Psychology, 22,* 36-71.

Schoutrop, M. J. A., Lange, A., Brosschot, J., & Everaerd, W. (1997). Overcoming traumatic events by means of writing assignments. In A. Vingerhoets, F. van Bussel, & J. Boelhouwer (Eds.), *The (Non)expression of emotions in health and disease* (pp. 279-289). Tilburg, The Netherlands: Tilburg University Press.

Schwartz, G.E., & Kline, J.P. (1995). Repression, emotional disclosure, and health: Theoretical, empirical, and clinical considerations. In J.W. Pennebaker (Ed.), *Emotion, disclosure, and health* (pp 177-194). Washington, DC: American Psychological Association.

Schwarz, N. (1990). Feelings as information: Informational and motivational functions of affective states. In E.T. Higgins & R.M. Sorrentino (Eds.), *Handbook of motivation and cognition: Foundations of social behavior, Vol 2* (pp. 527-561). New York: Guilford.

Seligman, M. E. P. (2000). Positive psychology. In J. E. Gillman (Ed.), *Science of optimism and hope: Research essays in honor of Martin E. P. Seligman,* pp. 415-429. Philadelphia, PA, US: Templeton Foundation Press.

Selye, H. (1978). *The stress of life.* Oxford, England: McGraw Hill.

Sheese, B. E., Brown, E. L., & Graziano, W. G. (2004). Emotional expression in cyberspace: Searching for moderators of the Pennebaker disclosure effect via email. *Health Psychology, 23,* 457-464.

Singer, J. A., & Salovey, P. (1993). *The remembered self: Emotion and memory in personality.* New York, NY: Free Press.

Sloan, D.M. & Marx, B.P. (2004a). Taking pen to hand: Evaluating theories underlying the written disclosure paradigm. *Clinical Psychology: Science & Practice, 11,* 121-137.

Sloan, D. M., & Marx, B. P. (2004b). A closer examination of the structured written disclosure procedure. *Journal of Consulting & Clinical Psychology, 72,* 165-175.

Smith, M.L., Glass, G.V., & Miller, R.L. (1980). *The benefits of psychotherapy.* Baltimore: Johns Hopkins University Press.

Smyth, J.M. (1998). Written emotional expression: Effect sizes, outcome types, and moderating variables. *Journal of Consulting and Clinical Psychology, 66,* 174-184.

Smyth, J. M., Stone, A. A., Hurewitz, A., & Kaell, A. (1999). Effects of writing about stressful experiences on symptom reduction in patients with asthma or rheumatoid arthritis: A randomized trial. *JAMA, 281,* 1304-1309.

Smyth, J.M., True, N., & Souto, J. (2001). Effects of writing about traumatic experiences: The necessity for narrative structuring. *Journal of Social and Clinical Psychology, 20,* 161-172.

Solano, L., Donati, V., Pecci, F., Persicheeti, S., & Colaci, A. (2003). Post-operative course after pailloma resection: Effects of written disclosure of the experience in subjects with different alexithymia levels. *Psychosomatic Medicine, 65,* 477-484.

Spera, S. P., Buhrfeind, E. D., & Pennebaker, J. W. (1994). Expressive writing and coping with job loss. *Academy of Management Journal, 37(3),* 722-733.

Springer, S. P., & Deutsch, G. (1998). *Left brain, right brain: Perspectives from cognitive neuroscience (5th ed.).* New York, NY: W. H. Freeman/Times Books/Henry Holt & Co.

Stanton, A. L., & Danoff-Burg, S. (2002). Emotional expression, expressive writing, and cancer. In S. J. Lepore, and J. M. Smyth (Eds.), *Writing cure: How expressive writing promotes health and emotional well-being,* pp. 31-51. Washington, DC: US. American Psychological Association.

Stone, L. (2003*). Expressive writing and perspective change: Applications to September 11.* Poster presented at the 2003 Conference for the Society for Personality and Social Psychology, Savannah, GA.

Sutker, P. B., Davis, J. M., Uddo, M., & Ditta, S. R. (1995). War zone stress, personal resources, and PTSD in Persian Gulf War returnees. *Journal of Abnormal Psychology, 104,* 444-452.

Taylor, L., Wallander, J., Anderson, D., Beasley, P., & Brown, R. (2003). Improving chronic disease utilization, health status, and adjustment in adolescents and young adults with cystic fibrosis. *Journal of Clinical Psychology in Medical Settings, 10,* 9-16.

Ullrich, P.A. & Lutgendorf, S.L. (2002). Journaling about stressful events: Effects of cognitive processing and emotional expression. *Annals of Behavioral Medicine, 24,* 244-250.

Vaidya, N. A., & Garfield, D. A. S. (2003). A comparison of personality characteristics of patients with posttraumatic stress disorder and substance dependence: Preliminary findings. *Journal of Nervous & Mental Disease, 191,* 616-618.

Vano, A.M., & Pennebaker, J.W. (1997). Emotion vocabulary in bilingual Hispanic children: Adjustment and behavioral effects. *Journal of Language and Social Psychology, 16(2),* 191-200.

Walker, B. L., Nail, L. M., & Croyle, R. T. (1999). Does emotional expression make a difference in reactions to breast cancer? *Oncology Nursing Forum, 26,* 1025-1032.

Watson, D., & Clark, L.A. (1984). Negative affectivity: The disposition to experience aversive emotional states. *Psychological Bulletin, 96,* 465-490.

Wilson, T.D. (2002*). Strangers to ourselves: Discovering the adaptive unconscious.* Cambridge, MA: Belknap Press/Harvard University Press.

Wolpe, J. (1968). Psychotherapy by reciprocal inhibition. *Conditional Reflex, 3,* 234-240.

Wortman, C. B., & Silver, R. C. (1989). The myths of coping with loss. *Journal of Consulting & Clinical Psychology, 57,* 349-357.

3

A Historical and Systematic Perspective about Distance Writing and Wellness

Luciano L'Abate

Keynote Address 2008 Wellness & Writing Connections Conference

Part I. Historical Background for Writing and Wellness

In this part, writing is considered within the (1) surge in the self-help movement in mental health, (2) advent of homework assignments, (3) context of a classification of writing, (4) classification of self-help practice exercises, (5) low-cost approaches to promote physical and mental health, and (6) introduction of technology in the mental health field.

Distance Writing Within the Self-Help Movement in Mental Health

With the help of the Internet, distance writing and self-help are now an everyday occurrence (Harwood & L'Abate, in press; Lange et al., 2003; Ritterband et al., 2003a, Ritterband et al, 2003b; Watkins & Clum,

2008). Information about help and how to get it is now at the fingertips of almost anyone who can write using a computer. Now even the phone can take the place of the computer. Help is continuously exchanged through self-help groups, chat rooms, formal and informal, structured and unstructured treatments in health promotion, prevention of illness, psychotherapy, and rehabilitation (Table 1).

Table 1: An Outline of Self-help Approaches in Mental Health

I. Self-support approaches initiated and maintained entirely by participants
   A. Nutrition and diets
   B. Exercise
   C. Face-to-face groups, AA
   D. Online chat groups
II. Self-help approaches initiated, administered, guided, maintained, and monitored by professionals for participants
   A. Bibliotherapy
   B. Distance writing
   C. Online therapy
   D. Manuals
   E. Miscellaneous (movies, videos, popular psychology books)
III. Self-help (adjutant/additional) approaches for specific conditions with professional help
   A. Anxieties
   B. Depressions
   C. Eating disorders
   D. Addictions
   E. Personality disorders
   F. Severe psychopathology
   G. Medical conditions
IV. Conclusion: The new paradigm in mental health: Self-help and/or distance writing online first and, if and when necessary, distance writing together with face-to-face interventions.

The Importance of Working at a Distance from Participants

The notion that we do not need to see participants to help them is still relatively foreign if not repugnant to many mental heath professionals who prefer presence and words to writing. Instead, I have argued that only by working at a distance from participants can we be truly objective and avoid personal whims and wills that may affect our judgment (L'Abate, 2008c). After all, many, if not most, medical treatments occur at a distance. After receiving two knee replacements, I had to undergo a series of physical exercises; otherwise my legs would not have been able to walk. After being operated on for a tumor in the lower abdomen, I had to undergo one year of a daily anti-cancer oral medication. After developing dizziness and vertigo, the symptoms disappeared when I learned to perform daily eye and body exercises administered by a physical therapist to begin with and then by following a manual with proper instructions.

Treatment, therefore, occurred under control of, but at a distance from, a physician. After the initial operations and a few visits, I did not have to see the physician anymore. The responsibility to see that I would be able to walk and be healthier remained on my shoulders, at a distance from the supervising physician, through exercises and proper medication.

I believe, therefore, that psychological treatment should occur at a distance from the therapist through administration of written interactive practice exercises interspersed with control visits with the therapist to check and receive feedback on whether or whatever homework has been completed, not necessarily face-to-face (L'Abate, 2008c, 2008d). We now have the technology to help many participants with a minimum contact with a therapist (L'Abate & Bliwise, 2008; L'Abate & Harwood, 2008). More of this point below.

The Advent of Homework Assignments in Mental Health

The last few years have seen a growth in the literature about homework assignments with a variety of populations in clinical and non-clinical conditions (Kazantzis et al., 2005; Kazantzis & L'Abate, 2007;

L'Abate, 1977, 1986; L'Abate & De Giacomo, 2003; L'Abate & McHenry, 1983). Most practice exercises in these and many other sources that employ homework assignments involve writing. Better treatment outcome is associated with specific therapist behaviors (e.g., setting concrete goals and discussing barriers to completing homework), characteristics of the homework task (e.g., using written reminders of the homework) and client involvement in the discussion (Detweiler-Bedell & Whisman, 2005).

A Classification of Distance Writing

This classification is presented in Table 2 (L'Abate, 2001, 2002, 2008b).

Table 2: A Classification of Distance Writing

A. **Automatic:** of questionable usefulness as a fad and in need of more controlled research before considering its use.

B. **Dictionary-aided:** basic to many self-help practice exercises (L'Abate, 2008).

C. **Expressive:** as in "Pennebaker's Paradigm" writing about hurts and traumas heretofore not shared with others for 15 minutes a day for four consecutive days. The literature on this approach is extensive and available online from Dr. Pennebaker's web pages.

D. **Focused:** as in autobiographies to be mailed or sent online (L'Abate, 2007, in press).

E. **Guided:** as in answering written questions in writing, after completion of autobiography, journal, or other homework assignments.

F. **Open-ended:** as in personal information gathered through diaries or journals.

G. **Programmed:** as in protocols or practice exercises for targeted clinical (children and youth, single individuals, couples, and families) and non-targeted conditions for life-long learning in non-clinical participants (www.mentalhealthhelp.com).

From this classification, two approaches will be highlighted: (1) a classification of self-help protocols, workbooks, or practice exercises, and (2) dictionary-based writing.

A Classification of Interactive Self-Help Practice Exercises

This classification is presented in Table 3 (L'Abate, 2001, 2002, 2004a, 2004b, 2008b; L'Abate & De Giacomo, 2003).

However, according to Clum and Watkins (2008) in regard to devising effective self-help programs, they concluded:

In one real sense we have no better idea today (about) how

Table 3: A Classification of Interactive Exercises in Mental Health

1. Composition of participants: singles (adults, children, youth), couples, families, groups.
2. Reason for referral: concern(s), diagnosis(es), single versus dual or multiple, problem(s), symptom(s).
3. Level and type of functionality: DSM-IV or Reason for Referral
   a. Functional; No diagnosis
   b. Externalizations; Axis II. Cluster B
   c. Internalization: Axis II. Cluster C
   d. Borderline: Axis II. Cluster A
   e. Severe: Axis I.
4. Practice exercises for specific symptoms versus general conditions.
5. Symptom-free versus symptom-related & diagnosis-linked.
6. Theory-derived, theory-related, theory-independent.
7. Format: (a) fixed (nomothetic); (b) flexible (idiographic); and (c) mixed (nomothetic and idiographic).
8. Style: linear versus circular (paradoxical).
9. Derivation: single versus multiple score tests, e.g. BDI vs. MMPI-2.
10. Content: clinical (addictions, affective disorders, Axis I and Axis II: Clusters A, B, & C etc.) and non-clinical (for life-long learning in individuals, couples, and families).

to write a self-help book than we did 30 years ago… As empiricists, therefore, we must conclude that we simply do not know how to present therapeutic content in ways to maximize behavior change (p. 421). …Additionally, no information is provided on the venue of the treatment approach — e.g., book, tape, or Internet — likely to prove more effective. We do not know what steps are important and in what order they should be presented. This deficiency is largely related to the lack of formal assessment of the many self-help offerings that exist in a given domain, a deficiency that is at least partially remediable (p. 422). …Assessment is an effective change agent for several reasons. Assessment informs whether the individual seeking change is using the recommended strategies to produce that change (p. 424).

These authors went on to expand on the importance of assessment as a way to produce change. However, they did not consider two important issues in trying to produce change for the better:

(1) Distance writing as the most important medium of communication and healing, in some cases more cost-effective than talk. For instance, the major approach reviewed thoroughly in their excellent book (Watkins and Clum, 2008) is bibliotherapy. However, from the best that can be surmised, this approach is based strictly on passive reading and little if any interaction with a professional helper. For instance, there is only one reference to written self-help materials for smoking cessation (pp. 273-278) but not to distance writing as a medium of communication and healing.

(2) A continuous interaction at a distance from a professional, who responds routinely and interactively to the completion of practice exercises on a weekly or biweekly basis. This process involves feedback loops, which are considered in Watkins and Clum's work solely for self-administered treatments (pp. 52-54), goal attainment (pp. 60-61), its function (p. 63), and personalized use (pp. 260-261). Furthermore, this feedback is apparently administered verbally rather than in writing,

making it difficult to keep a record of what is happening during this process.

I have argued (L'Abate, 2004b, pp. 3-64) that when a practice exercise is administered to individuals as homework, there are at least two new feedback loops that are missing in most talk-based treatments: (a) having to respond in writing to items and questions contained in a written practice exercise, a requirement to think about relevant to one's life and not just emote, (b) receiving feedback about one's answers from a professional helper, either verbally or in writing. In couples, there are at least two additional loops (a) comparing one's answers with those of a partner by oneself, and (b) comparing, contrasting, and discussing those answers face-to-face with a partner even before receiving feedback from a professional helper (L'Abate, in press-b).

What is important in Clum and Watkins' foregoing statement is the function of the initial assessment/evaluation and linking specific evaluation with specific treatment, something that I have advocated from day one (L'Abate, 1986, 1990, 1992) but which has still a long way to go. Instead of passively inert qualities, most psychological and psychiatric tests can be linked dynamically to treatment through dictionary-based writing as well as through psychiatric diagnosis and reasons for referral.

Dictionary-Based Writing

Quite a few practice exercises produced over the years of clinical practice (L'Abate, 2008b) require the use of the dictionary because I believe that this process is necessary and helpful to think more clearly, especially in dealing with people whose impulsivity lands them in jail or worse, or whose emotional upsets land them in a hospital or worse (L'Abate. 2007a). In addition, the use of the dictionary should allow them to achieve some distance from emotionally charged issues. Whether this belief is supported by evidence remains to be seen, as discussed further below. Whether the dictionary or no dictionary is necessary, however, the process that follows Clum and Watkins's foregoing recommendations also remains to be seen. For instance: (1) take any single item psychological test, such as Beck's Depression Inventory, or dimensions from a multiple score test, such as the Minnesota Multiphasic Personality Inventory (MMPI-2) among many others; (2) ask participants to define those terms and give two examples, with or without the use of a dictionary, even though I recommend it, and (3) rank-order those items according to how those items apply to them, from the one item or dimension that applies to them the most to items or dimensions that least apply to them.

This rank-order becomes a treatment plan because participants can now complete a standard practice exercise that requires them to answer, in writing of course, questions related to history, origin, frequency, duration, intensity, personal and relational functionality of a particular symptom rated as most important by participants. After completion of this first practice exercise, further homework follows the same sequence derived from the rank-order. Here, then, is how evaluation is linked directly to treatment in ways that would be impossible to implement through talk, what I have called *prescriptive evaluation* (L'Abate, 1990), linking evaluation with interventions — practically impossible to achieve through talk.

These practice exercises include most clinical conditions derived directly from many psychological tests and lists of symptoms from the *Diagnostic and Statistical Manual of Mental Disorders* published by the American Psychiatric Association for individuals, and from relational tests for conflictful couples and families. There are also practice exercises for non-clinical conditions and life-long learning for individuals, couples, and families without a diagnosable psychiatric condition (L'Abate, 2008c). (More of this below.) However, one more avenue needs to be considered.

Low-cost Approaches to Promote Physical and Mental Health

These approaches are available in L'Abate (2007b), as outlined in Table 1. From this approach I developed an experimental rating questionnaire (shown on page 63) that should help differentiate participants according to levels of functioning established by what participants specifically do and not according to how they answer on a personality test (L'Abate, 2008c, in press-b). This approach would follow what is now called a stepped procedure that I advocated years ago as "successive sieves" or hurdles (L'Abate, 1990, in press-b). Keep in mind that most psychological tests are directed toward pathology and do not enter into what participants do 24 hours a day. This questionnaire allows us to find information usually not available in most psychological tests.

Table 4: Toward a Technology of Mental Health: Tentative Contents

Introduction:

Chapter 1. The growth of technology in psychology, psychiatry, and mental health: An historical background for the application of technology to traditional in-class learning as well as independent learning, in clinical, scientific, and professional practice settings. (Nancy G. Bliwise and Luciano L'Abate)

Section I. Face-to-face Technology

Chapter 2. Biofeedback approaches

Chapter 3. Memory training. (Henry Mahncke, PositScience)

Chapter 4. Personal response systems

Chapter 5. Multimedia

Chapter 6. Virtual reality

Chapter 7. Transcranial magnetic stimulation

Section II. Distance technology

Chapter 8. Toward a technology of distance writing. (Luciano L'Abate)

Chapter 9. Animation

Chapter 10. Tutorials

Chapter 11. Conferencing

Chapter 12. Wikis and blogs

Chapter 13. Technology with non-human participants. (David Washburn, GSU)

Section III. Conclusion

Chapter 14. Implications of technology for the science and practice of psychology, psychiatry, and mental health. (Luciano L'Abate & Nancy G. Bliwise)

Introduction of Mental Health Technology

Last but not least, we need to consider that technology has dominated the whole of American society from its very outset in most aspects of our lives (Klein, 2007; Marx & Mazlich, 2007). It inevitable, therefore, that this technology, whether some psychotherapists like it or not, is and will become an important part of clinical psychology, psychiatry, and mental health (L'Abate & Bliwise, 2008; L'Abate & Harwood, 2008), as summarized in Table 4. Implications of this technology as part of a revolution in mental health are incalculable and it would take too much time to discuss them here.

Part II. Systematic Background for the Use of Writing and Wellness

Systematic means a replicable sequence of clearly defined and enunciated steps that can be followed by professionals as well as by participants.

Importance of Structure and Replicability in Writing and Wellness

Since the beginning of my career I have remained convinced about the need to verify my guesses, hunches, or hypotheses about intimate relationships and how to improve them to see whether they were correct (valid) or incorrect (invalid) (L'Abate, 1976, 1986, 1990, 1992). That means that whatever is written about helping people needs to be verified by someone else rather than oneself. Whatever needs to be verified must be set in a replicable structure, as by creating enrichment programs for couples and families with *verbatim* instructions (L'Abate, 1977; L'Abate & Weinstein, 1987; L'Abate & Young, 1987). Without replicability there is no way to separate facts from fictions, reality from fantasy, sanity from insanity, anecdotal impressions from verified empirical evidence, and narcissistic self-interest from altruistic interest in the welfare of our clients, consumers, participants, or patients.

Constructive Pattern Checklist of Behaviors Necessary
to Discriminate Levels of Functioning in Individuals, Couples, and Families

Instructions

Frequency means how often a behavior occurs from minimal (1) to maximal (5)

Duration means how long a behavior lasts from short (1) to long (5)

Intensity means how strong a behavior is from weak (1) to very strong (5)

Satisfaction means how much pleasure a behavior produces from little (1) to great (5).

Circle the number that best represents how often, how long, how strong, and how satisfying a behavior listed below is from 1 to 5.

If an activity is not included in this list, there are two available spaces where its name can be written.

Please note that this questionnaire is still experimental and it has not been validated.

Individuals:	Frequency	Duration	Intensity	Satisfaction
Nutrition: Weight, height, diet, vitamins, supplements, herbs	1 2 3 4 5	1 2 3 4 5	1 2 3 4 5	1 2 3 4 5
Physical activities: Exercise, sports, hunting, games	1 2 3 4 5	1 2 3 4 5	1 2 3 4 5	1 2 3 4 5

Pleasant and pleasurable activities: Hobbies, collecting, gardening, & similar activities	1 2 3 4 5	1 2 3 4 5	1 2 3 4 5
Reading: Preferred books, magazines, newspapers	1 2 3 4 5	1 2 3 4 5	1 2 3 4 5
Television: How much time spent, programs watched, reliance on tapes, disks, etc.	1 2 3 4 5	1 2 3 4 5	1 2 3 4 5
Computer and Internet Use: Enrichment, education, extra home, school/work interests	1 2 3 4 5	1 2 3 4 5	1 2 3 4 5
Friendships: Nature of friends and frequency of meetings	1 2 3 4 5	1 2 3 4 5	1 2 3 4 5
Correspondence: Writing versus computer-driven e-mails, etc.	1 2 3 4 5	1 2 3 4 5	1 2 3 4 5
Use of Car: Strictly for work and shopping purposes, joy riding/vacations	1 2 3 4 5	1 2 3 4 5	1 2 3 4 5
Abuse: Alcohol, smoking, drugs, Internet	1 2 3 4 5	1 2 3 4 5	1 2 3 4 5
Volunteering: Where, when, for how long?	1 2 3 4 5	1 2 3 4 5	1 2 3 4 5
Other _____	1 2 3 4 5	1 2 3 4 5	1 2 3 4 5
Other _____	1 2 3 4 5	1 2 3 4 5	1 2 3 4 5

Couples and Families:	Frequency	Duration	Intensity	Satisfaction
Attending movies, plays, concerts, symphonies, or operas.	1 2 3 4 5	1 2 3 4 5	1 2 3 4 5	1 2 3 4 5
Camping and hiking	1 2 3 4 5	1 2 3 4 5	1 2 3 4 5	1 2 3 4 5
Cooking together	1 2 3 4 5	1 2 3 4 5	1 2 3 4 5	1 2 3 4 5
Eating together	1 2 3 4 5	1 2 3 4 5	1 2 3 4 5	1 2 3 4 5
Eating out	1 2 3 4 5	1 2 3 4 5	1 2 3 4 5	1 2 3 4 5
Playing cards or board games	1 2 3 4 5	1 2 3 4 5	1 2 3 4 5	1 2 3 4 5
Shopping together	1 2 3 4 5	1 2 3 4 5	1 2 3 4 5	1 2 3 4 5
Vacations	1 2 3 4 5	1 2 3 4 5	1 2 3 4 5	1 2 3 4 5
Watching at home together vs. apart: movies, DVD, TV	1 2 3 4 5	1 2 3 4 5	1 2 3 4 5	1 2 3 4 5
Other _____	1 2 3 4 5	1 2 3 4 5	1 2 3 4 5	1 2 3 4 5
Other _____	1 2 3 4 5	1 2 3 4 5	1 2 3 4 5	1 2 3 4 5

Feel free to add comments that relate to the activities listed by adding more information about these activities.

For instance, based on my clinical impressions, I made an egregious error by claiming repeatedly that written homework practice exercises were cost-effective by reducing the number of therapy sessions (L'Abate, Gahnal, & Hansen, 1986). However, when we went over our 25 years of part-time private practice with individuals, couples, and families, we actually found the opposite: practice exercise administration increased significantly the number of therapy sessions in participants who received written homework versus those who did not receive them (L'Abate, L'Abate, & Maino, 2005). These results were somewhat contradicted by Damian Goldstein in Buenos Aires using a problem-solving workbook with decompensating women with personality disorders in a charity hospital (L'Abate & Goldstein, 2007). Therefore, the jury is still out on cost-effectiveness of homework and written practice exercises.

An even more egregious error may lie in my claiming the usefulness of the dictionary in helping participants "think" through a variety of definitions in many practice exercises created over the last two decades, as described above (L'Abate, 2007a, 2008b, in press-b). A recent study with undergraduates at the University of Padua failed to show main effects or interactions of dictionary administration versus no dictionary (Eleonora Maino, personal communication, June 10, 2008). Of course, one single study is not sufficient to validate or invalidate my original claim. More evidence will be necessary to support or impugn the possibly erroneous nature of that claim, that is, to help participants to think in better ways than it would be possible without a dictionary. I feel that without a dictionary many participants would flounder and eventually give up. The dictionary, therefore, would serve as a prosthetic tool to help participants think more clearly and more directly. Whether this hunch is valid or not needs to be verified by someone other than myself.

The first application of the dictionary dealt with definitions of hurt feelings that anecdotally produced significant emotional reactions in Italian undergraduates, requiring the signing of an Informed Consent Form. We will have to see what results will come from administering the same homework to addicts and inmates (Eleonora Maino, personal communication, June 10, 2008). We expect explosions and anger in this kind of population, if my hypothesis is correct that these as well as other troubled individuals in general avoid and have avoided hurt feelings most of their lives through denial, repression, and suppression (Bonanno et al., 2005; L'Abate, 2008b, in press; Roemer et al., 2005). Consequently, the jury about the use of the dictionary in writing is still out (L'Abate, in press-a). The first series of practice exercises dealt with the nature of hurt feelings. A second series of practice exercises deals with the causes of hurt feelings (L'Abate, 2008b).

Very likely, the use of the dictionary might work with some participants better than others, with certain practice exercises better than others, and with certain populations better than others. We cannot claim that any method of intervention will produce pall-mall positive effects on everybody. We need to specify how a particular approach will work with specific individuals, under what relational conditions, and at what cost. For instance, low literacy is a recognized barrier to efficient and effective health care. In mental health low literacy may have additional detrimental effects. Chronic mental illness may lead to deterioration in literacy by limiting opportunities for reading and writing, as well as for formal education and vocational training (Sentell & Skumway, 2003). Therefore, the dictionary may be a possible avenue of entrance into a treatment modality and possible enhancement of people who have difficulty with words and writing.

Rationale for the Usefulness of Writing to Promote Wellness

For some years, De Giacomo, his collaborators, and I have been involved in studying the effects of selected phrases that seem relevant to participants (De Giacomo et al., 2007, 2008, submitted for publication, a & b; L'Abate & De Giacomo, 2003). At the same time, Duane M. Rumbaugh, my former boss at GSU and a noted primatologist, was proposing a salience theory of learning that essentially debunks Skinner's mechanistic and simplistic response-reinforcement model. Rumbaugh posited an Amalgam of underlying internal sensations that become salient when matched with related and relevant environmental stimulations. Additionally, philosophers like Fredrick Schick wrote about the Ambiguity of language while Ludwig Wittgenstein wrote about the Arbitrariness of language. Consequently, we expanded Pennebaker's notion (Pennebaker & Chung, 2007) about going from an Analogic to Digital process when we talk or write. This model is derived from Pennebaker's expressive writing paradigm and from his even more exciting research on word usage. The progression from Analogic to Digital is a model strongly supported by Pinker's work (2007). This progression indicates that language and, of course, writing, involves a digital process: putting into words unspoken experiences that are essentially analogic at the internal experiential level (De Giacomo, L'Abate, Pennebaker, & Rumbaugh, 2008).

Putting two and two together from various sources, an Ambiguous, Analogic Amalgam or an Amorphous internal mass, I am convinced that what was called by all these scholars and researchers, that is: an ill-defined or undefined amorphous mass constitutes what Freud called our unconscious along a dimension of awareness ranging from extreme unconscious to semi-conscious to pre-conscious and to conscious (Bargh & Williams, 2007; Fitzsimons & Bargh, 2004; Kinsbourne, 2005; L'Abate, 2008a, in press-a; Laird & Strout, 2007; Ohman, 1993, 2000; Stegge & Terwogt, 2007; Wiens & Ohman, 2007).

The Importance and Dangers of Addressing Hurt Feelings in Writing

What does this mysterious unconscious consists of? It is the *ambiguous, undefined, amorphous amalgam* depository of our salient, pent-up, avoided, denied, repressed, and suppressed hurt feelings inevitably accumulated during the course our lifetime. We are all subject to being hurt by and to hurt those we love and who love us. We may be hurt physically by strangers, of course, either accidentally or by design.

However, those hurts do not count as much as those produced to and by those we love.

Consequently, when we ask people to write or talk about a topic such as traumas in Pennebaker's paradigm, or hurt feelings, as done by Eleonora Maino, what are we doing? I propose that we are tapping and giving digital words to a heretofore ambiguous, ill-defined, unclear mass of salient memories and feelings that have not yet had the chance to be expressed and shared with loved ones. This unconscious, semi-conscious, pre-conscious, and at times conscious mass consists of hurt feelings, a topic that has been consistently avoided by scientific researchers and mental health professionals. We may want to approach pleasure and we may try to avoid pain but we may not succeed in the pursuit of either goal (L'Abate, 2008a, in press-a).

In functional individuals and relationships hurt feelings are approached, expressed, and shared with loved ones (family and friends), verbally, non-verbally, as in crying together, or in writing, allowing these feelings to dissipate and disappear over time through a process of intimacy, the sharing of joys and of hurt feelings as well as fears of being hurt. In dysfunctional individuals and relationships hurt feelings are avoided through ridicule, put-downs, and abuse (Bonanno et al., 2005; L'Abate, 1997; Roemer et al., 2005). Consequently, in these individuals and their immediate, proximal relationships hurt feelings are kept inside to fester and to damage individuals and their intimate relationships. There is little if any intimacy in these dysfunctional relationships, except at funerals or weddings (L'Abate, 2005).

Gogol (1842) described the surge of the unconscious better than anyone else I know, many years earlier than Freud. When Chichikov, the social psychopathic hero of his story, was found out for all his past misdeeds, imprisoned, and without any hope of getting out of prison, he was trying to explain his behavior to his benefactor Mourazov:

> Chichikov now felt welling up in him hitherto unfamiliar and inexplicable feelings, it was as something was striving to come to light, something remote and out of the depths — something

belonging to his childhood years which had been repressed by the harsh and formal upbringing he had received, by the unaffectionate and sad character of his childhood years, by the desert-like emptiness of his home life, by the isolation of his family life which was poor and beggarly in its initial impressions... And it was as though this repressed something, long daunted by the harsh glance of fate, which had stared at him gloomily through a misty snow-covered window, was now striving to set itself free (p. 451).

I cannot think of any scientific or professional writing expressing this process better than Gogol.

Current Research on Hurt Feelings in Italy

If I may be allowed a personal note, since my retirement from teaching and from private practice, I consider myself lucky to have collaborators like Mario Cusinato and his collaborators at the University of Padua and Piero De Giacomo and his co-workers at the University of Bari. They have helped me evaluate the validity of various models in relational competence theory with 50+ doctoral dissertations (Cusinato et al., 2008) as well as programmed writing or practice exercises. In Padua, these collaborators have been using undergraduates, addicts, or inmates, while in Bari they have employed psychiatric patients. These populations are no longer available to me. The interest and enthusiasm of these colleagues in working with me have made the last years of my life worth living, allowing me to produce and to publish beyond my wildest expectations.

Discussion

The bottom line about writing is whether it produces positive or negative changes in participants who use it. In addition to a meta-analysis of self-help, mental health practice exercises that produced significant effect sizes (Smyth & L'Abate, 2001), my professional experience with programmed writing has usually been focused on decreasing the impulsivity of acting-out youth and incarcerated inmates (L'Abate, 1992, 2008b). Some participants I have also seen face-to-face professionally, therefore it would be difficult to evaluate whether any changes that might have occurred for the better were due to the relationship or to written practice exercises. However, I have been able to work with two inmates I have never seen face-to-face. Both were evaluated before and after termination of written homework practice exercises. Both showed positive changes, at least psychometrically and by self-report, one in lowering impulsivity and the other decreasing the initial level of depression that was the reason for referral. In other words, I believe that behavior, functional and dysfunctional can be improved through distance writing without ever seeing participants face-to-face, as it is already occurring every day on the Internet (L'Abate, 2008b).

If distance writing can be demonstrated to be more cost-effective than talk, then we can expect and predict that given two different methods to help troubled people positively, we should choose the least expensive first, such as distance writing, before initiating, instituting, or switching to the more expensive method such as talk (L'Abate, 2007a, 2008b, in press-b).

Conclusion

There is no doubt in my mind that writing will become the predominant medium of intervention in mental health promotion, prevention, psychotherapy, and rehabilitation in this century because talk is too expensive and too difficult to record, replicate, analyze, and codify. That does not mean and is not meant to mean that talk is not important. It is meant to mean that to help people in trouble we need to rely on as many media and approaches as are available to us and to them. All three media — verbal, written, and non-verbal — are equally important and we should use all three as much as necessary, sensitively and responsibly (L'Abate, 2002). After devoting the first two decades of my professional career to talk and the next two decades to writing, in the fifth decade of my life, I am now working on the third non-verbal medium of communication: play across the life cycle (L'Abate, in press-c).

References

Bargh, J. A., & Williams, L. E. (2007). The nonconscious regulation of emotions. In J. J. Gross (Ed.), *Handbook of emotion regulation* (pp. 429-444). New York: Guilford.

Bonanno, G. A., Papa, A., Lalande, K., Zhang, N., et al. (2005). Grief processing and deliberate grief avoidance: A prospective comparison of bereaved spouses and parents in the United States and in the People's Republic of China. *Journal of Consulting & Clinical Psychology, 73*, 86-98.

Clum, G. A., & Watkins, P. L. (2008). Self-help therapies: Retrospect and prospect. In P. L. Watkins & G. A. Clum (Eds.), *Handbook of self-help therapies* (pp. 419-436). New York: Rutledge.

Cusinato, M., Maino, E., Colesso, W., Scilletta, C., & L'Abate, L. (2008). Evidence for a hierarchical theory of relational competence. Manuscript submitted for publication.

De Giacomo, P., L'Abate, L., Margari, F., De Giacomo, A., Santamo, W., & Masellis, R. (2008). Sentences with strong psychological impact in psychotherapy: Research in progress. *Journal of Contemporary Psychotherapy, 38*, 65-72.

De Giacomo, P., L'Abate, L, Santamato, W., Sgobio, A., Tarquinio, C., De Giacomo, A., Iadicicco, R., & Masellis, R. (2007). Compass sentences with strong psychological impact in family therapy: Preliminary investigations. *Journal of Family Psychotherapy, 18*, 45-69.

De Giacomo, P., L'Abate, L., Pennebaker, J. M., & Rumbaugh, D. M. (2008). Amplifications and applications of Pennebaker's analogic to digital model in health promotion, prevention, and psychotherapy. Manuscript submitted for publication.

Detweiler-Bedell, J. B., & Whisman, M. A. (2005). A lesson in assigning homework: Therapist, client, and task characteristics in cognitive therapy for depression. *Professional Psychology: Research and Practice, 36*, 219-223.

Fitzsimons, G.M., & Bargh, J. A. (2004). Automatic self-regulation. In R. F. Baumeister & K. D. Vohs (Eds), *Handbook of self-regulation: Research, theory, and applications* (pp. 151-170). New York: Guilford.

Gogol, N. (1842/1948). *Dead souls*. New York: Pantheon Books.

Harwood, T. M., & L'Abate, L.. (in press). *The self-help movement in mental health: A critical evaluation*. New York: Springer.

Kazantzis, N., Deane, F. P., Ronan, K. R., L'Abate, L. (Eds). (2005). *Using homework assignments in cognitive behavior therapy*. New York; Routledge.

Kazantzis, N., & L'Abate, L. (Eds.). (2007). *Handbook of homework assignments in psychotherapy: Theory, research, and prevention*. New York: Springer.

Kinsbourne, M. (2005). A continuum of self-consciousness that emerges in phylogeny and ontogeny. In H. S., Terrace, & J. Metcalfe (Eds.). *The missing link in cognition: Origins of self-reflective consciousness* (pp. 142-156). New York: Oxford University Press.

Klein, M. (2007). *The power makers: Steam, electricity, and the men who invented modern America*. New York: Bloomsbury.

L'Abate, L. (1976). *Understanding and helping the individual in the family*. New York: Grune & Stratton.

L'Abate, L. (1977). *Enrichment: Structured interventions with couples, families, and groups*. Washington, DC: University Press of America.

L'Abate, L. (1986). *Systematic family therapy*. New York: Brunner/Mazel.

L'Abate, L. (1990). *Building family competence: Primary and secondary prevention strategies.* Newbury Park, CA: Sage.

L'Abate, L. (1992). *Programmed writing: A self-administered approach for interventions with individuals, couples, and families.* Pacific Grove, CA: Brooks/Cole.

L'Abate, L. (2005). *Personality in intimate relationships: Socialization and psycho-pathology.* New York: Springer.

L'Abate, L. (Ed.). (2001). *Distance writing and computer-assisted interventions in psychiatry and mental health.* Westport, CT: Ablex.

L'Abate, L. 2002). *Beyond psychotherapy: Programmed writing and structured computer-assisted interventions.* Westport, CT: Ablex.

L'Abate, L. (2003). *Family Psychology III: Theory-building, theory-testing, and psychological interventions.* Lanham, MD: University Press of America.

L'Abate, L. (Ed.). (2004a). *A guide to self-help mental health practice exercises for clinicians and researchers.* Binghamton, NY: Haworth.

L'Abate, L. (Ed.). (2004b). *Using practice exercises in prevention, psychotherapy, and rehabilitation: A resource for clinicians and researchers.* Binghamton,, NY: Haworth.

L'Abate, L. (2007a). A completely preposterous proposal: The dictionary as an initial vehicle of behavior change in the family. *The Family Psychologist, 23,* 39-43.

L'Abate, L. (Ed.). (2007b). *Low-cost interventions to promote physical and mental health: Theory, research, and practice,* New York: Springer.

L'Abate, L. (2008a). *Hurt feelings: The fundamental but neglected affects.* Manuscript submitted for publication.

L'Abate, L. (2008b). *Sourcebook of interactive exercises in mental health.* New York: Springer.

L'Abate, L. (Ed.). (2008c). *Toward a science of clinical psychology: Laboratory evaluations and interventions.* Hauppauge, NY: Nova Science Publishers.

L'Abate, L. (2008d). Working at a distance from participants: Writing and nonverbal media. In L. L'Abate (Ed.), *Toward a science of clinical psychology: Laboratory evaluations and interventions* (pp. 355-383). Hauppauge, NY: Nova Science Publishers.

L'Abate, L. (in press-a). Hurt feelings: The last taboo for researchers and clinicians? In L. Vangelisti (Ed.), *Handbook of hurt feelings in close relationships* (pp. 000-000). New York: Cambridge University Press.

L'Abate, L. (in press-b). Proposal for including distance writing in couple therapy. *Journal of Couple & Relationship Therapy.*

L'Abate, L. (in press-c). *The Praeger handbook of play across the life cycle: Fun from infancy to old age.* Westport, CT: Praeger.

L'Abate, L, & Bliwise, N. G. (2008). *Handbook of technology in psychology, psychiatry, and mental health.* Proposal submitted for editorial consideration.

L'Abate. L., & De Giacomo, P. (2003). *Improving intimate relationships: Integration of theoretical models with preventions and psychotherapy applications.* Westport, CT: Praeger.

L'Abate, L., Ganahl, G., & Hansen, J. C. (1986). *Methods of family therapy.* Englewood Cliffs, NJ: Prentice-Hall.

L'Abate, L., & Goldstein, J. (2007). Practice exercises to promote mental health and life-long learning. In L. L'Abate (Ed.), *Low-cost approaches to promote physical and mental health: Theory, research, and Practice* (pp. 285-303). New York: Springer.

L'Abate, L., & Harwood, T. M. (2008). *Toward a technology for clinical psychology: The future is now.* Manuscript submitted for publication.

L'Abate, L., L'Abate, B. L., & Maino, E. (2005). A review of 25 years of part-time professional practice: Practice exercises and length of psychotherapy. *American Journal of Family Therapy, 33,* 19-31.

L'Abate, L., & McHenry, S. (1983). *Handbook of marital interventions.* New York: Grune & Stratton.

L'Abate, L. & S. E. Weinstein, S. E. (1987). *Structured enrichment programs for couples and families.* New York: Brunner/Mazel.

L'Abate, L., & Young, L. (1987). *Casebook of structured enrichment programs for couples and families.* New York: Brunner/Mazel.

Laird, J. D., & Strout, S. (2007). Emotional behaviors as emotional stimuli. In J. A. Coan & J. B. Allen (Eds.), *Handbook of emotion elicitation and assessment* (pp. 54-64). New York: Oxford University Press.

Lange, A., Rietdijk, D., Hudcovicova, M., van de Ven, J-P, et al., (2003). Interplay: A controlled randomized trial of the standardized treatment of posttraumatic stress through the Internet. *Journal of Consulting & Clinical Psychology, 71,* 901-909.

Marx, L., & Mazlich, B. (Eds.). (2007). *A culture of improvement: Technology and the Western Millennium.* Cambridge, MA: MIT Press.

Ohman, A. (1993). Fear and anxiety as emotional phenomena: Clinical phenomenology, evolutionary perspectives, and information-processing mechanisms. In M. Lewis & J. M. Haviland (Eds.), *Handbook of emotions* (pp. 511-536). New York: Guilford.

Ohman, A. (2000). Fear and anxiety: Evolutionary, cognitive, and clinical perspectives. In M. Lewis & J. M. Haviland-Jones (Eds.), *Handbook of emotions. Second Edition* (pp. 573-593). New York: Guilford.

Pennebaker, J. W., & Chung, C. K. (2007). Expressive writing, emotional upheavals, and health. In H. Friedman & B. Silver (Eds.), *Handbook of health psychology* (pp. 263-284). New York: Oxford University Press.

Pinker, S. (2007). *The stuff of thought: Language as a window into human nature.* New York: Viking.

Ritterband, L. M., Cox, D. J., Walker, L. S., Kovatchev, B., et al. (2003a). An Internet intervention as adjunctive therapy for pediatric encopresis. *Journal of Consulting & Clinical Psychology, 71,* 910-917.

Ritterband, L. M., Gonder-Frederick, L. A., Cox, D. J., Clifton, A. D., et al. (2003b). Internet interventions: In review, in use, and into the future. *Professional Psychology: Research & Practice, 34,* 527-534.

Roemer, L., Salter, K., Raffa, S. D., & Orsillo, S. M. (2005). Fear and avoidance of internal experience in GAD: Preliminary tests of a conceptual model. *Cognitive Therapy & Research, 29,* 71-88.

Sentell, T. L., & Skumway, M. A. (2003). Low literacy and mental illness in a nationally representative sample. *Journal of Nervous & Mental Disease, 191,* 459-552.

Watkins, P.L. & Clum, G.A. (Eds.). (2008). *Handbook of self-help therapies.* New York: Rutledge.

Part Two:
Genres of Wellness and Writing Connections

4

Poetry Therapy, a Healing Art: History and Practice

Debbie McCulliss

Poetry therapy touches and affirms our humanity.
— Nicholas Mazza

History

Creative self-expression has been an important part of healing since the beginning of history. Biblical poetry such as the Psalms and the Song of Solomon speaks of love and offers comfort amid suffering. In primitive time shamans and healers chanted poetry for the well-being of the tribe or individual during religious rites (Poetry as Healer, 2006). In ancient Egypt, sacred words were chanted in rituals to promote healing or words were written on papyrus and then dissolved into a solution so that the words could be physically ingested by the patient and take effect as quickly as possible (Poetry Therapy, 2009). Chanting was thought to help bring about change in self, others, or the environment. In ancient Greece, medicine and the arts were entwined; Apollo was the god of both poetry and medicine. Aristotle discussed catharsis in *Poetics*, expounding his belief that literature had the capacity to stir up emotions and purge unhealthy feelings, to renew and heal the human spirit (Kaster &

Burroughs, 1993). The Greeks designated libraries as healing places and left poems in shrines in remembrance of their healing. In ancient Rome, psychological healing took place in temple theatres dedicated to Aesculapius, the god of medicine and healing. Historically, the first Poetry Therapist on record was Soranus, a Roman physician, who in the first century A.D. prescribed tragedy for his manic patients and comedy for those who were depressed (Poetry Therapy, 2009).

William Wordsworth, an English poet, wrote the following lines in 1807 in "Ode on Intimations of Immorality from Recollections of Early Childhood":

> To me alone, there came a thought of grief:
> A timely utterance gave that thought relief
> And I again am strong.

Whether it was his intention or not, these words appear to reinforce the idea that poetry can provide an emotional release and perhaps an emotional cure. Benjamin Rush MD, the "Father of American Psychiatry," believed in the healing effect of literature, as he was the first American to prescribe poetry as an adjunct to mental health care at Pennsylvania Hospital, the first hospital in the United States. It was here, around 1810, that Rush designed a grand library where self-directed patients could go to the library and read, write, or publish poetry to gain insight into personal issues. Many of the poems were published in their own newspaper, *The Illuminator* (Poetry Therapy, 2009).

Beginnings, organizations, publications: In 1916 Samuel McChord Crothers, essayist, first used the term "bibliotherapy" to describe literature that may have a therapeutic effect in an article, "A Literary Clinic," that appeared in the *Atlantic Monthly* (1916, v.118, pp. 291-301). In the 1920s, hospital librarians who saw the value in bibliotherapy, searched out and selected reading materials specifically for their potential to help psychiatric patients understand themselves by drawing them out of themselves. There was no facilitated discussion of the reader's personal reaction to the material.

In the 1950s, Eli Greifer, a pharmacist, attorney, and poet, began a "poemtherapy" group at Creedmore State Hospital in New York City. However, it was Greifer and Smiley Blanton, psychiatrist, who gave Poetry Therapy its name when they proposed poetry as a tool to be used in an interactive process between therapist and client. Reading bibliotherapy became interactive bibliotherapy/poetry therapy. Greifer, with supervision from psychiatrists Jack J. Leedy, and Sam Spector, established the first formal United States poetry therapy group at Cumberland Hospital in Brooklyn, New York, in 1959. Guided reading was used to learn about and develop insight into illness, stimulate catharsis, and aid in the healing process.

The popularity of poetry therapy was gaining momentum. As a take-off from his work at Cumberland, Dr. Leedy's love of poetry therapy led to the creation of the Association for Poetry Therapy (APT) in 1969. Morris R. Morrison, PhD, poet, educator, and author of *Poetry as Therapy* (1986), drafted the initial standards for certification in this fledgling field. Morrison was also the founder of the American Academy of Poetry Therapy in Austin, Texas.

In 1973, California psychologist and widely published poet, Arthur Lerner, PTR,[1] author of *Poetry in the Therapeutic Experience*, founded and directed the Poetry Therapy Institute. This was a nonprofit organization devoted to the study and practice of poetry therapy. The following year, Sister Arleen McCarty Hynes created the first comprehensive poetry therapy training program, utilizing Morrison's standards. A librarian at St. Elizabeth's Hospital in Washington, DC, her work was encouraged and supported by Dr. Kenneth Gorelick, a dedicated psychiatrist who contributed greatly to the field.

During these same years, a multitude of books on the subject were published. *The Healing Power of Poetry*, a book on poetry therapy and

---

[1] In 2006, the abbreviated designation for Registered Poetry Therapist — RPT — was changed to avoid confusion with Registered Physical Therapists (RPTs) and Registered Play Therapists (also RPTs).

its therapeutic value, was written by Blanton in 1960 based on several years of practice; Greifer published a pamphlet, *Principles of Poetry Therapy*, in 1963. Leedy continued Greifer's work and compiled and edited two major works in the field of poetry therapy, *Poetry Therapy: The Use of Poetry in the Treatment of Emotional Disorders (1969)* and *Poetry, the Healer (1973).* Books published in 1978 that further advanced the field of bibliotherapy/poetry therapy include *Bibliotherapy: A Guide to Theory and Practice* and *Bibliotherapy Source Book* by Rhea Joyce Rubin and *Poetry in the Therapeutic Experience,* a book on practice, theory, and research, by Lerner.

Poetry therapy received additional support and acknowledgment as a distinct field under the auspice of The National Coalition of Arts Therapies Association. Formed in 1979, this coalition of six professional associations was dedicated to the advancement of the arts as therapeutic modalities.

In 1981, APT became the National Association of Poetry Therapy (NAPT), a non-profit membership organization that represents poetry therapists. Today, the mission of NAPT is to bring together diverse practitioners to promote growth and healing through language, symbol, and story with individuals, couples, families, groups, and communities in different settings, worldwide. The *Museletter* was created to serve as the official newsletter of the NAPT. The Association and NAPT Foundation support the field through annual conferences, publications, publicity, fellowship, resource sharing, grants, scholarships, and special projects.

One such project was *Giving Sorrow Words: Poems of Strength and Solace*, an anthology of original poems by internationally renowned poets including Lawrence Ferlinghetti, Billy Collins, Ellen Bass, Robert Bly, Lucille Clifton, Denise Levertov, and Naomi Shihab Nye. It was written in response to the terrorist attacks on September 11, 2001, and published in 2002, as a resource to the global community.

In 1985, chapters from both of Leedy's books were published in *Poetry as Healer: Mending the Troubled Mind.* In 1986, Hynes and her daughter, Mary Hynes-Berry, wrote the first comprehensive text,

Bibliotherapy — The Interactive Process: A Handbook, a landmark book in the field of biblio-poetry therapy and a primary textbook in the certification program.

In 2000, the National Federation for Biblio/Poetry Therapy, an organization created to address current educational standards of excellence in the field, became the only organization in the field of poetry therapy to grant credentialing. Poetry therapists are required to be grounded in psychology and literature, as well as group dynamics. In order to obtain the Certified Applied Poetry Facilitator (CAPF) designation, non-mental-health-related professionals must successfully complete a 440-hour developmental training program that includes 120 facilitation hours. Licensed mental health professionals who complete the 440-hour program are designated as Certified Poetry Therapists (CPT). Successful completion of a 975-hour clinical training program that includes 300 facilitation hours is required for clinical therapists to become a Poetry Therapist-Registered (PTR).

For more than twenty years, Mazza has been the dedicated editor of NAPT's *Journal of Poetry Therapy: The Interdisciplinary Journal of Practice, Theory, Research and Education*, a comprehensive source of current theory, research, and techniques. He published *Poetry Therapy: Theory and Practice* in 2003, presenting a unified model for the effective practice of poetry therapy. In the same year, NAPT executive members, Geri Giebel Chavis, PhD, CPT, and Lila Lizabeth Weisberger, MS, PTR, published *The Healing Fountain: Poetry Therapy for Life's Journey*. In 2007, *Layers of Possibility: Healing Poetry from the National Association for Poetry Therapy Members* was published.

Practice: Poetry Therapy in Action

Poetry therapy is an interactive, structured process. Sherry Reiter, CSW, PTR, RDT, and past president of NAPT, wrote in her 1977 report, "Poetry Therapy: Testimony on Capitol Hill," that the basic goal of poetry therapy is to promote change. Although there are threads of connection and application between psychology and poetry therapy, specific goals of poetry therapy are therapeutic, not diagnostic like those of psychiatry or psychological counseling, and include:

- To improve the capacity to respond to vivid images and concepts, and the feelings aroused by them;
- To enhance self-understanding and accuracy in self-perception;
- To increase awareness of interpersonal relationships;
- To heighten reality orientation;
- To develop creativity, self-expression, and greater self-esteem;
- To encourage positive thinking and creative problem-solving;
- To strengthen communication, particularly listening and speaking skills;
- To integrate the different aspects of the self for psychological wholeness;
- To ventilate overpowering emotions and release tension;
- To find new meaning through new ideas, insights, and/or information; and
- To help participants experience the liberating and nourishing qualities of beauty. (*Journal of Poetry Therapy*, Vol. 10, No. 3, 1997)

Choosing literature and poems: T. S. Elliot, in his poem, *We Shall Not Cease* (from Little Gidding), writes

> We shall not cease from exploration
> And the end of all our exploring
> Will be to arrive where we started
> And know the place for the first time.

These words summarize what a facilitator hopes to effect in a poetry therapy session: leading a client back to oneself. To that extent, there are countless forms of literature besides poetry that can be used in poetry therapy, including short stories, storytelling, articles, fables, myths, fairy tales, plays, novels, memoirs, journal writing, songs, and videos. Literature is not chosen for literary merit, but as a tool for awareness and self-discovery. This is what makes the work distinct from teaching. When used for therapeutic purposes, literature is discussed as an independent entity serving as a catalyst for guided dialogue. It evokes feeling responses for discussion and must be powerful in content and relevance to participants. Literature should have evocative value, be easily understood, use simple, clear language and universal subject matter, thereby increasing accessibility and bridging cross-cultural gaps. It is positive, stimulates the senses through concrete imagery, is short enough to hold attention, and always offers hope. The facilitator should be very familiar with the poem but the literature carries itself, almost like a co-facilitator.

It is important to note choosing the right poem is critical and *not all poems can be used for therapeutic purposes.* The repetition of words or images carries weight. Line breaks and white space provide breath and can underscore esthetic and/or physical involvement, metaphor helps language move beyond the literal, rhythm is related to emotion, cadence is carried in the sound, pitches, and beat of the words and can help shift a reader from one place to another, and similes assert a likeness between unlike things while drawing attention to their differences. Poems do not have to rhyme.

Poetry therapy always involves projection onto the poem so it is difficult to facilitate one's own poem without a high risk of transference and counter-transference. Among the many classic and contemporary poems that can be used for therapeutic and/or educational purposes, are *The Guest House*, Rumi; *The Road Not Taken*, Robert Frost; *The Journey*, Mary Oliver; and *Talking to Grief*, Denise Levertov.

Leadership, facilitation, group specifics, and examples: Poetry therapy lends itself to different styles of leadership. Credentialed facilitators are professional, self-confident, perceptive, sensitive, empathetic, genuine, nonjudgmental, accepting, respectful, and skilled listeners. Guidelines for facilitators include: don't force, don't push, don't take control, don't show favoritism, and always put the desires of participants as individuals first (rather than themselves or the group as an entity). Personal disclosure is okay as part of the process as long as it is mindful and contained in a teachable moment. It is important to remember that the process of growth may be slow and almost imperceptible. The facilitator's personal satisfaction is not the primary goal of facilitating a session; the facilitator's primary goal is further growth and self-understanding for each participant through the use of literature/poetry.

Poetry therapy has been shown to be successful in many different populations. Developmental poetry therapy uses literature and creative writing to promote growth and development in healthy populations, for example, adolescents and seniors and others managing various developmental or situational challenges, such as war veterans or prisoners. Clinical poetry therapy uses literature and creative writing to promote healing and growth in populations requiring treatment for a variety of illnesses and conditions including those that do not respond to traditional modalities, for example, Alzheimer's and cancer patients, and people suffering from depression.

To better address group and individual needs, it is helpful to speak to each interested person ahead of time to screen, clarify the purpose of the group, identify expectations, and flush out any major misconceptions. When organizing a group, size is a factor. The optimal group size is typically eight or less to ensure that everyone will have a chance to participate and that the material and any issues can be examined in sufficient depth in the course of a session. As different populations, as well as individuals within these populations, have different therapeutic goals and needs, a facilitation plan is prepared ahead of time specific to each group.

A non-threatening atmosphere — a sacred space — is necessary for participants to feel safe and supported to bring up and share thoughts, feelings, and ideas openly and honestly. Sessions take place in a suitable quiet, convenient, and accessible location (public areas are not recommended). Comfort needs such as temperature of the room, lighting, restroom availability, writing surface, room set-up, and seating arrangements (typically circle format) are addressed. Sessions are held at regularly scheduled intervals and are sixty to ninety minutes long. They can be shorter when indicated, for example, when working with children or the ill. The group and facilitator together will determine the number of sessions and can choose to terminate the group when the purpose of the group has been achieved.

At the first meeting, a handout of ground rules is distributed followed by a welcome and introductions. A norm of confidentiality and group rules are established including: what is said in the group stays in the group and respect for each other (arriving on time and not leaving early, turning off cell phones). Helpful introductions may include the use of nametags that participants can draw personally symbolic images on or having participants say their name and one thing unique to them that most people don't know.

For a series of sessions, poems are structured under the umbrella of one theme, such as empowerment or identity, and meet overarching goals. However, original plans are sometimes abandoned to meet the needs of the group. In situations where there may be frequent turnover of participants, special adaptations will need to be made to avoid a sense of superficiality and fragmentation. Referrals are made as needed to appropriate mental health professionals.

Typically, a session begins with a call for silence or with the ringing of a bell. Starting rituals may include the use of background music or candles, keeping in mind some people may be sensitive to certain smells. This would be followed by warm-up prompts. One or two warm-up prompts related to the selected material or theme for the session help participants transition the mind, be present, focus, and engage more deeply with the material. Resources in the poetic toolbox, used in connection with the initial warm-up prompts, that are usually well received include: entrance meditations, visualization, drawing, collage, writing exercises, journal-writing techniques, arts and crafts, picking words from a bowl, or realia (objects connected to poems/exercises) such as stones, sea shells, and postcards. Colored pens, pencils, markers, and paper can be kept on hand.

Participants are encouraged to share their creative writing, drawing, or their poems, genuine feeling reactions, and unique interpretations throughout the session. They can reveal as much or as little as they want. Although the act of self-expression does not always lead to therapeutic self-understanding, self-expression and self-exploration are encouraged. For some, this may include full self-disclosure. Participants are encouraged to give themselves permission to be open to the experience, engage themselves fully, and accept the process. Each person is given equal opportunity to speak freely and be listened to without interruptions or interpretation from others. Silence is okay, crying is okay, but side conversations are not acceptable. Energy for the group should be redirected if the silence is a resistant, nervous, or defiant silence.

During the first stage of the interactive process, poems are distributed facedown to each participant, and then turned over to be read by everyone at the same time. The poems are then read two or three times by one or more participants from beginning to end or by stanza or line. Poems are not to be read silently. Hearing one's voice out loud, moments of silence, reading emotionally rather than intellectually, and taking in the words visually when reading are all important aspects of poetry therapy. Recognition happens when participants identify with the selection or become aware of something for the first time. "Aha" moments may be experienced when one recognizes existential truths.

The great English poet Lord Byron once said, "Poetry is the lava of the imagination whose eruptions prevent the earthquake." William Blake, poet, painter, and mystic, in his poem, *I Was Angry with My Friend*, calls for expression of feelings directly and honestly

> I was angry with my friend:
> I told my wrath,
> My wrath did end.
> I was angry with my foe:
> I told it not,
> My wrath did grow.

Amy Christman, poet and poetry therapy trainee, in her poem, *Make Use of Suffering*, writes

Choose
to either bury or nurture the
suffering that forms the chrysalis
from which you must finally emerge.

Examination, the second stage of the interactive process, happens when the poem is discussed. The facilitator asks questions that probe, focus, explore reactions and responses, and invite application to the self — questions that may take the dialogue deeper, such as, "What does the poem mean to you? What's your best guess for what this poem is saying to you? What does a specific line, phrase, or word trigger in you? Where did this poem land in you? What word or phrase do you most connect with? Where do you see yourself in this poem?"

Juxtaposition, the third stage of the interactive process, happens when participants gain insight from exploring the interplay between contrast and comparisons. For example, Robert Frost's poem *The Road Not Taken* is about coming to a fork in the road and having to make a choice. While this particular message seems straightforward, participants may come to different interpretations; there is no single best interpretation of any poem. In fact, poems don't necessarily have to be understood. A negative reaction to a poem is okay. Participants may be asked, "Which line do you dislike the most, the least?" Participants can be encouraged to write about what they didn't like about the poem, what words they would change, or what it would take for them to like the poem. The key is asking the "right" questions, which means active listening and flexibility on the part of the facilitator.

A session often ends after the facilitator suggests a couple more writing prompts, inviting participants to ponder and let their thoughts flow through their pens. All writing is done in timed spurts, typically five to ten minutes. Sessions are ended with prompts that, unlike prompts offered in the body of the session, direct focus back outward instead of continuing inward — closing the circle/process rather than deepening/opening it further. This allows for a winding down, a conscious movement back into reality.

At the end of the session, the facilitator can ask, "What one word comes to mind that you take away from this session?" The last session of a series could be celebrated through careful selection of a poem such as *The Healing Time*, by Pesha Joyce Gertler, poet and educator, *The Writing Group* by Perie Longo, PhD, PTR, or *The Larger Circle* by Wendell Berry.

Formal evaluation can be obtained through a summary evaluation. Questions can be asked: "What did you learn about yourself? What did you like best/least? Was what you expected to gain out of this group obtained? or How was the group for you today?" Observations can be made including the following: steady attendance; little turnover; promptness on arrival, leaving on time; active participation; body language; eye contact, active listening, increase in socialization, mutual support, reassurance, and compassion; openness, self-disclosure, degree of insight, and depth of responses; improved self-esteem, clarity on a personal issue, physical or emotional healing, positive feelings, and identified change or personal growth; or a satisfying, affirming or validating experience is reported.

The answers to these questions and the observations made leads to the fourth and final stage of the interactive process. This happens when participants' feelings and concepts are genuinely experienced in the real world.

In conclusion, poetry therapy is a unique and powerful form of communication and is effective if:

- Participants feel affirmed, noticed, seen, connected, understood, and empowered;
- Trust is established;
- Containment provides safety;
- Attitudes and perspectives are changed;
- Energy is shifted;
- Synergy occurs;
- Commonality is experienced; the truth of one's own experience is reflected back in a recognizable form;

- Emotions are inspired, stimulated, or evoked;
- Self-perceptions are more accurate;
- Discernment is practiced;
- Risks are taken;
- Self-esteem is improved;
- Experiences and perspectives are shared;
- Voices are heard;
- Self-expression manifests itself; and
- Action is taken.

Mary Caprio, 2005-2007 NAPT Vice-President, sums poetry therapy up in her poem, *Perhaps You Too Have Found Yourself.*

> I can tell you that poetry saved my life
> not so long ago and know that you
> will nod in understanding, not give me
> the quizzical look I find elsewhere,
> for you too have seen how much power
> can be packaged in small containers.
> Perhaps you too have treaded water
> as long as you could and celebrated
> the miracle of a rope of words landing
> by your hands, hooking your heart and
> guiding you not just to shore but to a new shore,
> a beach where the sand cushions your tired feet
> and sea gulls cry out in iambic pentameter.
>
> Perhaps you too have found yourself
> between the lines, living in the margins
> between what is and what was,
> and on the edge of what could be.
> The cry of the wild geese offers redemption
> to people like us, and even though
> we might introduce ourselves —

> I am Nobody, who are you? — we feel
> a bit of a smile now as we say it
> recognizing one another as survivors,
> kindred spirits who reached for a rope,
> and grasping it were saved, so now
> we can hold this rope out to others,
> inviting them to dwell with us
> here in this house of infinite possibility.
>
> (*Museletter*, 2005, p. 16)

References

Bolton, G. Field V., and Thompson K. Editors. (2006). *Writing Works: A Resource Handbook for Therapeutic Writing Workshops and Activities*. London: Jessica Kingsley Publishers.

Baldwin, C. (1994). *Calling the Circle: The First and Future Culture*. New York: Bantam.

Bioethics Discussion Blog. http://bioethicsdiscussion.blogspot.com/2005/06/poetry-in-medicine-2.html. Retrieved May 2008.

Chavis, G. G., & Weisberger, L. L. (2003). *The Healing Fountain: Poetry Therapy for Life's Journey*. St. Cloud, Minnesota: North Star Press.

Fox, J. (1997). *Poetic Medicine: The Healing Art of Poem-Making*. New York: Putnam.

Holy Bible, King James Version, "Psalms" and "Song of Solomon."

Hynes, AM. and Hynes-Berry, M. (1994). *Biblio/Poetry Therapy: The Interactive Process: A Handbook*. St. Cloud, Minnesota: North Star Press.

Kastner M. & Burroughs H. (1993). *Alternative Healing: The Complete A-Z Guide to Over 160 Different Alternative Therapies*. La Mesa, California: Halcyon Publishing.

Leedy, JJ. (1985). *Poetry As Healer: Mending the Troubled Mind*. New York: Vanguard Press.

Longo, P.J. Sanctuary Psychiatric Center's Information Network. www.spcsb.org/advoc/poetrytx.html. Retrieved July 2006,

Mazza, N. (2003). *Poetry Therapy: Theory and Practice*. New York: Brunner-Routledge.

Moyers, B. (1995). *The Language of Life: A Festival of Poets*. New York: Broadway Books.

Museletter. (2005). Volume XXVI, No. 2, July 2005, p. 16. National Association of Poetry Therapy.

National Association of Poetry Therapy. (2009), www.poetrytherapy.org.

Pennebaker, J. (1990). *Opening Up: The Healing Power of Expressing Emotions*. New York: The Guilford Press.

Poetry as Healer. (2006). http://www.breakoutofthebox.com/poetryashealer.htm. Retrieved August 2006

Poetry Therapy. (2009). A Brief Overview of Poetry Therapy. www.poetrytherapy.org/articles/pt.htm

Rhythm and Emotion in Poetry. (2005). *Journal of Poetry Therapy: The Interdisciplinary Journal of Practice, Theory, Research, and Education*, Volume 18, No. 4. December.

Yalom I. (1995). *The Theory and Practice of Group Psychotherapy, Fourth Edition*. New York: Basic Books.

5

Writing Illness — Writing Healing: Exercises in Writing to Heal

Leatha Kendrick

The healing process begins when patients tell of symptoms or even fears of illness — first to themselves, then to loved ones, and finally to health professionals. That illness and suffering must be told is becoming clear, not only in treating trauma survivors but in ordinary general medicine. The powerful narratives of illness that have recently been published by patients ... demonstrate how critical is the telling of pain and suffering, enabling patients to give voice to what they endure and to frame the illness so as to escape dominion by it... Without these narrative acts, the patient cannot himself or herself grasp what the events of illness mean.

— *Rita Charon*, Narrative Medicine, 66.

I became interested in the interaction of writing and healing when I faced a major illness. Though I determined to explore every avenue that might possibly offer a cure for my cancer, I did not want to write about it. On the contrary, I wanted with everything in me to refuse its reality.

As a writer, I had experienced how the act of creating poems or narratives created or revealed realities I had not articulated before. To write of illness, then, would be to lend it a psychic reality I resisted. Just seeing that scribbled "*CA*" next to "Diagnosis" on the orders for my first labs had made me blush with shame because this label defined who I was within the world I was entering. I wanted to erase those incriminating letters — to declare them a mistake. In the weeks following my diagnosis I would not even write about it in my journal.

Besides, I did not want to add to "the literature of illness" in any way. As a reader, I had had little patience with illness narratives. Most of them seemed unbearably depressing to me — why add any more misery to my life? And I felt that many of them traded on the cheap literary thrill of reading about someone else's extreme situation — sort of a daytime TV version of literature that (like daytime TV talk shows) was definitely not for me!

And, as a writing teacher, I felt that "writing as therapy" rarely yielded writing anyone would want to read. I'd had enough experience with bad poetry and half-baked stories whose writers claimed had been "therapeutic" to write. I wanted no part of it. I had just published my first book of poems, and I wanted to be known as a careful craftsman in my work. In fact, perhaps the hardest thing for me to overcome in accepting that writing could have healing properties was resistance to what I then understood about "writing as therapy."

Paradoxically, until I was diagnosed with cancer, I understood that writing was somehow essential to my well-being and that when I was not writing I was perpetually out of sorts. I had even noticed that the yearly respiratory infections of my youth and young adulthood had virtually disappeared in the years since I had committed myself to writing as a vocation. But to claim that writing was therapy? No. Writing was my art and craft, my profession. Not simply a way to "spill my guts."

I had a lot to learn about writing and healing.

* * * * *

People who wrote about their deepest thoughts and feelings surrounding a trauma evidenced an impressive drop in illness visits [to the student health center] after the study compared with the other groups. In the months before the experiment, everyone in all the groups went to the health center for illness at the same rate. After the experiment, however, the average person who wrote about their deepest thoughts and feelings went fewer than 0.5 times — a 50% drop in the monthly visitation rate. People who wrote just about their emotions surrounding the trauma [without describing the event itself], just about the facts of the trauma [without speaking of their feelings], or about superficial topics averaged visiting the health center almost 1.5 times per person... [In a further experiment] people who wrote about their deepest thoughts and feelings surrounding traumatic experiences evidenced heightened immune function compared to those who wrote about superficial topics. Although the effect was most pronounced after the last day of writing, it tended to persist six weeks after the study. — James Pennebaker, *Opening Up — The Healing Power of Expressing Emotions*, pp. 34, 37.

When I was first diagnosed with cancer I read to save my life — I read anything I thought would provide useful and applicable information: books on how to survive treatment, articles on treatment modalities, books on alternative therapies, volumes on how psychic health (or disease) might manifest itself in the body. I quickly amassed a notebook of clippings, lists of sources, sections of my test results, and doctors' notes. I lugged this tome with me from clinic to clinic, oncologist to radiologist in search of my (MY) cure — which I was pretty sure would not look exactly like anyone else's.

Though the reading I did was helpful, motivating, grounding, it was not *healing*. What the books lacked — though it took me a while to realize this — was what I came to call "a poetry of experience." The books I had read were written by doctors, theorists, activists, but mostly not by the sufferers themselves — or if there were snippets of sufferers' stories, they were not rendered vividly, with an attention to language and the tools of language — metaphor, allegory, drama, scene, imagery. The books were written clinically or academically — to inform, but not arouse emotion (though they often aroused anxiety and dread in me as I read).

Despite everything, I had slowly begun to write about my cancer in an indirect way. I had to spend a lot of time in pretty grim waiting rooms around this time, going for second opinions and for various tests to assess the biology of my cancer. I carried a yellow pad on which I had written my questions and which I could use for notes. As I sat, I began to "doodle" (my term for partially formed bits of writing) what I saw and felt and overheard as I sat through these agonizing hours. The writing calmed me. It was one way I kept from succumbing to the panic that threatened to overtake me. Of course, none of this writing was to be for publication.

Some of my waiting room notes did end up turning into a poem, however, that after many revisions, I titled "Second Opinion."

Second Opinion
We're four women waiting among a shifting set of others
in radiology's store-front lobby — three daughters
and a mother linked by blood and laughter
over *Cosmo Girl*'s "most embarrassing
moments" (trail of toilet paper from the back of slacks,
the inevitable period started when you're wearing white,
a student asking her teacher, "If your quizzies are hard,
what about your testes?") Lyda loves that last one —
my funny last one — she's the performer, the mime.
Thank god, she's mine, feeding me one-liners.

The middle one, Eliza, brought my x-rays here,
and parked the car. She works the crossword,
all attention like her father but she's part of me,
my watching self. And Leslie, eldest, watches over us all,

rails against this three hour wait, tries to breach
the impersonal walls of disinterest in our fate. She was first
to nurse from this right breast, that pressed and prodded,
and later slicked with gel will echo sound onto a screen
to show the probable malignancy. I'm going to lose it —

the breast — and along with it the cancer, too, I hope.
The receptionist gives us a hard look when we laugh.
We're linked, silvery with a happiness
glinting out even in this waiting place.
I finger the necklace I've just bought, touch
the curative moonstone, murmuring "hope" —
I want to believe in sudden remission,
in some way to avert what we are certainly
headed for. What I can believe in
is the healing of their fingers laced through mine.

The poem let me grieve, but it made me laugh, remembering. It was a huge release. And revising it only deepened my pleasure in the poem as a "made" thing and my re-experiencing of that horrible, wonderful moment in one of those waiting rooms.

A couple of months after I'd written the poem (in February, 2001, about five months into my treatment), one of my closest writing friends suggested that I try to write about the relationship between writing and healing, since I was aiming my research on cancer toward the topic. From the time of my diagnosis (initially a Stage IV cancer), I'd spent many hours each week doing research — at first as a way to keep from actually writing about my experience and to distance myself from its reality. (Research to keep from writing had worked in grad school, after all!) My friend pointed out that Virginia Woolf had written about illness, and Susan Sontag, and other writers whom I admired. I could write a grant to fund the work since I'd taken a leave from my college teaching to research and survive the treatment. With misgivings, I submitted an intent to apply and wrote the grant. Putting together a bibliography pushed me to search for anything that was out there on the topic.

When I first looked into how writing related to healing, the most prominent and prolific authority was James Pennebaker, whose 1988 study on writing and healing resulted in his book, originally titled *Opening Up, the Healing Power of Confiding in Others*. I found a used copy online and bought it, fascinated that Pennebaker had found hard data to support the idea that writing could enact sustained changes in health — increased immune activity, decreased pain, fewer visits to health care providers. The way I read it, Pennebaker's research depended not on the mere act of writing itself, but on writing about what mattered in a way that produced a concrete, coherent narrative that linked feelings with events. His findings made me want to know more. Could I apply the prompts I used in my college creative writing classes to help students generate concretely rendered poems and stories as a means to evoke healing writing up for those who'd suffered trauma?

I proposed to create a writing workshop for people who had suffered some kind of trauma or who were dealing with a chronic debilitating condition or a terminal diagnosis. I would research the relationship between writing and healing, present it succinctly, and devise a writing workbook of exercises and suggestions for writing that would help participants write concretely and vividly. In addition I hoped to produce a book that collected the finished (revised and polished) writing of workshop participants.

I got the grant. In June of 2001, I began to prepare a workshop curriculum.

* * * * *

In *Legacy of the Heart,* Wayne Muller observes that "our own wounds can be vehicles for exploring our essential nature, revealing the deepest textures of our heart and soul, if only we will sit with them, open ourselves to the pain, … without holding back, without blame."

Virginia Woolf said that the moments of profound insight that come from writing about our soulful, thoughtful examinations of our psychic wounds should be called "shocks." For they force us into an awareness about ourselves and our relationship to others and our place in the world that we wouldn't otherwise have had. They realign the essential nature of our being. — Louise DeSalvo, *Writing as a Way of Healing,* 4-5.

As wounded, people may be cared for, but as storytellers, they care for others. The ill and all those who suffer, can also be healers. Their injuries become the source of the potency of their stories… But telling does not come easy, and neither does listening. Seriously ill people are wounded not just in body but in voice. They need to become storytellers in order to recover the voices that illness and its treatment often take away. — Arthur Frank, *The Wounded Storyteller,* xii.

In my early refusal to tell the story of my cancer, in my sense of having disappeared into the *"CA"* diagnosis on my lab orders, in my first interactions with caregivers, and even in the books I read to understand my disease, I was experiencing what Arthur W. Frank names "narrative surrender." I found no voice for my felt experience and no place in the medical protocols where I could try to articulate that experience. To write about it was to give it a life outside myself and to admit to the shame and fear I felt. I was not sure I could keep myself together if I allowed the cancer a life on the page. So I was silenced.

It was when I began to read Frank and Louise De Salvo (literary theorists turned explicators of illness narratives), that I first began *as a writer* to understand how the way one told a story related to the healing power of that story.

In her book *Writing as a Way of Healing* Louise De Salvo picked up where Pennebaker left off. In addition, she emphasized the importance of self-care while doing "risky writing" and insisted on how important it is to link inner experience with a disciplined description of outer circumstances and to balance positive with negative to achieve the rounded telling characteristic of good narrative writing.

Let me repeat these important tenets:

1. self care
2. inner emotions linked to disciplined description of outer objects and events
3. positive and negative revelations: light drawn along with shadow to give a truly three-dimensional telling

De Salvo's book and Frank's, both heavily dependent on a "lit crit" approach to writing, completed Pennebaker's work for me as a teacher. Their collective insistence that the way you told a story was crucial to whether or not the writing had healing potential affirmed my instinct that the superficial writing that often passed for "therapeutic" was not only bad writing, but was not truly therapeutic. In short, healing writing depends on craft.

About this time I bought a copy of *Writing on the Margins*, Hilda Raz's brilliant editing of breast cancer writing by women poets. Only as I sank into these narratives and poems did I begin to feel the healing power of writing. This was accomplished writing, attentive to craft, unblinking in rendering the *felt* reality of cancer, balancing inner states with vivid descriptions of exterior drama and scene. Here the emotions of illness were not only acknowledged but embodied in recreating the details of highly charged moments. This writing engaged me the way any good novel or poem does, releasing emotions I had held pent up. The narratives in this book suggested ways I could write and topics I could address. The link between reading and writing was direct and nurturing, affirming my conviction that the best writing teacher is good literature. Saul Bellow asserted that "a writer is a reader who's been moved to emulation."

* * * * *

The worksheets that follow grew out of my experience as a teacher, writer, and cancer patient. Their foundation is the reading I've briefly summarized. They represent the writing that that reading freed me to do and the ways I have taught other writers over the last seven years to render their own experiences.

Exercise 1: Beginning — The Thorn

Write about what you want to write about — what will not leave you alone.

It may seem small or trivial. It may seem way too large. It may not seem to be what you "ought" to write about, but it is the heart of something. Trust it. It's the thorn whose pricking makes you know you are alive! It's the reason you're here.

What images keep coming to you that don't seem important? Write them!

> Seasoned writers train themselves to value and capture their tiny moments of inspiration; beginning writers often devalue theirs and do not pay attention to them. One sure way to help our creative work is to train ourselves to pay attention to these gifts when they come to us. In doing creative work, we can learn a particular kind of alertness and sensitivity to the way our creative spirit works and to what we're experiencing… We must learn that many mighty works have developed from the simplest of images. At this stage, we can help our writing process by not censoring whatever comes into our imagination and by writing down these ideas and capturing them in some way so that we can elaborate upon them and develop them and see where they will take us. — DeSalvo, *Writing as a Way of Healing,* 130-1.

Try to write for fifteen minutes without stopping.

Later on, come back to what was bothering you, if you want, and write again, only this time take the thorn and put it back on its bush. In other words, recall the time, the place, the sky — maybe a road or a room that was home to what made you write this piece.

Make the pricking of its feeling physical by narrating one moment stolen out of the flow around your "thorn."

Exercise 2 — The Moment of Change

We are all engaged in a futile struggle to maintain ourselves in our own image. — Mark Epstein, *Thoughts without a Thinker*

The question "why" strangles us. Only the questions "What is happening?" and "Who is this happening to?" seem to set us free. — Stephen Levine, *Meetings at the Edge*

Recall a moment when you realized that nothing would ever be the same again. Or maybe you could not realize anything then, but you see now that something shifted in your sense of who you were at a certain moment in the past. Perhaps at the time you were paralyzed, numb. Now you can stand outside that moment. Now you can speak for yourself.

1. What do you see? (If you can, describe the setting. Where were you? What is under your feet? What is above you? Who is there? What is the light like?)
2. As you describe this moment, as you *place* it (recall its setting), tell how you felt.
3. Show us what you are doing. What are the others in the scene doing?
4. Can you recall what anyone said?
5. Balance *inner* with *outer*.

Remember that you are safe. You are standing in a place beyond that moment. You have survived.

If you begin to feel unsafe, stop writing about that moment. If you want, you can freewrite about whatever comes to mind.

When the writing time is up, if you want to, you can read your writing in the group. Hearing what I have just written is sometimes the best way for me to let the feelings in it go.

Exercise 3 — The Map

Work. Relax. Don't think.

1) Map or sketch a significant place.

A place where you realized something important

OR

A place where some big change occurred in your life

OR

The place that most defines you

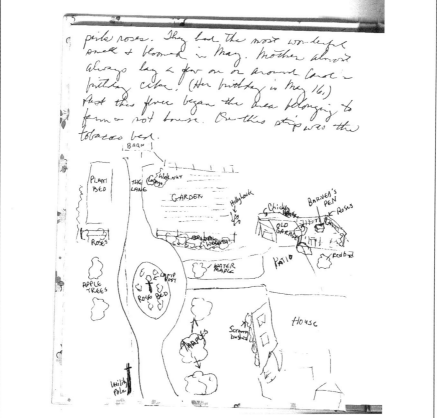

A map from my 1989 journal. I wrote two short stories from this and several poems over the course of more than 15 years. The latest poem was published in a collection in 2008, nineteen years after the drawing.

Don't Fret about the drawing — this is only for you! Let your hand or arm *feel* the way. Stick with what comes to mind no matter how "wrong" it seems.

2) Label the places as you recall and draw them

If you want to, locate sensory memories and label them on your map or drawing.

Include each sense: Push yourself and you will tumble into memory. Let go. It's safe here.

> The writer in the midst of writing, like the penitent in the midst of prayer — finds the self falling away. Or getting out of the way. Only when we slip out of our writer bodies do we truly don the skin of story. — Jane Yolen

* * * * *

What happened as a result of the grant I received? Well, in addition to reading about healing writing, I created the workbook I'd hoped for and I taught my first writing-to-heal class, which I called "Writing through Crisis." The course description invited anyone who'd experienced a trauma or ongoing crisis they wanted to explore through writing to register for the class. That six week series was scheduled to begin at the Carnegie Center for Literacy and Learning (a community writing and literacy center) on September 11, 2001.

That evening, uncertain if anyone would show up, I decided to go over to the Carnegie Center prepared to teach, just in case. Eleven people had registered, nine showed up that night. All of them completed the course. The nine included a woman suffering from crippling arthritis, a young pregnant woman who had lost her first child and wanted to honor him before her next child was born, a young man suffering from chronic depression, a woman newly through a turbulent divorce, and a seventy-year-old woman who wanted to explore why she felt so disconnected from her experience. We wrote in class every week. We read. We talked about what worked in the writing. We tried to revise what we'd written to make it better, stronger, truer. And at the end of the eight-week class, we invited a book artist to teach us how to make handmade books from the collected stories I had had typeset and copied.

Teaching that class was a life-changing experience for me. I have never been able to go back to writing or teaching as I did before that fall, when, just three months out from the end of my own first-time treatment for cancer, I wrote and suffered and refined myself as a writer and teacher with nine amazing and completely ordinary people who taught me to trust the power of writing as a way of healing.

As I wrote, alone and with my students, I crafted poems that not only articulated my cancer experience, but — most importantly — led me to insights I would not otherwise have had. The poems themselves taught me about my strengths, my resilience. They gave voice to a part of me that was feistier and happier, more generous to herself and others than I could have imagined in those first dark days of the diagnosis. They are collected and published in two volumes now — books I have shared with my caregivers and with other cancer patients. I make sure that each new doctor (yes, I am still in treatment, eight years later) gets copies. In fact, one of the books is dedicated to my oncology nurse at the practice where I eventually settled for the bulk of my treatment — the first caregiver who laid her hand on my shoulder and acknowledged, "This must be very hard."

References

Charon, Rita. *Narrative Medicine — Honoring the Stories of Illness.* Oxford: Oxford University Press, 2006.

DeSalvo, Louise. *Writing as a Way of Healing — How Telling Our Stories Transforms Our Lives.* Boston: Beacon Press, 1999.

Frank, Arthur W. *The Wounded Storyteller — Body, Illness, and Ethics.* Chicago: The University of Chicago Press, 1995.

Kendrick, Leatha. *Second Opinion.* Cincinnati, OH: David Robert Books, 2008.

Pennebaker, James W. *Opening Up: The Healing Power of Expressing Emotions.* New York: The Guilford Press, 1997.

6

"Writing with the Ink of Light on the Tablet of the Spirit":
Coping with Chronic Pain & Other Health Challenges

Gail Radley

A startling thought struck me when I learned I'd be leading a workshop on wellness and writing — how *lucky* I was to have fibromyalgia so I could participate! I understand that having health issues wasn't a prerequisite. And I'd rush to agree that fibromyalgia is more plague than prize. In fact, fibromyalgia has plagued me since before the diagnosis was first used — nearly all of my adult life. During that time, I wandered from specialist to specialist and dabbled in numerous alternative modalities and home remedies. While having a name for my symptoms was oddly comforting, even without promise of cure, I soon began hearing that it was "garbage pail" diagnosis, not a *real* disease, that the pain was in my head. (Now that researchers are discovering brain differences with fibromyalgia, perhaps that disparaging "all in your head" comment held some truth.) Wherever the pain originates, it is persistent and resistant to relief. When fibromyalgia is complicated with degenerating disks and arthritis, as mine is, daily life is more taxing.

Fibromyalgia is hardly something to celebrate. Why, then, did I feel lucky?

My response, it turns out, is not unusual in those with long-term or chronic illness. Surgeon Bernie S. Siegel relates that his patient Greta, for example, called her cancer "the best thing that ever happened," because she found meaning in it which translated into purpose. Human beings are meaning-makers. Perhaps one of the greatest psychological tortures is feeling that we exist in a chaotic world, victims to meaningless suffering which we can neither control nor modify. Finding meaning is key. To find meaning is to discover purpose, to control, or at least modify, suffering. It is mind-mastery over the chaos, a despair antidote. Psychiatrist Viktor Frankl, a Holocaust survivor, argues that "suffering ceases to be suffering … at the moment it finds a meaning" (p. 179). He proposes that "Nietzsche's words, 'He who has a *why* to live can bear with most any *how*' could be the guiding motto for all psychotherapeutic and psychohygienic efforts regarding prisoners" (p. 121).

The prisoners that Frankl had in mind were those whose bodies were trapped. But those with compromised health are trapped *by* their bodies. The keys to freedom are in reach for both types of captives. 'Abdu'l-Bahá (Central Figure of the Bahá'í Faith), who spent forty years in prison and exile, claimed, "There is no prison but the prison of self" (quoted in Chamberlain, p. 24). The self that imprisons feels unconnected to others, sees only the present, and cannot envision growth or larger purpose.

To make meaning and find purpose, we must expand our vision. Expanding vision means stepping into the realm of spirituality, into belief in something larger than ourselves — whether in God, a philosophy, value, or cause — and acting on that belief. Siegel adds that spirituality involves a "belief in some meaning or order in the universe" (p. 177). On its grandest scale, we see spirituality in action in the founders of the world's religions and echoed by innumerable others who accepted suffering because they envisioned benefit to humanity.

Perhaps, though, this is too grand a scale. We find spiritually based action behind those who volunteer serve in soup kitchens, fight for social justice — and attend conferences, sacrificing time and money in the name of helping others. An expanded, spiritual vision also enables the ill to taste gratitude. Just as Greta found worth in her cancer because it enabled her to "help someone else" (quoted in Siegel, p. 135), I felt gratitude that perhaps my struggle with fibromyalgia could prove useful. Nothing is as enlivening as a strong purpose, a feeling of contributing.

Yet purpose need not be focused outward to help the sufferer. Though she would eventually share the fruits of her growth in *Alchemy of Illness,* Kat Duff discovered in Chronic Fatigue Syndrome a profound personal tutor. "Even at my sickest," she wrote, "when I was spending the majority of the daylight hours in bed aching, I knew my illness was showing me facets of truth that I had missed" (p. 43). Like Duff, many have emerged from illness with greater understanding of themselves and their strengths. However, even when the focus is inward, the results extend to others. Explaining the connections between individuals, 'Abdu'l-Bahá observes that "if pain or injury afflicts any member of that body, it must inevitably result in suffering for all the rest" (p. 39). The reverse is equally true. Growth attained during illness affects how we *are* in the world, what beliefs and energy we bring to it. We cannot create an isolated ripple. We are part of the whole; the rest of the pond ripples with us.

No matter the "size" of the purpose we discover, we find it by expanding our vision, that is, by growing. The two are synonymous. The difficulty is that chronic and long-term illnesses tend to stop growth. They drag on, with little, if any, improvement, leaving a trail of failed remedies that invites depression. Depression further decreases the likelihood of recovery. If illness is the prison, depression is the guard, conspiring to keep us *feeling* locked in. Overcoming depression is hard work. Suggestions to "look on the bright side" or "count blessings" will not open the cell doors. Usually, we must explore our confines before escaping them, whether they're primarily physical or emotional. We must describe the shadows and restrictions, our anger, depression, and even denial. That such reactions to illness resemble Elizabeth Kübler-Ross's initial stages in death and dying should be no surprise. Chronic illness is a death sentence of sorts; we mourn the loss of the healthier self and must learn to accept the delicate, dependent replacement.

Writing offers a powerful, adaptable tool not only to begin that process, but also to encourage growth and discovery. Many a teenager has latched onto a diary or journal for relief from the pressures of feeling *stuck* between childhood and adulthood. Countless adults also journal to ponder shifts in thoughts and feelings. An occasional journaler myself, I find that it quiets the whirl of thoughts cycling through my mind; once on the page, they seem to stand still, one step removed. Adults with mental, emotional, and/or physical illness might be reminded of how useful diaries can be. Consider the diary of Anne Frank, which she named Kitty, as if writing to an ever-available, understanding pal. Kitty never judged Anne. Family and friends, conversely, don't always understand or listen. Sometimes people doubt or discount our pain. This is particularly true when the patient *looks* well, as with fibromyalgia or chronic fatigue. I used to wish for a "pain-o-meter" on my forehead, to make plain the degree of pain I was soldiering through. I wasn't after accommodation or fuss, just acknowledgement. Writing is a way of exorcising negative feelings — and, when it's made public, of getting acknowledgement. This longing to have one's situation recognized might help explain the popularity of Internet diaries (and is part of the allure of publishing generally). In chat rooms and on blogs, for example, despite potential embarrassment and indifferent, bad, or downright dangerous responses, teens unburden their souls as their parents had done only in locked diaries.

Poetry, with its compressed language and forms that bestow significance to each line, is another form that attracts sufferers of every type. Poetry implicitly invites writers to pack meaning into symbols that may be highly personal and inexplicable to readers. Yet, because the authors find their symbols feel so potent and satisfying, they assume the lack is the readers' rather than theirs. No matter. Writing needn't be aesthetically wonderful to help the writer. In fact, the first (and only) rule

I give my students for impromptu class writing is that it doesn't have to be great. Since it's unrevised, it *shouldn't* be perfect. Polished pieces take work — work that many are not inclined to do, particularly with poems, which seem to flow — or bleed — directly from heart to page. Except to professionals, revising a poem may feel sacrilegious, like selling their souls. I ask students to *freewrite*, to follow their thoughts without worrying about writing well. With license to write "badly," students can focus on simply getting ideas down. Revisions are a separate step — and perhaps an unnecessary one in therapeutic writing.

When therapeutic work is shared, we should be supportive of the emotional content, rather than attending to literary worth. We should recognize the courage sharing what may be still raw and painful takes. At my home, we held a monthly poetry reading for years. Purely social in intent, we had dinner and shared poems or short inspirational readings. Most attendees weren't writers, but some used the opportunity to read their writing, and most of that was cathartic. This group seemed to know instinctively that every effort deserved encouragement. Thus, a neophyte recounting her troubles in strained rhyme and a serious poet both received enthusiastic applause. Those most challenged by the performance flushed with pleasure and pride as they surrendered the "hot seat," I suspect feeling less alone for sharing. Indeed, face-to-face sharing seems to legitimize and pronounce feelings acceptable. I seldom write poetry unless I'm in, as I say, "a high growth period." But when my parents were in care facilities, diagnosed with Alzheimer's, poetry seemed to be the natural voice for what had been nameless emotions. Though I'd never read my poems to an audience, I mustered my courage. Having a "public" venue eased my grief over the situation, making me feel as if others were helping to carry the load.

Similarly, feeling frustrated over my unending pain, I wrote a poem called "Progression," sharing it later at poetry night. In the first half of poem, subtitled "Message to My Body," I "divorced" my body, explaining that this was "not a death wish, but a wish/for a never-ending out-of-body experience" (pp. 10-11).

However, simply writing and sharing may not be sufficient to get us to a healthier place. In fact, precisely because of the potency of writing, we may find our misery amplified. "Creating consistency is one thing writing is good for, and one reason it is dangerous," neurologist Alice W. Flaherty notes (p. 215). There's danger of remaining stuck in the Now, when writing about traumatic events. Susan K. Lutgendorf and Philip Ullrich even suggest that "the effects of" writing about emotions *only* may be "similar to the effects of uncontrolled exposure to a traumatic event" (p. 182). They add that such writing may cause the writers "to relive the physiological and emotional activation of the trauma during its recall" but if they are focused solely on emotions, "they may not be able to work through the trauma to reach a state of resolution from which they have a different perspective" (p. 182). We are, say Joshua M. Smyth and Melanie A. Greenberg, "forcing the encoding of the traumatic memory into narrative language" (p. 151). Without getting beyond part one of my poem, I might have felt stuck in longing for separation from the physical world. So, if writing is to be healing, it needs to somehow move us beyond where we are.

I managed to move beyond by pondering the problem from a new perspective in part two of my poem, "To Pain":

> Or suppose I were to enter you
> Willingly, as one does a House of Horrors,
> if not delighting in the spasms of terror,
> at least relishing the reminder:
> I am alive!
> With every jangling nerve,
> knotted muscle, throbbing pain,
> I live!
> Suppose I were to take your hand
> as I might a friend's, to clasp you to my heart,
> as an enemy forgiven. Suppose
> I were to seek to know you
> as fully as I know myself —

> your every wince, your tugging for attention.
> Even more, suppose I were to greet you
> as a lover, kneel at your feet as a suppliant,
> learn from you?
> Suppose, just suppose, we were to walk
> the rest of our days together, not with struggle,
> but with radiant acquiescence?

The expression "radiant acquiescence," which comes from the Bahá'í Writings, has some relationship to acceptance, Kübler-Ross's final stage — a stage which not everyone attains. Kübler-Ross describes acceptance as a time when the terminally ill have "found some peace," (p. 220) indicating an end to the struggle. "Acceptance," she explains, "should not be mistaken for a happy stage. It is almost void of feelings…" (p. 219). It is to accept, as they are fond of saying in Alcoholics Anonymous, the things they cannot change, to resign oneself. Yet there is no need to rule out happiness, even in the face of pain and incurable ailments. In fact, radiant acquiescence is rich with feelings, going beyond resignation or acceptance. Radiance signifies glowing, joyfulness. Not a Pollyannaish denial of reality, it represents a peak moment of gratitude in which one can see the positives in an apparently negative situation — including not only that sense of purpose, but subtler gains in personal growth, perhaps, or simply of utter contentment. Described as "the shining pathway out of the 'greater prison of self'" (Chamberlain, p. 24), it is not a state that most of us can maintain. Radiant acquiescence — even more than acceptance — is a slippery commodity. But knowing it is there, reaching it occasionally, is enough to shift perspectives significantly.

My poem to my body not only helped me think differently about pain, it also helped me to *experience* radiant acquiescence. More recently, I wrote a letter "To My Dear Thin Neck," focusing on what it has done for me, rather than solely on what a royal pain in the neck it is. Poetry and letter writing suggest another technique — writing a dialogue, as play, poem, or story, to let the illness speak. The writer might ask pain why it's there, what it has to say, even what it needs in order to leave. A fully engaged writer "hears" and records what the pain has to teach. The "pain" will likely have a few questions for the writer, too, inviting a debate that may have surprising results.

Variations of Kübler-Ross's stages have been offered and we now recognize that the stages are neither as distinct nor progress as orderly as her writings suggest. We may cycle backward, leap over a stage, or experience two simultaneously. Still, Kübler-Ross provides a useful framework for considering the sorts of emotions one might experience when facing unwanted change. Writing prompts might be devised from them — or another model — to help clients explore their varied emotions and encourage growth. While an individual could use the prompts for journaling, the ideal would probably be a series of group sessions, so that clients could write and then discuss. The value of writing first is that individuals, given the assurance that they have the right *not* to share their writing, may surface ideas that had only been vague, unexamined feelings. Whatever they *choose* to share will help create community, bring acknowledgement and acceptance, and further insight.

According to Kübler-Ross, the first stage is denial. Clients might describe their feelings when they received their diagnosis or realized their pain just wasn't going away. Suggest that they write what they've never told anyone. While the chronically ill may logically continue doctor and remedy shopping, Kübler-Ross sees it as part of denial. Whether logic- or denial-driven, though, the many dead ends take a significant emotional, physical, and financial toll; writing may help air frustration and disappointment and reawaken realistic hope. Stage two, anger, includes the "why me" question, the feeling that we are victims of a great injustice, so writers might be encouraged write or list the reasons this shouldn't have happened to them and elaborate on how unfair it is.

Next, in the bargaining phase, dying patients generally seek additional time from God in exchange for a promise of service. Someone with chronic pain or illness may seek a cure or even a brief respite. Writing a letter to God about what they would be willing to do or give up should their wish be granted seems a natural assignment. In doing so, clients explore the magnitude of their condition and its "worth" in relation to other aspects of their lives. For example, would they give up all their vacations for a cure? Their need to be in charge? Their desire to succeed? Their children? That the ailment is *not* the center point quickly becomes clear. The bargaining phase is reminiscent of a psychodrama technique in which the clients "enter" an imaginary magic shop where they are invited to trade something of value for their desire. Shaping the prompt this way may work better for those who either don't believe in God or who feel uncomfortable petitioning. A variation is meeting with the sage. What questions might they ask a sage and what answers might they receive? Clients should avoid platitudes, listening instead for their inner wisdom. The sage might offer a drink from the Cup of Wisdom. What are the contents of that cup? How does it taste? What emotions does it inspire? Either version might best be written as dialogue.

When bargain seeking fails, depression is natural. Because it's difficult and worrisome to see someone struggling through this stage, we're tempted to hurry them along. This usually backfires. We wouldn't tell a person who'd just lost a loved one to "snap out of it" or "count their blessings." To do so disrespects the lost relationship. It also likely leaves the individual feeling more isolated and despondent. Mourners need time. A person with a long-term or chronic condition has lost the person closest to her, herself — or at least that healthier version of herself — a significant loss. Plans shift, dreams vanish, vitality is sapped. Daily life is disrupted in very tangible ways and, most importantly, her image of herself as capable, independent, and ready to tackle life is assaulted. "Normal life" may be gone forever. Just as a person might feel angry about the injustice, so might she feel depressed.

We help mourners by listening and comforting — when they let us. What of the stuffers, the introverts, the people who shut the windows to their souls, and crumble quietly within, where no one will see or hear? These are the people who settle into depression and lose the path out. Numerous researchers testify to the influence of emotions on physical health; Harald C. Traue, for example, found that when they suppressed their emotions, even unconsciously, his chronic pain patients had "an intensified experience of these feelings and an increased physiological response," (p. 171) i.e. muscle tension and pain. Clearly, it is better for people to record their stories on paper rather than in their musculature and cells.

Indeed, for introverted patients, writing may be a required preliminary to face-to-face disclosure; it may even be the first time they truly acknowledge their feelings. Create a meditative atmosphere. Invite participants to relax, eyes closed, and visualize before writing. You might start with a short relaxation exercise, adding a script like the following as a prompt. "It is late at night. You are finally able to be alone with your thoughts in a place that feels safe, comfortable, and private, perhaps in the quiet of your favorite room. The lights are off and with the soft glow of the moon the room has become shadows and shapes, soft, comfortable, familiar. Or you're atop a mountain with only the stars in the vast night sky for company. You're glad because now is the unburdening time. There's something you've been carrying around so for long… You see it now, a heavy, dark bundle of thoughts and feelings, you haven't wanted to share — it never felt safe or right to share, until now… Now you know you can put it into words, and, when you do, you'll be freer and lighter. And so, opening your eyes, you pick up your pen and begin."

Finally, to nudge clients toward the acceptance — or radiant acquiescence — stage, encourage them to freewrite about both the coping methods they've learned and the good things that have resulted from their illness, including personal growth. The simple title, "In Praise of Pain" [or Illness], may be spark enough. In a small group, after freewriting, the group might create a group poem. Begin with a given line like, "The path of pain has not been easy, / but because of pain…." Each person contributes one or two positive ideas, incorporating "because of pain." For example, the poem might develop this way:

> The path of pain has not been easy,
> but because of pain, I notice the little things.
> Because of pain, I've learned my strength.

When the finished poem is read aloud, individuals may discover more positives to ponder, replacing what may have been a litany of complaints with one of pride and gratitude. These will be the words of survivors and conquerors, rather than victims. Because, as Flaherty noted, writing creates "consistency," the poem will strengthen these positive thoughts.

Memoirists may find the Kübler-Ross-inspired prompts and activities useful in highlighting feelings associated with various stages. Many guides are available offering techniques for recalling significant times in life, exploring their meaning, and shaping them into effective prose. Ruth Kanin's "Wheel of Life," is one. The wheel — a pie chart with eight equal sections — creates an organized visual of one's life. The first seven slices represent the years lived, with ages recorded. Writers note important events in each slice, noting the emotional tone each period, e.g. sad, ambitious, hopeful. Cold-blooded accounts of events seldom engage readers. Moreover, researchers believe they rob writing of its healing potential. Emotions invest moments with meaning. Writing autobiography is only partly about telling our stories. Autobiography — even this charting exercise — helps us make sense of our lives, discover themes, and illuminate cause-effect relationships. Often, autobiography reminds us that illness and suffering, while consuming, are not our lives' entirety. Nor are they the whole of our present. The eighth slice, begging to be filled with realizable goals, is a motivator: we are writing our futures now.

The wheel idea can chart the life of an illness, too. Taking the positive view, call it "The Wellness Wheel." Use the same wheel divided into eight, reserving that eighth slice for our healthier future. The first slice might represent the time before illness and the second, illness's beginning. Slice three might begin with the diagnosis and first treatment approach. That leaves four more slices, representing either equal time spans from that first treatment effort to the present or the major treatments and/or stages in our illness — thoughts and feelings included.

To write a life story is to write narrative. The beauty of narrative, fiction or nonfiction, is that it drives its writer toward a resolution, even when the ending is unknown. The ending needn't be perfect, but the most satisfying endings include growth, hope, and/or purpose, even if predicting more struggle. In other words, in stories, things happen. Stories represent movement and growth, the antidote to stagnant depression. Depression represents loss of faith, in the largest sense — loss of faith in doctors and their remedies, in life to give us a fair shake, in ourselves to cope, and, yes, sometimes in God. The system — however we perceive that system — has failed us, and now we are stuck. We need faith to carry on, to trust in the unknown future. Furthermore, research backs the common sense understandings that having faith in ourselves increases positive feelings, diminishes negative ones, and contributes to health. When faith is shaky or broken, stories can carry us to a land that is higher, drier, and healthier, where we can pause, reflect on our progress, and ready ourselves to step forward. When we keep that "eighth slice" open to a better future, even our own stories can accomplish this, and with greater relevancy.

The healing potential of visualization also relates to writing this eighth slice. Psychologists, counselors, motivational speakers, coaches are among many advising a simple, but effective strategy: visualize success. While we explore wellness and writing, other true believers suggest we visualize wellness. Even patients with apparently incurable cancer shrink their tumors, achieving what no doctor's scalpel could. It works because, as Siegel writes, our bodies "cannot distinguish between a vivid mental experience and an actual physical experience" (p. 153). The greater the ability to visualize in detail, the greater the likelihood of success. As with writing, the downside is that visualizing negative times may temporarily worsen related symptoms, because the body reacts much as it originally did. When symptoms flare, it's important to remember that we're involved in a *process*; illness probably didn't descend on us all at once and is unlikely to leave that way. However, as we find the words to describe our experience, *including our emotions*, Smyth and Greenberg indicate, we are less likely to continue carrying the emotions' impact on bodies. We learn to let the negative go, emotionally and physically, as we write, and whether naturally or through progressive prompts, we begin using more "insight words (e.g., understand, realize)" which are "associated with more health improvement" (pp. 151-2). In the process of gaining insight (discovering its *meaning* for us), we begin writing and visualizing radiant acquiescence, a state of such inner and outward relaxation that it should well make up for an earlier, temporary increase of symptoms.

Beyond all this, there's a feel-good aspect to writing generally. Neurologist Alice W. Flaherty points out there is an increasing body of scientific evidence that joy produced by quite diverse sources "activates the same brain systems, many of them opiate systems" (p. 212). She goes on the make a connection between joy and "creative inspiration" (present in nonfiction as well as fiction writing), adding that we don't have to be truly inspired to feel the heady joy of that state (ibid.). As I tell my students, writing begets writing; one simple reason is that, once we cross the threshold of resistance and begin, we experience a sort of joy in the flow of ideas. Joy, Flaherty insists, "is inextricably intertwined with creative inspiration" (ibid.). Perhaps this is why some find writing addictive!

The crux is that anyone can gain the physical and emotional benefits of writing. Joy and writing both trigger the energized sense of creative inspiration. When that energy drives us toward a growth and process-oriented perspective on life — and illness, we begin to find meaning and purpose where chaos once reigned. Arriving there, we realize that, while we can't control everything, we can control our reactions. We are writing our futures, literally and figuratively. And, if we choose it, if we write toward radiant acquiescence, we find ourselves, as Bahá'u'lláh (the Prophet-Founder of the Bahá'í Faith) prescribes, writing "with the ink of light on the tablet of [our] spirit" (*Arabic Hidden Words* #71).

References

'Abdu'l-Bahá. *Secret of Divine Civilization.* Wilmette, IL: Bahá'í Publishing Trust, 1975.
Bahá'u'lláh. *The Hidden Words.* Wilmette, IL: Bahá'í Publishing Trust, 1954.
Chamberlin, Soroya. 'Abdu'l-Bahá *on Divine Philosophy.* Boston: Tudor, 1918.
Duff, Kat. *The Alchemy of Illness.* New York: Pantheon, 1993.
Flaherty, Alice W. *The Midnight Disease.* Boston: Houghton Mifflin, 2004.
Frankl, Viktor. *Man's Search for Meaning.* New York: Pocket, 1963.
Kanin, Ruth. *Write the Story of Your Life.* New York: Hawthorn/Dutton, 1981.
Kübler-Ross, Elizabeth. "On Coping with Death." *Opposing Viewpoints Sources: Death/Dying. Vol. 1. Bruno Leone, et al., eds.* pp. 213-220. St. Paul: Greenhaven, 1984.
Lutgendorf, Susan K. and Philip Ullrich. "Cognitive Processing, Disclosure and Health: Psychological and Physiological Mechanisms." *The Writing Cure.* Ed. Stephen J. Lepore and Joshua M. Smyth. pp. 177-196. Washington, DC: American Psychological Association, 2002.
Siegel, Bernie S., M.D. *Love, Medicine and Miracles.* New York: Harper, 1986
Smyth, Joshua M. and Melanie A. Greenberg. "Scriptotherapy." *Psychodynamic Perspectives on Sickness and Health,* Eds. Paul Raphael Duberstein and Joseph M. Masling. pp. 121-160. Washington, DC: American Psychological Association, 2000.
Traue, Harald. "Inhibition and Muscle Tension in Myogenic Pain." *Emotion, Disclosure and Health.* Ed. James Pennebaker. pp. 155-175. Washington, DC: American Psychological Association, 1995.

7

My Son's Name Was Michael — Not Elijah

Fran Dorf

Fourteen years after her son's death, a writer reflects on the process and consequences of turning her grief into fiction.

On a beautiful summer day in June 2000, shortly after the publication of my third novel, *Saving Elijah*, a casual acquaintance stopped me on the sidewalk in front of Starbucks. We exchanged a few pleasantries, and then she hit me with this: "Did you *really* have an affair? And your husband took you back?"

I looked at her, speechless. *Saving Elijah*, to describe it as the aggressively sensational Putnam cover copy did, is about a woman named Dinah, who while keeping vigil over her comatose five-year-old son, Elijah, "meets a seductive spirit in the hospital corridor outside the pediatric intensive care unit, one with a startling connection to her past, who claims he can make her child well again — if she's willing to pay the price." Near the end of the novel Dinah has a brief, desperate affair, so the question wasn't totally off the wall, but I still wanted to shake her and scream, "DINAH IS A *CHARACTER*, YOU IDIOT." Luckily I was not only speechless I was paralyzed.

Before publication I had decided not to even try to keep secret that I had turned a very raw personal trauma into fiction. In publicity materials I had revealed that my novel was "inspired" by the loss of my son, choosing the words as carefully as I had every word in the book. There was no way to hide it, certainly not in my small New England city, where it was well known that I had lost Michael. Seven hundred kind souls, locals mostly, attended his funeral six years before, the woman in front of Starbucks probably among them.

The "official" reviews had so far been excellent, if not as plentiful as I hoped for. Most critics praised the book as moving and effective, and appreciated its serious intent, *and its* wise-talking, hate-spewing, blaspheming, special literary device. I knew my decision to publish an unconventional novel to which some might have a negative critical reaction, was emotionally risky, and I felt prepared.

An answer was in order, but my mouth refused to move. If this woman assumed I was Dinah and was looking for juicy gossip, why go for the unimportant affair episode? After all, this is a novel that takes on removal of a child's life support. Wasn't she *dying* to know if my husband and I had faced that question? Had I invited frivolous questions by cloaking a novel about serious matters in supernatural garb? Why couldn't I do that? Ann Rice wrote about a blood-sucking vampire after her daughter died of leukemia. Toni Morrison's *Beloved* featured a ghost. Oh, don't be ridiculous. I'm not Ann Rice, let alone Toni Morrison. Where did I get off expecting people to take this work "seriously?" My previous books had been labeled "suspense," and *Saving Elijah* could easily be mistaken for suspense, or even horror. All the Borders stores shelved it with the mysteries, too bad for the reader who came expecting a mystery. Maybe I should have stuck with memoir, or even a more conventional novel, because some were going to find this book too raw, or not raw enough, or not up to the task artistically, or an unseemly juxtaposition of the serious and the outrageous —

Wait, I was getting hysterical. If I was going to get through the next few months, which the great writer, Carol Shields, in a *Washington Post* essay some years back, called the "fragile" time, when writers are at their most vulnerable, I was going to have to be a lot tougher than this. I couldn't be paralyzed at the first awkward question sighting.

Okay then. Why not ask if *I* had met a ghost in the hospital corridor who offered a Faustian bargain to save my son? Ah, would that it were so!

Thomas Mann, in *Death in Venice*, said it's not a good idea for readers to know the source of a writer's fiction, and I generally agree. Yet if my son hadn't died, I would *never* have written a novel about a dying child, *or* grief. I wouldn't have had the nerve. Or the interest. But I had something important to share, and nothing left to lose. And once I had written the book it seemed not only impossible but absurd to deny my experience. Surviving the loss felt like the major accomplishment of my life; writing the novel paled in comparison, although even then, at some psychological level, I realized that actually writing the novel had been a key component of my survival.

So why didn't I write a memoir, when the life and death of Michael Max Dorf, who died before his fourth birthday, was so compelling in its own right? As I look back, I see now that my decision to write *Saving Elijah*, while partly a creative choice, was probably inevitable — a crucial, unavoidable step in the psychological process called "grief work." Obviously not every bereaved mother can write a novel, and in that sense the step was uniquely mine, but grief work itself is universal, and never-ending — no matter how many times we hear that misused word "closure." A review of my story will be enlightening for anyone who seeks serenity, in the Buddhist sense; instructive for anyone interested in grief or the creative process; and potent testimony to the therapeutic power of writing.

At the time my husband and I adopted Michael in 1990, we'd been married for twelve years. We had a daughter and were blessed in many ways, but we'd also had more than our share of ups and downs, beginning early with my husband's bout with cancer. He survived, and we wanted a second child, but were unable to conceive. We finally contracted with a birth mother and, by corresponding with her, became attached to the child before he was born two months prematurely in a hospital many miles from our home. We went ahead with the adoption when he was one day old because we felt it would have been morally inexcusable to leave him there because he might have problems. Michael was beautiful, enthusiastic, and loving, with the face of an angel, but he had many, many problems.

Some years before, I had gone back to school for a master's degree in psychology, but about midway through, around 1987, I began writing, resurrecting a hobby I'd had as a teenager, when I kept a journal and wrote poetry and fiction. I also had an undergraduate degree in journalism, but had given up creative writing as impractical.

My first novel, a psychological "suspense thriller," was published in 1990, the same year we adopted Michael. Three and a half years later on the day he became ill, December 7, 1993, my own version of Pearl Harbor Day, I was forty-one years old. A paperback of my second novel had just been published, and I was already working on a third to fulfill a two-book deal. In the previous six weeks, for reasons that remain mysterious and fascinating, I had been writing faster than I had ever done, and had over a hundred pages of a novel about the kidnapping of two-year-old. I called the child Elijah, and his parents, Sam and Dinah Galligan. Sam, an advertising executive from a Catholic family, and Dinah, an overachieving Jewish psychologist with a narcissistic mother, were coming to fictional life. Equally mysteriously, I spent very few pages advancing the kidnapping plot, and many on what I imagined to be the couple's grief and terror. Prescience perhaps. Or maybe only an expression of my fears for my troubled son. (There are always at least two explanations for coincidental events; a person is either drawn to supernatural explanations, or not. I am a fascinated skeptic; all my novels, though primarily psychological, have employed supernatural elements.)

That afternoon, I put Michael down for his nap, and went out to work in my office in our detached garage, listening for anything unusual on the monitor. At around four I went to wake him up, and found him having a seizure, an event I later fictionalized in the novel, sticking in this case relatively close to the facts.

He never woke up. We arrived with our baggage in Hell. He died six months later. Sometime during this period, or maybe shortly after he died — I can't even remember when now — I banged out the rest of the kidnapping novel. I switched point of view to the kidnapper, took her on a bizarre sojourn with a Montana cult, and never returned to the parents. What a sight I must have been, out there in my office pounding away on the computer, a frantic, wild-eyed zombie in a bathrobe, since I hardly ever got dressed. Though each of my other novels had taken several years to write, *Enemy Kissed* took about three more weeks. It was violent, incoherent book; the publisher rejected it, and I lost my two-book deal. Did I think I could plow through such a loss and carry on with business as usual? Grief makes you insane. It really does.

I retreated to my house and spent the next two years in my bathrobe, crying or staring vacantly at the walls, vaguely aware of my daughter and husband coming and going, floaters in my field of vision. Like most writers I had always been a voracious reader, but I even stopped reading, partly the result of inability to concentrate, a common grief reaction. Eventually I dragged myself to a therapist, then a grief support group, where I made a lot of bitter jokes. I was the life of the grief party. But I also listened, and heard.

Many people suggested I keep a journal, but I got angry at any advice. Writing a journal seemed illogical, anyway. How do you write a scream? What words convey weeping, rage, terror, paralysis, self-recrimination, failure, the physical pain of grief? And how could someone who hadn't been there presume to say how I should cope? I hated all the suggestions, those people who mean well but whom I've come to call the de-legitimizers of grief: the babblers *(Let's talk about anything, anything except your horror)*; advice givers *(Concentrate on your other children; Adopt another child; It's time to get past it now, why don't you?)*; pain-minimizers *(God must have wanted him; He's in a better place; You did everything you could*); lesson-learners (*Everything happens for a reason);* and pseudo-empathizers *(I know just how you feel).*

One day I bought a school composition book at the supermarket, secretly, because I didn't want anyone to know that I had taken that step, which seemed like a betrayal to Michael. You cling stubbornly to your grief, because grief is all you have of the lost one. Buying that journal was a major accomplishment. My first entry came a few weeks later. I scrawled the words "Help me" over and over until they dissolved into unrecognizable strokes. A few weeks later, I described a trip to the bank I had to abort due to unbidden tears. Grief was a faucet that I couldn't turn off. I wrote that down. Grief was a thundering, hissing, four thousand pound monster I was condemned like Sisyphus to lug around on my back for the rest of my life. I wrote that down. Like most writers I have always been a fan of metaphors.

I began writing whenever I could bring myself to do it. Publishing was the furthest thing from my mind and I was concerned only with getting to the next moment; and since no one would ever see my journal, I didn't have to think about content, form, logic, style, syntax, grammar, appropriateness.

One day I recounted a story I'd heard in my support group; another day I flatly described what Michael's seizure looked like; another I riffed on eyes, and tears, and eye torture, reviving an old dream I used to have about people poking things in my eyes. I heaped abuse on myself for all the acting out with drugs and boys I did as a teenager. Maybe that was why I had lost my son. I recorded a recurring dream in which I would find myself in an empty house, running from room to room, looking frantically for him. I talked about whether it was better to sleep then be awake. (It was a draw; both were excruciating.) I wrote a letter to my son's birth mother (a version of which I eventually sent), and spewed bile against an ex-friend I ran into in the cheese aisle, who had abandoned me, what a superficial person after all I had done for her, blah, blah, blah. I wrote a list of all the words Michael had said in his life, maybe ten in all. I compiled timelines of which tests he'd had, and when; and made lists of the foods he'd been willing to eat. Maybe I'd had the wrong tests, fed him the wrong things. I talked about a bereaved mother I'd met who found non-bereaved people so lacking in compassion that she refused to be friends with anyone who hadn't also lost a child. I wrote about my friends and my perceived enemies, less about my friends. I attacked my therapist's motives and ability. I named names. I wrote snippets, poem-like things, lists, memories, narratives, syllogisms, metaphors. One day's entry was, *If my cells are one part Rachel, one part Michael, and the crucial Michael-piece of each nucleus has been sliced off at the cellular level, doesn't the missing piece of each cell defile the whole structure? I must be a creature defiled.* (Eventually something like this became a piece of Dinah's interior monologue.)

I gave voice to the depths — no matter how ugly, inaccurate, tasteless, tactless, ungrateful, bitter, or hurtful. One of the first coherent things I wrote was this, which also found its way to *Saving Elijah*:

> I am a clobbered egg
> ex orb exploded,
> white shard in your eye,
> it hurts.
> There there.
> This sweet yellow yolk
> rots now,
> threaded with bloodeous black,
> glutinous maximus,
> sweet rot drips
> all over the imported linen,
> sticky on the gold rimmed China,
> soiled with the grotesque muck of my child's grave.
> There with my child, so cold.
> I sweat this stuff in your face,
> All placid and complacent as a baby's toes.
> I yield up nothing you want.

No angel wings,
No down for your bed,
No meat.

One creepy, paranoid, and erroneous outburst blamed my husband for everything because he hadn't thought enough about what we were getting into when we adopted Michael. In another I groused against my poor wounded daughter, and the teacher who stepped in to help her, though it was apparent to everyone, including me in my more lucid moments, that I had all but removed myself from my living child's life.

Disorganized, unfiltered ravings. Raw and bleeding. A big, glutinous, tortured, repetitive, insane, self-flagellating, unreadable mess.

As I wrote I suspect I began to subconsciously crave the typing rhythm again, fingers flying over the keys as fast as I can think. Long hand felt so slow. I had written the first draft of my first novel in 1988 on a Selectric typewriter, the manuscript stiff with whiteout, before finally taking my husband's suggestion that I try the newly invented miracle called a computer, and producing the next six or seven drafts on an early PC.

When I crept back to the computer in my garage office, I was, without realizing, it taking yet another step. I was beginning to enter the acceptance phase of what Elizabeth Kübler-Ross, in her groundbreaking work, *On Death and Dying*, called the five stages of loss, often misunderstood, but valid: denial, anger, bargaining, depression, acceptance. More recently, psychologists have noted that true grief work may not even commence until the acceptance stage, when the bereaved begins to reinvest in life without the lost one, and take into account theoretical models and orientations; personal, circumstantial, and cultural variables; the degree of relationship to the deceased; the problem of re-traumatization; and oscillation back and forth between adaptive and bereaved mind states. Many of these models can appropriately provide a framework and language for my own halting emotional progression.

It occurred to me as I continued to type disconnected journal entries three years after the death of my son that being bereaved is not an occupation. Did I want an occupation? Did I want to even live? I was a wife (though the marriage was shaky), and still Rachel's mother, but what was I going to be, now that I was no longer Michael's mother too? I was beginning to understand, through self-observation and observation of other bereaved, the way grief shatters the ego. This popular term, real despite being a psychological construct, can be understood in this context as the mechanism that regulates a human being's sense of self and self-worth, the way one has learned to negotiate the world. Okay then, why not go back to school and get an MSW to add to my psychology master's, a licensable degree with which I could hang out a shingle, perhaps counsel the bereaved? I'd admired the way the social worker led the grief support group, even coping with cynical, distraught, angry, tortured, bitter, joke-cracking me. But did I want to do *anything*, beyond grieving my son?

Yes. Save my marriage. Take my daughter back. Personally, I think a bereaved mother (or father) must, at a time of her choosing, make a conscious decision to go on living; you can easily go on being paralyzed with grief forever.

Beyond that? Ten years before, I'd put most of my occupation eggs in the writing basket; I'd studied craft, worked hard, and while I hadn't written a best seller I'd achieved success many writers only dream of. Could I just go back to that? Maybe in order to feel like a whole person again, I needed to. I'd gotten used to moving through the world as a writer. But what would I write about, when I couldn't see anything but grief?

One of the biggest surprises you get as a bereaved person is how unprepared many people are to cope with your grief, how some even run for the hills. The Buddhist definition of compassion is in my view the best one: *Compassion is willingness to be close to suffering.* Some people are gifted in this regard; they're willing, and know what to do and say instinctively, or are prepared to learn if they care enough. It takes commitment and stamina to sit close to all that anger and pain. Like so many other bereaved I'd met, I had some friends who stuck by me, and some who abandoned me to my misery. It's hard when you're already feeling isolated and lost to conclude that people aren't coming around because something is wrong with you. Not coming around when a friend is bereaved is like kicking a bleeding dog. (By the way, I no longer resent the abandoners. It is they and not I who missed something by walking away, something instructive, deeply human, profound.) But if so many people naturally turn away from grief, how could I write the truth and still attract readers?

Asking questions meant I was still alive. Asking what I might write for publication was a major step toward reinvestment in life. For one thing, it conceived a future that didn't involve sitting around in a bathrobe, staring vacantly at walls.

While unfiltered journaling is a valuable healing tool, publishing work is another matter. My journal was incoherent, hateful, nearly indecipherable. To publish such a journal would be like broadcasting your therapy sessions on television, what trainee therapists call a process recording. Or worse. Okay, so I'd write a memoir. I'd begin to filter, conceive, order, and make the hard choices a memoirist, like a fiction writer, must make about what to include and how to organize and express the material — context, voice, point of view, tone, theme.

I labored on that for several months, but found that I couldn't write honestly. There was my young daughter and husband to consider, and a birth mother. I didn't want to risk a libel suit by respected doctors and others who might feel maligned. I didn't want to name names — even with a disclaimer. Or re-traumatize myself by opening my psyche and actions to public scrutiny. (Perhaps that's what I did in the end, because more readers than I expected assumed I am Dinah anyway, and that I faced the same struggles and choices as she does. Even fiction writers who don't explain their sources face readers' assumptions. Still, you have to be brave, and let characters become whoever they need to become, just like children, even if Aunt Susie thinks she recognizes herself and never speaks to you again. See Phillip Roth for details.)

It may seem quaint in this era when so many people blog their souls, tell the most hideous secrets before hooting television audiences, that a writer might not want to do that. I switched back to fiction partly because I was more familiar with that form, and partly because I wanted to hide to some extent, but mostly because I wanted to speak to what I had heard and learned about the psychological commonality of grief, not my own particularly. (Fiction writers *get* to universal themes by being very specific, but let's leave that aside here.) In retrospect, I can see more clearly: I needed to write about *another* bereaved mother because only by corroborating even the most hideous aspects of my own grief could I affirm their legitimacy and thus feel human again. In any case, what would be the point of identifying what awful things *I* had said and thought, which friend abandoned me, which doctor patronized me, what issues were problematic in my marriage, and so on? The point I wanted to make was that many couples split after losing a child; have friends who abandon; encounter many people who say and do exactly the wrong thing; have negative experiences with doctors. (Some also have wonderful doctors; we had some of those too.) I wanted the reader to understand "grief," not necessarily *my* grief. I could disguise all that as it specifically related to my own life, maybe thinly, as they say, but in a novel I could also add, subtract, invent, and alter as necessary for the story I would create during the fictional process.

Okay, so I'd write a novel. Why not pick up with Sam and Dinah and their son, Elijah? If I hadn't adequately portrayed their grief, I could do better now. I could have stuck with the kidnapping, but a reader coming to an abduction novel might have expectations I had no intention of fulfilling, and, in any case, I had an interest in showing the devastation wrought by the arrogance of some physicians on the ill and their families. How closely I would stick to the facts, medical and otherwise, how closely my psychological issues and background would overlap with Dinah's, I would determine as I went along, applying what I knew about the way grief works on the ego, psyche, family.

I struggled for a while with that plan, but now, whenever Dinah sounded authentic, she also sounded narcissistic and hateful, railing against the world and God, weeping and whining, snapping at her mother, children, friends, husband. What reader would want to spend time with that story, inside that head? All right then, maybe we come into the novel two years after Dinah's son has died, when she is beginning to recover —

But I didn't want to write a novel about a mother recovering. A mother never "recovers." I wanted to write a novel about the thick of maternal grief.

By this time I was reading every self help grief book I could get my hands on, along with memoirs and novels about grief. So many of the novels felt inauthentic, or came at the fictional problem from outside the mother's head, presenting maternal grief from someone *else's* point of view, daughter, son, husband, friend. Maybe some of these authors had lost a child, I don't know, but made the less problematic (some might say nearly impossible) fictional choice. Why did I think I could come closer? I don't believe that a man can't write effectively from a woman's point of view, a young person can't create a believable old one. I don't know why, I just did. Or maybe I felt that enduring the loss was justification enough to try. But I worried about whether I had the facility with words to evoke what a bereaved mother feels without either whitewashing the truth, or alienating the reader?

Oh forget it. Maybe I should concentrate on getting *out* of the grieving mother's head. Since I needed an occupation now to feel whole again, I'd go back to school for an MSW on top of my MA in psychology, become a therapist, and if I still wanted to be a writer in five years, I'd write detective novels, as the bereaved mother does in John Irving's *A Widow for One Year.* I tossed the idea of becoming a therapist around in my head, and yet couldn't resist the pull of writing. Nor could I write about anything else. And wasn't it better to write while I was still inside it, so I wouldn't have to draw only on memory, but on living emotion?

I had never been a writer who outlines plot in advance. I always tried to develop character and plot simultaneously, so as not to allow plot to dictate as it does in many "genre" novels, mainly because I know too much about human beings and their psychology to be interested in characters that don't seem human. I always wrote scene by scene, allowing characters to bubble up from my inner psyche, so as not to force a character in a direction already prescribed to fit a plot, which has a character-flattening affect. As a result, I often found myself writing some bit of business into a scene without knowing exactly why, only to discover the explanation later. For example, I had no idea why I had named that kidnapped boy Elijah in what was essentially an early draft of *Saving Elijah.* I only realized this later, when I discovered the conciliating role Elijah has in the Bible. I believe that name bubbled up from my unconscious, or, to use the Jungian term, the collective unconscious.

I had decided to have Dinah run into an old boyfriend in the hospital while she kept vigil over her dying son. Two years later, as she is realizing her marriage is no longer working — as part of *her* "reinvestment" — she calls this man and begins an affair. If I started the novel then, I could do the hospital scenes in flashback, and not make the reader spend too much time where she didn't want to be, in a hospital with a dying child.

I tried to work on the opening scene when she calls the man, but couldn't make it work, so I tried the hospital flashback and really got going on that, but when I brought Dinah out to the corridor to run into the man, the scene fell flat. Why was this guy there? Was he not working because the whole thing was too much of a coincidence?

Saving Elijah, plot and all, was conceived in that moment. Maybe this man *wasn't* there. Maybe he wasn't a living character, but a figment of her imagination, a ghost, spirit, god, or devil, any of which can appear to the beholder in any form. That wouldn't be an imposed coincidence; that would be psychologically sound. Dinah *might* be thinking about someone in her life about whom she's conflicted, say, an early boyfriend who died in a motorcycle accident from which she herself was spared. I'd certainly thought about choices I made in *my* life. And why was this figment there? He's there to offer Dinah what she wants most, what even all the arrogant doctors can't offer her. What does she want? She wants what *any* mother wants; she wants her boy to *live*.

Of *course*. The fiction writer must identify what each character wants. The ghost could personify the psychological *process* of grief, and pose all the ugly, painful questions a bereaved mother asks herself, a structure later praised by one reviewer as a "tough-minded interrogative approach." The ghost could be a living metaphor for motherly "bargaining," as Kübler-Ross called it, stand in for the ugly, cruel, solitary, narcissistic truth of grief; take that burden off Dinah so the reader could sympathize with her. The ghost could help the reader viscerally understand that grief makes you wonder if you're going insane, by presenting a character only Dinah seems to see, and a maybe-it's-true/maybe-not scenario. The ghost could show grief in all its rawness, yet make it palatable, even entertaining.

A talking ghost would go beyond the supernatural elements I'd previously worked with, but by giving my imagination free rein I took yet another step toward "reinvestment." And once I conceived the ghost and put him in that corridor it was as if I started channeling him from some unknown ethereal realm. I still wrote the book scene by scene without outline and, even as I approached the end of the first draft many months later, wasn't sure whether I was going to save Elijah or not.

But one thing I did know, and still do: I constructed the structure out of my deepest grief: equal parts terror, sorrow, rage, hope, wishful thinking, catharsis, honesty, experience, intellect, knowledge of psychology, and imagination.

And how emotionally satisfying — very close to a peak experience — it was to write the moment when Dinah, watching over her comatose son, first hears the ghost's song, leaves her boy's bedside to go into the corridor, and sees a being that only she can see, who says he can save her son.

The woman in front of Starbucks was only the first of a long line of questioners who wanted me to personally explain which parts are "true," as if I could do that line by line. Is my husband Catholic? (No.) Was my mother as impossible as Dinah's mother is? (My mother died years ago.) Was my first boyfriend a sick bastard like Seth? (Ha Ha.)

I came up with an appropriately "literary" answer, true, if evasive: Fiction is a pot of soup whose ingredients might include almost anything seen, heard, felt, read, imagined, experienced, or dreamed, and just as the long cooking process profoundly transforms raw ingredients, so does the fictionalizing process transform specific events. You can't isolate a particular herb in a bubbling puree of carrot.

With that answer I managed to satisfy all but the most persistent of questioners, but there were still surprises, many of which felt like re-traumatization at the time: the "friend" who'd witnessed my loss and said nothing about the novel beyond that she didn't "like that sort of stuff," meaning, I guess, ghost stories; the men who said their wives loved it but would never read it themselves; the people who used neutral words like "interesting" or who didn't say anything at all. (Shields' essay offered comfort through similarity of experience.)

I had always thought that dealing with negative critical reaction was going to be the major emotional danger of the undertaking. It was, but not only because some seemed to fail to appreciate the literary merit of my work, which had been my chief worry, but because those who didn't get it failed to understand the truths I'd wanted — felt compelled — to convey. I see now that reactions to my novel often echoed reactions to my grief; they were about the reactor and not me. Sure, some found my book artistically lacking, but some are also intimidated by writers, snobby about the parameters and form of "literary" fiction, immovably appalled by outrageous and/or supernatural plots, or unwilling to read a book about a dying child. Just as some people are naturally compassion-ate, some insensitive, some stupid.

I've come to separate the cathartic writing experience from the occasionally anxiety-producing, re-traumatizing publishing experience, yet I appreciate each for its own lessons. How could I ever forget the radio announcer who, like so many others in the media, interviewed me after reading only the publicity materials? "We have with us Fran Dorf," he said on the air, "who has written a novel inspired by the loss of her son. *Hmmm.* Last week we had another parent who had lost a child on the show. I guess there's a lot of that going around these days." I got through that Jackie Gleason moment, and when I hung up called the publicist and told her I was through promoting my book.

Picasso said, "Art is a lie that helps you tell the truth." I believe *Saving Elijah,* by personifying grief in the form of that ghost, by essentially making an extended metaphor for the process of grief, tells truths about grief that couldn't be told in a memoir, or at least is the best expression of what *I* wanted to say about grief. I would argue that although not a single scene literally occurred, every single word is true. Though I sometimes now feel as if I carry two (lopsided) burdens, part Michael, part Elijah, I stand by the novel. I also have come to fervently believe that writing as a practice can help us understand, integrate, intellectualize, compartmentalize, and express even our most traumatic life experiences. The long process helped me begin to find the way to reinvest in my life without my son, and in effect SAVED MY LIFE.

About two years after publication, I became friendly with a woman I met in a gym, a respected surgeon. On her own she picked up my book, whose jacket doesn't say anything about my sources; she had no idea I lost a son. The next time I saw her in the gym, she said, "Your book was amazing. I can't believe you wrote that without spending a lot of time in a PICU. So real and true."

Real and true in a book in which the future is foretold, the Angel of Death shows up, and one of the main characters is a malodorous ghost who slings insults, gyrates his pelvis Elvis-style, and mocks everyone and everything, including doctors and God.

The question I'm most often asked now when I confess that I lost a child AND wrote a novel inspired by the experience is why I didn't write a memoir. (Depending on who asks, I might leave out one or the other of those facts.) I could have, I suppose. A carefully constructed memoir can give a reader unique access to someone else's singular experience, possibly fostering empathy, learning, understanding, growth. But reading a memoir can also make us feel safe, even smug, in the essential "otherness" of the author's experience. Like the millions who gawk at a celebrity's all-too-human troubles, or hoot at bad behavior on Jerry Springer, the woman at Starbucks could think, "Well, I would NEVER have had an affair." You wish, lady. You have no idea what you would do if your child died, let alone what *I* would do.

Reinvested in writing fiction as a profession, I finished another novel in 2004, but my agent was unable to sell it. He suggested that in this increasingly difficult, best-seller-oriented publishing environment it's going to be very difficult for me to sell another novel to a big publisher, because *Saving Elijah* didn't make back its very large advance. Perhaps the ghost seduced the publisher into thinking the book would sell like a horror blockbuster, paying me too much for what was essentially a literary undertaking. Maybe I didn't receive many reviews because critics were trying to spare me a critical slam that would land atop the emotional pain I'd suffered already. If that's so, I appreciate the kindness. On the other hand, I remember one reviewer who said the book was destined to make Fran Dorf "a household name." Perhaps it was emotionally best for me that *Saving Elijah* didn't make me a "household name." And that the story proved too difficult to adapt for a film, despite the efforts of actress Emma Thompson, who optioned the book for a year, and then the persistence and hard work of the independent producer who optioned the film for three years after that. Any of the two treatments and three scripts that came from those efforts would have resulted in a film that sensationalized the story, missed its point entirely, and broken my heart all over again, this time VERY publicly.

Household names can easily become targets of our insatiable, voyeuristic media and public. Consider James Frey's *A Million Little Pieces*, a work that in my opinion succeeds as fiction, tells important truths about addiction, and speaks, as all good fiction does, to the universality of experience, but falls short of the accuracy required for a memoir — as Mr. Frey found out so painfully and publicly. (Mr. Frey's decision to stretch truth and call his book a memoir, no doubt with encouragement from bottom-line-loving agents and publishers in an era when memoir is far outselling fiction, probably says more about the addictive personality than even the book itself does.) The cynic might say of Mr. Frey, or any other target who has achieved a certain measure of success, "Don't feel sorry for him, he's laughing all the way to the bank." I don't think it's that simple. And compassion for the target of the week doesn't even make the punditry's list of considerations. In this coarse and shameless culture, nothing is off limits. Consider the appalling derogatory remarks directed at Cindy Sheehan, who lost a son in Iraq.

I continue to reinvest in different ways. I write to make sense of the world, but now only when the spirit moves me — poetry, essays, articles, a blog called *The Bruised Muse* (www.bruisedmuse.com). I'm a regular contributor to Open to Hope, an online resource center for people who have experienced loss affiliated with the national organization Compassionate Friends. I'm not writing fiction now, although I can't say this is a permanent condition. I've learned to assume nothing is permanent. I got about halfway through an MSW degree in the year before my novel came out, then quit to devote myself to finishing, editing, and publishing my book. I'm finishing that degree now.

In the seven years since the publication of "Saving Elijah," using my reading, training in psychology, and experience as a clinician and writer, I've developed a workshop I call "Write-To-Heal." Its goal is to help people identify, express, integrate, and even transform the complex, difficult emotions surrounding grief, loss, and/or trauma. The workshop employs fictional and interrogative techniques, some arising out of themes developed in *"Saving Elijah,"* to deepen and clarify self-knowledge, and a constantly evolving series of exercises to stimulate the imagination and generate meaningful story, memoir, metaphor, and/or image. Some of the exercises encourage individual expression, some nurture group healing, community, and support. When I help people write for healing, I encourage them to banish all self-censorship, because, as I discovered, it's only by giving voice to the most despicable feelings we have that we can begin to let them go, or at least make some sort of peace with them. (Of course, this censor-banishing advice is also useful for the writer of any first draft.) Some of the exercises in the workshop I've developed myself, some I've adopted from other teachers, writers, researchers, and experts in this field such as James Pennebaker, Susan Zimmerman, Susan Bray, and John Fox. Although many of the experts in this field are wary of sharing, and I always make it optional, I've found that sharing in a trusted group provides validation of feelings that can be beneficial, particularly for bereaved parents, who are often concerned about their sanity, as I was. I've conducted workshops with many different groups, including the bereaved, addicted, and homeless. I tailor the workshop to the needs and interests of the participants, and it is accessible to anyone. I've found that people are amazed at their own power, and come away from the workshop with a sense of renewal, hope, strength, and growth.

Life goes on. My husband and I are still together. My daughter, who was twelve at the time of Michael's death, is now a grown woman, pursuing a PhD in psychology. Last summer she married a young man we love like a son, and we were thrilled to make them a wedding. Michael wasn't there.

I miss him. I expect I'll think of that fine little boy as I draw my last breath. For all my powers of imagination, I can't even begin to imagine what he would be like now, at eighteen years old. Maybe someday I'll write more about him. The writer decides what to write, and then makes a choice whether to send that out into the universe, and when and how. The universe responds.

I'll never forget the woman in a bookstore where I was doing a reading who asked, "What's your novel about?" "A woman trying to save her dying son," I said. "Grief." The woman lowered her eyes and backed up like a car in reverse, tires screeching. "Oh no," she whispered, eyes wide. "I can't go there."

Sometimes now I go to the place where my son is buried and place stones on the brass and marble marker that says: **Mikey, BELOVED SON AND BROTHER**. After fourteen years, grief is no longer a thundering, hissing monster. Grief is quiet now, like the hollow thud of rock on stone.

8

A Spirit Laid Down in Chapters: Telling Your Story with Personal Essay

Emily Simerly

There are hundreds, maybe thousands, of books on how to write memoirs. Within these books are thousands of questions to prompt anyone, anywhere to write about their life. So this presentation, although it will prompt you to write, will free you from specific questions and take you to a deeper part of your self, a place that is more free-flowing from your unconscious. It is not free association, exactly, because I will be doing readings from my work and the work of others that will elicit certain feelings within you, and from those feelings, I hope you will move to events in your own life that connect to the feelings you are having. I am calling this a Be-In, which is a word from the late 1960s for a gathering of people who were expressing who they were. Be-Ins were freeing experiences, freeing from the weight of social norms and edicts. They were also called Happenings. They were *very* fun.

This is a time you can spend a little like children who are having a bedtime story read to them and then thinking about it or writing about it. I so remember my eighth grade English teacher, who used to start every class with the phrase, "As we live and breathe and have our being…" I hope that you will "have your being" here today. There will be six readings, and whatever you write after each reading can be a part of a chapter of your own personal life history. By the end of this workshop, you will have six "chapters."

I work in a maximum-security men's prison where I work with a variety of inmates of all races and crimes. I work on Death Row; I work in our High Maximum Security building that houses inmates who not only did not make it in the free world, they haven't even made it in prison. These are inmates who have multiple incidents with security that have led to multiple disciplinary reports. They have all had fights with security. Some of them have killed staff or other inmates while in prison. Some of them have also been extremely self-injurious, with such unusual behavior as cutting their throats, cutting their arms, and fishing out arteries in their arms so they can spray the walls, swallowing objects like razor blades, and inserting objects into wounds and even into their private parts.

The question for me is, why do I thrive in this environment? I am constantly on the go to this emergency or that, or to this intense therapy session, or to a meeting to work on inmate care. I would like to say it is my humanitarianism. When people ask me to volunteer for something, I say, "No thanks, I give at the office." But that's only a part of it. My work is not a calling for me, but it is a perfect niche. A large part of the reason I love working in such a place is the vast sea of drama and intrigue on which every prison rocks.

Several years ago, in an effort to get my friends and everyone else in general to understand why I loved working in a prison, I wrote an article that was published in *Voices* and excerpted in *The Georgia Psychologist*. It says exactly what I feel about my work. It is titled, "I Come from Privilege."

It's time now to begin the Be-In. Get comfortable in your seat, whatever that means for you. Let the seat support you so your mind can focus or wander to its heart's desire. After the reading, I will give some other "non-instructions" for you to follow or not. Close your eyes if you'd like, and let the bubbles come up from your unconscious.

I Come from Privilege

I come from privilege. I left there about an hour ago. When I'm there I'm reminded that I'm privileged because I see miracles happen daily. This privilege is a maximum-security men's prison in middle Georgia. In our own rich world, where we have the Blackberry and the mountain house and all the acquired assets, prison is one place that reminds us of the inhumanity that exists in other spheres. Most people I know, including therapists, have no sympathy for criminals. With prisoners, it's not an I and Thou, it's an Us and Them. The incarcerated folk are a good repository for our revenge needs, our sense of righteous anger, our moral superiority. It's easy to look down on a group who seem so justly to deserve their current fate. Inmates are the lowest caste in our country. They are our Untouchables.

I work in a prison but that doesn't mean I'm immune to those feelings. Historically, I have identified with victims and fairness. I struggle every day with my views of one inmate or another, views that include the person as a human being and the act or acts he committed to get to where I am. Not lapsing into those classist, moralist, scornful feelings is a daily activity for me. It's awkward that bringing up the best in myself, pushing back feelings of derogation, has to be an active process. But working with inmates puts me in a position of knowing them as human beings, and that makes it much, much harder to look at them in a negatively polarized way. How can I look down on a "client?" Wouldn't that come through in the work we call therapy? Would you be able to have a healthy healing relationship with someone who felt superior to you? Me neither.

As a psychologist working in a prison, I get a lot of privileges. Yes, there is managed care in prison, but it is actually quite helpful. Managed care follows the Georgia Department of

Corrections guidelines and requirements, and these have been well thought out. I get to do group and individual therapy. I get to supervise a variety of counselors. I get to do program oversight. It's very rich, a description used recently by an inmate when he spontaneously described therapy. He and I had been working together for about six months and progress is slow but deep. He has not received parole in two tries and still sits in prison, not because of his relatively minor charge of commercial burglary, but because of his behavior. And he is fully responsible for his anger, entitlement, and dangerousness. But he is smart enough to know, as he said, "If I had been able to get this kind of therapy before, I might be out by now." And then he said, "Therapy with you is like living in a rich neighborhood. You know you might have to live in a poor neighborhood again, but you'll take some of what you learned in the rich neighborhood with you."

And yes, I may one day have sway towards his parole, so the cynical (and smart) among you say he is just buttering me up. My cat, Marvin Roy, will tell you we're all listening for the sound of the can opener. That's one of the fascinating things about working in a prison — the truth is, I don't know if he's telling the truth. But if he is, isn't it a great image? And if he's not, isn't it a great lie? In other words, either way, I win. I was taught in graduate school at Georgia State University to work towards, recognize, and value authenticity. I do that every day in prison. If the prisoners are not authentic, that's a choice they are making. But they can't get away from authenticity being presented to them, and I believe that every bit of good that is put out into the world is a hit, none of it a miss.

Another inmate I work with is ill with AIDS. He calls himself trailer trash, and he has a speech impediment and a quite low IQ. But I sit mesmerized by him in group as he confronts others much better off than he about their self-destructive behavior, as he talks about his constant suicidal thought, as he thanks the group for letting him talk about his shame. This same inmate, who cannot take the cocktail medicines that are so helpful against HIV, occasionally comes for an individual session. At the last one, we talked about telling his family and how hard that will be and about his hopes for the future. As he was leaving, he got to the door and turned to me and said, "Thank you for helping me be human again. It makes dying easier."

The statement cast the light of life onto the stark gray of concrete blocks, the authoritative glare of fluorescent lighting, and the unforgiving barbed wire surrounding us. Thomas P. Malone was right when he said 20 years ago that psychopathology could be thought of as nonexperience. What that inmate was telling me was that the experience of being taken as a human being made him feel like a human being. That his crime, his class, his illness all had been transcended in the moment of meeting, inside the barbed wire, inside the concrete block walls, under the glare of fluorescent lights. Transcendence and miracles.

All the old things still work not matter where you are — the things we learned in school, the things we've seen along the way. What William Faulkner talked about in his 1950 Nobel Prize acceptance speech is still true — that we will prevail because we have a soul, a spirit that is capable of compassion and sacrifice and endurance:

> The poet's, the writer's, duty is to write about these things. It is his privilege to help man endure by lifting his heart, by reminding him of the courage and honor and hope and pride and compassion and pity and sacrifice which have been the glory of his past. The poet's voice need not merely be the record or man, it can be one of the props, the pillars to help him endure and prevail.

I submit that that this is the therapist's duty as well. To prop up the heart until the heart has healed enough to beat on its own.

So when I walk among the dispossessed and the disenfranchised, I don't forget the damage they have done or the damage that was done to them. I use it all in the service of the heart. Hearts live in prison, too.

Yes — I come from privilege.

Now is the time for you to reflect and write a few words that come to you as you listened to this essay from prison. Let your mind or heart or gut go to your hand and express the thoughts and feelings from them on paper. Be mindful. In several minutes, the Buddha bell will bring you back to another reading.

(Buddha bell tones.)

My brother, Terry Simerly, PhD, has had a private psychotherapy practice in Manhattan for many years, beginning back in the 1970s. My brother is gay and was living in Manhattan during the heyday of the human rights movements. During the 1980s and early 1990s, he ministered to many men who were dying of AIDS. When the worst of it was said and done, he had ushered over 100 men to their deaths. Though they were unlucky to die, they were lucky to have someone so skilled and kind as my brother to walk that difficult path with them.

In 1992, in a journal called *Pilgrimage: Psychotherapy and Personal Exploration,* my brother wrote about his experiences. The editor's note about his piece said, "It has taken a long time to find someone willing to share both the pain and the satisfaction of working with those suffering from AIDS. I am very pleased to welcome Terry Simerly to our pages and am most appreciative of his honesty and courage in presenting the powerful account of his work with AIDS patients. Terry writes, 'I have been in private practice in New York City since 1977. I live and work in a sunny loft in midtown Manhattan.'"

Terry titled his essay "I Am Not Resigned" from a poem by Edna St. Vincent Millay called "*Dirge without Music.*" The full quote is "Quietly they go, the intelligent, the witty, the brave. I know. But I do not approve. And I am not resigned."

Terry divided his piece into categories that, when I reread it for this presentation, made me like I was reliving that crisis all over again, with so many, many losses. But, like my brother said, it won't do to be resigned. He began his essay under the heading "The Age of Innocence," when being gay and free was so fun. He moved on from there to "The Long Haul." Then he began to get more personal about his view of his clients under the heading "The Hero's Journey" Knowing what was coming, he titled the next section "Toward the End." The last part is called "I Think It's Soon," and it is the story of my brother and two of his clients, all three of them going through the most difficult passage of life.

I Am Not Resigned

Most men do not want extreme measures taken if they are debilitated, and protect themselves against invasive procedures by signing a living will. Not so Michael, who was a fighter from start to finish. Toward the end, he requested a respirator though the use of it meant he could not talk. As he deteriorated, he would fight it when asleep; this necessitated the hospital staff paralyzing him with drugs to inhibit his movements. Frightened but not disoriented, he could only move his hands. I gave him a hand-size teddy bear to hold when no one was in the room with him. The bear served quite literally as a transitional bridge between him and me, and perhaps even between life and death.

One night his lover Rob called me from the hospital and said, "I think it's soon." Michael was in a coma, his breathing labored and heavy. Rob and I took turns talking to him and meditating, encouraging him to let go, crying softly and saying our good-byes. The room began to fill with a nameless joy; there was tingling in our hands for an hour afterwards from the physical contact with Michael. His spirit was lifting; mixed with the grief of the final good-bye was a profound and unforgettable joy.

His partner Rob began working with me soon after Michael's death. He was part of the second generation, mourners who themselves were sick. Coming to my office for the first time, knowing this was where Michael had talked about his illness and impending death, Rob could feel both Michael's presence and his absence. His year of grief work over Michael was a gift to me: it helped me grieve as well. It was months before Rob could change anything in their apartment; a year before he could imagine dating. He felt guilty when things began to have meaning again. He said he was afraid that if he went on with life, he'd lose Michael as a soul mate.

Because he so honestly felt and expressed his grief, after a year or so, he did begin living fully again. He had 18 months of relatively good health, and met a new lover. The last year was one of decline, several hospitalizations, numerous infections, occasional periods of reprieve. Now he is sometimes able to get to my office, but we are more likely to meet at his place or in the hospital. And just last week, knowing his strength is waning and tired of the struggle, he said to me, "I think it's soon." (pp. 8-9)

Now take time for meditation and writing. In time, I will help the Buddha call you back with his bell.

(Buddha bell tones.)

There is a book called *The Noonday Demon: An Atlas of Depression* by Andrew Solomon. Some of you may know this book. It is an aching description of the humanness of depression, covered with instances of those who live with depression, including the author, and some who have triumphed over it. One story in particular is about a Cambodian woman who lived during the Khmer Rouge devastation led by Pol Pot. I am old enough to remember this time, but it was distant to me even back then. After reading this section of *The Noonday Demon*, it is not distant any more.

Make yourselves comfortable in your chair as I read the story of Phaly Nuon:

From "The Noonday Demon"

We started with her own story. In the early seventies, Phaly Nuon worked for the Cambodian Department of the Treasury and Chamber of Commerce as a typist and shorthand secretary. In 1975, when Phnom Penh fell to Pol Pot and the Khmer Rouge, she was taken from her house with her husband and her children. Her husband was sent off to a location unknown to her, and she had no idea whether he was executed or remained alive. She was put to work in the countryside as a field laborer with her twelve-year-old daughter, her three-year-old son, and her newborn baby. The conditions were terrible and food was scarce, but she worked beside her fellows, "never telling them anything, and never smiling, as none of us ever smiled, because we knew that at any moment we could be put to death." After a few months, she and her family were packed off to another location. During the transfer, a group of soldiers tied her to a tree and made her watch while her daughter was gang-raped and then murdered. A few days later it was Phaly Nuon's turn. She was brought with some fellow laborers to a field outside of town. Then they tied her hands behind her back and roped her legs together. After forcing her to her knees, they tied her to a rod of bamboo, and they made her lean forward over a rice field, so that her legs had to be tensed or she would lose her balance. The idea was that when she finally dropped of exhaustion, she would fall forward into the mud and, unable to move, would drown in it. Her three-year-old son bellowed and cried beside her. The infant was tied to her so that he would drown in the muck when she fell: Phaly Nuon would be the murderer of her own baby.

Phaly Nuon told a lie. She said that she had, before the war, worked for one of the high-level members of the Khmer Rouge, that she had been his lover, that he would be angry if she were killed. Few people escaped the killing fields, but a captain who perhaps believed Phaly Nuon's story eventually said that he couldn't bear the sound of her children screaming and that bullets were too expensive to waste on killing her quickly, and he untied Phaly Nuon and told her to run. Her baby in one arm and the three-year-old in the other, she bolted deep into the jungle of northeastern Cambodia. She stayed in the jungle for three years, four months, and eighteen days. She never slept twice in the same place. As she wandered, she picked leaves and dug for roots to feel herself and her family, but food was hard to find and other, stronger foragers had often stripped the land bare. Severely malnourished, she began to waste away. Her breast milk soon ran dry, and the baby she could not feed died in her arms. She and her remaining child just barely held on to life and managed to get through the period of war.

By the time Phaly Nuon told me this, we had both moved to the floor between our seats, and she was weeping and rocking back and forth on the balls of her feet, while I sat with my knees under my chin and a hand on her shoulder in as much of an embrace as her trancelike state during her narrative would allow. She went on in a half-whisper. After the war was over, she found her husband. He had been severely beaten around the head and neck, resulting in significant mental deficit. She and her husband and her son were all placed in a border camp near Thailand, where thousands of people lived in temporary tented structures. They were physically and sexually abused by some of the workers at the camp, and helped by others. Phaly Nuon was one of the only educated people there and, knowing languages, she could talk to the aid workers. She became an important part of the life of the camp, and she and her family were given a wooden hut that passed for comparative luxury. "I helped with certain tasks at the time," she recalls. "All the time while I went around I saw women who were in very bad shape, many of them seeming paralyzed, not moving, not talking, not feeding or caring for their own children. I saw that though they had survived the war, they were now going to die from their depression, their utterly inca-pacitating posttraumatic stress." Phaly Nuon made a special request to the aid workers and set up her hut in the camp as a sort of psychotherapy center.

She used traditional Khmer medicine (made with varied pro-portions of more than a hundred herbs and leaves) as a first step. If that did not work or did not work sufficiently well, she would use occidental medicine if it was available, as it sometimes was. "I would hide away stashes of whatever antidepressants the aid workers could bring in," she said, "try to have enough for the worst cases." She would take her patients to meditate, keeping in her house a Buddhist shrine with flowers in front of it. She would seduce the women into openness. First, she would take about three hours to get each woman to tell her story. Then she would make regular follow-up visits to try to get more of the story, until she finally got the full trust of the depressed woman. "I had to know the stories these women had to tell," she explained, "because I wanted to understand very specifically what each one had to vanquish."

Once this initiation was concluded, she would move on to a formulaic system. "I take it in three steps," she said. "First, I teach them to forget. We have exercises we do each day, so that each day they can forget a little more of the things they will never forget entirely. During this time, I try to distract them with music or with embroidery or weaving, with concerts, with an occasional hour of television, with whatever seems to work, whatever they tell me they like. Depression is under the skin, all the surface of the body had the depression just below it, and we cannot take it out; but we can try to forget the depression even though it is right there.

"When their minds are cleared of what they have forgotten, when they have learned forgetfulness well, I teach them to work. Whatever kind of work they want to do, I will find a way to teach it to them. Some of them train to clean houses or take care of children. Others learn skills they can use with the orphans, and some begin toward a real profession. They must learn to do these things well and to have pride in them.

"And then when they have mastered work, at last, I teach them to love. I built a sort of lean-to and made it a steam bath, and now in Phnom Penh I have a similar one that I use, a little better built. I take them there so that they can become clean, and I teach them how to give one another manicures and pedicures and how to take care of their fingernails, because doing that makes them feel beautiful, and they want so much to feel beautiful. It also puts them in contact with the bodies of other people and makes them give up their bodies to the care of others. It rescues them from physical isolation, which is a usual affliction for them, and that leads to the breakdown of the emotional isolation. While they are together washing and putting on nail polish, they begin to talk together, and bit by bit they learn to trust one another, and by the end of it all, they have learned how to make friends, so that they will never have to be so lonely and so alone again. Their stories, which they have told to no one but me — they learn to tell those stories to one another."

Phaly Nuon later showed me the tools of her psychotherapy trade, the little bottle of colored enamel, the steam room, the sticks for pushing back cuticles, the emery boards, the towels. Grooming is one of the primary forms of socialization among primates, and this return to grooming as a socializing force among human beings struck me as curiously organic. I told her that I thought it was difficult to teach ourselves or each other how to forget, how to work, and how to love and be loved, but she said it was not complicated if you could do those three things yourself. She told me about how the women she has treated have become a community, and about how well they do with the orphans of whom they take care.

"There is a final step," she said to me after a long pause. "At the end I teach them the most important thing. I teach them that these three skills — forgetting, working, and loving — are not three separate skills, but part of one enormous whole, and that it is the practice of these things together, each as part of the others, that makes a difference It is the hardest thing to convey" — she laughed — "but they all come to understand this, and when they do — why, then they are ready to go into the world again." (pp. 34-37).

Now is the time for meditation and writing. The Buddha will let you know when to return.

(Buddha bell tones.)

Ben Okri is a Nigerian man who grew up in London. He is a poet and a writer of fiction. He is magic when he puts pen to paper. In 1991, after he published *The Famished Road*, I went to a reading he did in West Hollywood. It was an almost hypnotic event for me, listening to him read. He focused on African folklore, with the magic and the less clear distinctions between this world and whatever other ones exist. Here is part of the first chapter of *The Famished Road*. This piece is about letting yourself drift out into the infinite, about which we know nothing.

The Famished Road

In the beginning there was a river. The river became a road and the road branched out to the whole world. And because the road was once a river it was always hungry.

In that land of beginnings spirits mingled with the unborn. We could assume numerous forms. Many of us were birds. We knew no boundaries. There was much feasting, playing, and sorrowing. We feasted much because of the beautiful terrors of eternity. We played much because we were free. And we sorrowed much because there were always those amongst us who had just returned from the world of the Living. They had returned inconsolable for all the love they had left behind, all the suffering they hadn't redeemed, all that they hadn't understood, and for all that they had barely begun to learn before they were drawn back to the land of origins.

There was not one amongst us who looked forward to being born. We disliked the rigours of existence, the unfulfilled longings, the enshrined injustices of the world, the labyrinths of love, the ignorance of parents, the fact of dying, and the amazing indifference of the Living in the midst of the simple beauties of the universe. We feared the heartlessness of human beings, all of whom are born blind, few of whom ever learn to see.

Our king was a wonderful personage who sometimes appeared in the form of a great cat. He had a red beard and eyes of greenish sapphire. He had been born uncountable times and was a legend in all worlds, known by a hundred different names. It never mattered into what circumstances he was born. He always lived the most extraordinary of lives. One could pore over the great invisible books of lifetimes and recognise his genius through the recorded and unrecorded ages. Sometimes a man, sometimes a woman, he wrought incomparable achievements from every life. If there is anything common to all of his lives, the essence of his genius, it might well be the love of transformation, and the transformation of love into higher realities.

With our spirit companions, the ones with whom we had a special affinity, we were happy most of the time because we floated on the aquamarine air of love. We played with the fauns, the fairies, and the beautiful beings. Tender sibyls, benign sprites, and the serene presences of our ancestors were always with us, bathing us in the radiance of their diverse rainbows. There are many reasons why babies cry when they are born, and one of them is the sudden separation from the world of pure dreams, where all things are made of enchantment, and where there is no suffering.

The happier we were, the closer was our birth. As we approached another incarnation we made pacts that we would return to the spirit world at the first opportunity. We made these vows in fields of intense flowers and in the sweet-tasting of moonlight of that world. Those of us who made such vows were known among the Living as abiku, spirit-children. Not all people recognised us. We were the ones who kept coming and going, unwilling to come to terms with life. We had the ability to will our deaths. Our pacts were binding.

Those who broke their pacts were assailed by hallucinations and haunted by their companions. They would only find consolation when they returned to the world of the Unborn, the place of fountains, where their loved ones would be waiting for them silently.

Those of us who lingered in the world, seduced by the annunciation of wonderful event, went through life with beautiful and fated eyes, carrying within us the music of a lovely and tragic mythology. Our mouths utter obscure prophecies. Our minds are invaded by images of the future. We are the strange ones, with half of our beings always in the spirit world.

We were often recognised and our flesh marked with razor incisions. When we were born again to the same parents the marks, lingering on our new flesh, branded our souls in advance. Then the world would spin a web of fate around our lives. Those of us who died while still children tried to erase these marks, by making beauty spots or interesting discolorations of them. If we didn't succeed, and were recognised, we were greeted with howls of dread, and the weeping of mothers.

In not wanting to stay, we caused much pain to mothers. Their pain grew heavier with return. Their anguish became for us an added spiritual weight which quickens the cycle of rebirth. Each new birth was agony for us too, each shock of the raw world. Our cyclical rebellion made us resented by other spirits and ancestors. Disliked in the spirit world and branded amongst the Living, our unwillingness to stay affected all kinds of balances.

With passionate ritual offerings, our parents always tried to induce us to live. They also tried to get us to reveal where we had hidden the spirit token that bound us to the other world. We disdained the offerings and kept our tokens a fierce secret. And we remained indifferent to the long joyless parturition of mothers.

We longed for an early homecoming, to play by the river, in the grasslands, and in the magic caves. We longed to meditate on the sunlight and precious stones, and to be joyful in the eternal dew of the spirit. To be born is to come into the world weighed down with strange gifts of the soul, with enigmas and an inextinguishable sense of exile. So it was with me.

How many times had I come and gone through the dreaded gateway? How many times had I been born and died young? And how often to the same parents? I had no idea. So much of the dust of living was in me. But this time, somewhere in the interspace between the spirit world and the Living, I chose to stay. This meant breaking my pact and outwitting my companions. It wasn't because of the sacrifices, the burnt offerings of oils and yams and palm-nuts, or the blandishments, the short-lived promises of special treatment, or even because of the grief I had caused. It wasn't because of my horror of recognition either. Apart from a mark on my palm, I had managed to avoid being discovered. It may simply have been that I had grown tired of coming and going. It is terrible to forever remain in-between. It may also have been that I wanted to taste of this world, to feel it, suffer it, know it, to love it, to make a valuable contribution to it, and to have that sublime mood of eternity in me as I live the life to come. But I sometimes think it was a face that made me want to stay. I wanted to make happy the bruised face of the woman who would become my mother.

When the time arrived for the ceremonies of birth to begin, the fields at the crossroads were brilliant with lovely presences and iridescent beings. Our king led us to the first peak of the seven mountains. He spoke to us for a long time in silence. His cryptic words took flame in us. He loved speeches. With great severity, his sapphire eyes glowing, he said to me:

"You are a mischievous one. You will cause no end of trouble. You have to travel many roads before you find the river of your destiny. This life of yours will be full of riddles. You will be protected and you will never be alone."

We all went down to the great valley. It was an immemorial day of festivals. Wondrous spirits danced around us to the music of gods, uttering golden chants and lapis lazuli incantations to protect our souls across the interspaces and to prepare us for our first contact with blood and earth. Each one of us made the passage alone. Alone, we had to survive the crossing — survive the flames and the sea, the emergence into illusions. The exile had begun.

These are the myths of beginnings. These are stories and moods deep in those who are seeded in rich lands, who still believe in mysteries.

I was born not just because I had conceived a notion to stay, but because in between my coming and going the great cycles of time had finally tightened around my neck. I prayed for laughter, a life without hunger. I was answered with paradoxes. It remains an enigma how it came to be that I was born smiling.

Now begin your meditation and writing, and I will channel the Buddha bells to recall you to this space.

(Buddha bell tones.)

I wrote this next piece after a trip out to Tucson, Arizona. A friend of mine was on her clinical psychology internship there. I was thrilled with this trip to the desert, a place of beauty to me. I had first seen the desert in California in my twenties and felt suffering for the plants out there. It was a hardscrabble existence in every sense of the word. Also shocking for me was the outrageous difference that water could make in the landscape. Mars and Earth, more or less. When I came back to Georgia, I was asked to write an article for the journal *Voices*. The theme of the issue was psychotherapy and social issues. So I wrote an article I called "Desert Borders" that compared desert flora to borderline personality disorder. I picked part of this piece to describe what some call a sense of place. I think Southerners are born knowing what that means, but it is still useful practice describing it.

Desert Borders

The dry, hostile, prickly vista of the desert is as far from the warm, soft, wet furrow of the South Georgia I grew up in as a borderline is from an earth mother. I spent 20 years in the dampness that defines South Georgia. My early dreams and nightmares had to do with water and responsibility. The atmosphere begged for green growth — mildew and moss, lush grass and thick overhang were all a part of the verdant home I knew.

Many unknowing souls refer to the South as "backward" and "ignorant." I believe that the real truth about us is not that we are backward, but that we are primitive. We have not evolved in the way the rest of the country has — we are still in a transitional stage of evolution, where ontogeny has a shorter phylogeny to recapitulate. We still have the vestiges of gills in our jaws, so that when we are out running in the heavy aquarium of morning dew, we can filter oxygen out of the water that is supposed to be air. Our world had not forced as much adaptation. (p. 18)

Take some time to reflect on this short piece and the sense of place it invokes. In time, the Buddha will call you back.

(Buddha bell tones.)

Way back in the dark ages, when I was a junior grad student, I entered a student essay contest held by the journal *Voices*. The theme was "The Stages of Sages," so in the beginning, I didn't even think about it. I didn't know I wanted to be a therapist until I was 27, so I didn't think I had "stages." Then I realized one can have stages without knowing it. So I wrote about the stages I didn't know I'd had, and it all came together in the end of the piece.

Sit back, let the chair support you, do what makes you feel comfortable, and listen in.

When I was 27, my brother "suggested" that perhaps psychotherapy could help me with some problems I was having. With a typical duh response on my part, I said "Ok," little knowing the impact that was to come. I blithely entered into the therapy process. And I realized I did have stages.

Now, for the last time, get comfortable and listen to a truly personal essay

Every Road I Ever Took

My first memory, for instance. I'm two and a half years old and I'm standing at the curb with my blind father, holding his hand. It's a sunny day, and we are about to cross the street on the way to the barbershop so he can get his hair cut. He asks me if there are any cars coming. That is my task, to watch for cars so we can safely cross the street. In the first actually conscious moment of my life, I feel myself jerked out of the carefree and unaware innocence of childhood and plopped indecorously into the responsibilities of caretaking. Worse yet, as I heard his question I realized at that instant that I had indeed not been looking. I had no idea whether or not a car was coming. I was terrorized immediately, and as I felt the shame come up suddenly, I shut my throat to the guilt. With a two-and-a-half-year-old's will, I vowed never again to get caught not looking, always to be vigilant. And for most of my life, my conflicts with others often have a common theme: Why can't you see?

In this early stage, I learned symbiosis, dependence and independence, and the strength of early decisions. I also learned about the abilities of toddlers to respond to adult responsibilities, as well as the costs involved.

I'm six years old now, and my mother is late getting home from work. As it got later and later, I would realize she wasn't coming home for awhile. Nobody told me, but I figured out she had sort of run away from home. Adults would call it marital conflict, but for me it was sheer terror. She had left without telling me or my brother or father, and (we found out soon) had gone to stay for a few days with her sister. But I sit in the front yard, as it is happening, and every time I hear a car coming, I strain to look down the street hoping against hope that it's Mama. It never is, so after awhile I play a game. I imagine that if I keep my eyes closed until the next car gets almost to our driveway, then it will be her. If I can hold myself back when what I really most want to do is run to the street, maybe I'll be repaid by it being her. Maybe she'll turn in the driveway, and I won't have to be so scared. She doesn't, though.

The next night I think I hear her call my name from outside my dark bedroom window. I go and tell Daddy that I think I heard Mama calling to me from out in the bushes. He says he doesn't think she's out there, but I am very sure. So he picks me up and carries me outside and he and my brother and I look through the bushes for her. Of course, she's not there; it is simply a child's longing to see her mother again. In another few days, Daddy and I drove down to Florida to pick her up. I was so happy, so joyous to see her. Every time I looked at her, I cried. It didn't matter that she and I didn't get along or that my brother was her favored child. Mama was coming home.

In this stage I learned about superstition, magic, illusion, hope, terror, and the shock of separation.

I'm 22 and I've fallen in love with, of all things, a dog. Her name was Snazzy. My parents were temporarily keeping her for my uncle, and my father made the mistake of telling me my uncle had offered to give Snazzy to me. My father had told him no, that I was young and didn't need that much responsibility, and Daddy acted like that was the end of it. I argued with him about it, but he could not be swayed. So one weekend, I went to visit my parents in my hometown. As I was leaving on Sunday, I told my parents I wanted to put Snazzy in the backyard because she always looked so sad when I left. If she was out in the back-yard, I said, leaving would be easier. And so I left, waving as I drove away. I drove down the block, turned the corner, and came back up the alley behind my parents' house. I got out of the car, opened the back gate, and called softly to Snazzy. She looked as happy as I felt, as she flew down the yard towards me. I put her in my car and we tore off for Atlanta. That evening, my mother called me and said, "Do you have that dog?" I said, "Yes, I do. She's MY dog now!"

So began a 10-year love affair. The years went by with by such affection. Snazzy had been born in Washington State, but since she now lived down South, I thought she needed a South-ern name. So Snazzy became Snazzy Lou Ann Sue Ann Sue. Snazzy wrote songs like "Poochie Rama" and "Fry Me a Liver" and "Supercalifragisticdoggiehalitosis" and I sang them. She didn't have a veterinarian, she had a pediatrician. With Snazzy came a chance for me to mother as I had never been mothered, as I deeply longed to be mothered. With her came a chance to allow an innocence I felt I never had. There came a chance to support a dependence I wanted so much to experience. Most of all came a chance to love purely and without bounds; and what I was loving in many ways was me. I make no apologies for the relationship. It's the most fun I've ever had.

In this stage, I learned about determination, true love, mothering and me, loyalty, and again, symbiosis. And I learned in the end about letting go.

I'm 27 and I'm near the end of my very first hour as a client in psychotherapy. I brightly and naively ask my therapist, "Well, what do you think?" not even knowing exactly what I was asking. She said a number of things and then said that she noticed my mother and I had worked hard to give each other special presents. She thought my mother maybe had a hard time showing her love directly, or sometimes at all. It was almost as if that statement by my therapist gave my neck muscles a new ability, one that allowed me finally to turn and look squarely at a perception of my existence, a terrible truth I had been harboring for years but refused to look at. I walked out of that session with an invisible stranglehold on my throat and went quick and zombie-like to my car. Safely inside, I let go and sobbed, sobbed. All I would think was, "All this time my problem has been that my mother doesn't love me. How cliché." I felt like I was in a Woody Allen movie.

When I came back the following week, I began crying near the end of the session; the next week I cried in the middle, and the next week I cried near the beginning of the session. I felt the therapy room was a conditioned stimulus and I was a Pavlovian dog. With no seeming effort, therapy elicited tears of a lifetime. I was washed in magic in a real world. THAT was when I decided to become a psychotherapist. I left a "junior executive" job in business and an office on the 34th floor of a trendy new building downtown, where one whole wall of my office was a glass window, beneath which the business world lay at my feet. I never looked back.

In this stage I learned about risk, release, trust, and relief.

There have been many other stages and many other lessons, of course, all leading me to the same place. I can hear in my mind a song written by Bob McDill and Dickey Lee and sung best by Emmylou Harris. It's titled "Someone Like You," and it is a testimony to these stages. I didn't know until I was 27 years old that I wanted to be a therapist, and that didn't matter at all. This stage is called convergence:

No, I never wasted a minute of my time...

Cause every road I ever took led me to your side.

I can see clearly now, my whole life through,

I was just waiting for someone like you.

(Buddha bell tones.)

So now you have six chapters of your own called-up memories. Remember that many opportunities await you to unfold your life story. All of your senses are available and waiting for you to call for them. Don't forget the dark side — it dwells in all of us and might have a few things to tell that will not only surprise you but suddenly make a lot of things make sense. Or not. I wish I could be with you on your journey.

References

Okri, Ben. (1991). *The Famished Road*. Doubleday. (pp. 3-6)

Simerly, E. (1988). Every Road I Ever Took. *Voices: the Art and Science of Psychotherapy*, *24*(2), 51-54.

Simerly, E. (1990). Desert Borders. *Voices: the Art and Science of Psychotherapy*, *26*, (2), 18-22.

Simerly, E. (2001). I Come from Privilege. *Voices: the Art and Science of Psychotherapy*, *37*(3), 38-42.

Simerly, T. (1992). I Am Not Resigned. *Pilgrimage: Psychotherapy and Personal Exploration*, September/October, (2-9).

Solomon, Andrew. (2001). *The Noonday Demon*. Scribner. (pp. 32-37).

9

Writing the Personal Essay in Literary Form: One Writer's Journey Writing through the Death of a Child

Belinda Shoemaker

Speaker's introductory remarks: The use of writing as a tool to assist people working through pain and illness is becoming more common in the context of psychotherapy sessions. Teachers in community memoir writing workshops frequently find themselves in the position of assisting students work through deep hurts, and in coming to terms with illness and bereavement. A lot of what is written in these contexts, if published, could help a much wider audience going through similar experiences. The tendency for the writer in each of these situations is to write in journalistic form. Journal writing is unappealing, for the most part, to publishers.

It is this writer's contention that in order to appeal to a publisher, and to make the journey of writing toward wellness more accessible to a wider audience, these personal experiences need to be written as personal essays in literary form. In this paper an example of writing the personal essay in literary form is described in terms of one writer's experience writing through bereavement following the death of a child. Examples of personal essay styles are given from Brenda Miller and Suzanne Paulo's book Tell it Slant.

In July 2006, Jacqueline, an eight-year-old girl who lived with me was killed in a tragic accident. Jacqueline was my live-in caretaker's daughter. Her father, Pedro, was drunk. Jacqueline was sitting in the front seat of her father's truck. She was not wearing a seat belt. Pedro drove over a cliff a quarter of a mile from home. Jacqueline was killed instantly. As a writer, I decided to write my way through my grief. In this essay I will use excerpts from my essay, *Jacqueline's swing*, to illustrate how this story was written in literary form.

I consider myself fortunate that, as a writer, I have a medium that comes naturally to me through which I can express my grief. It is often said that we write to understand our lives, and/or the world in which we live. Writing is certainly one way in which I try to understand my world, be it consciously or unconsciously. Writing about painful experiences can be cathartic on a personal level, and contribute to the experience of catharsis for a wider audience experiencing personal pain. When I have performed readings of my essay, *Jacqueline's Swing*, I have observed the pain of others. People have told me how my words gave voice to their feelings and in some cases gave hope that pain would subside, leading to a healthier life.

In 2005, the author, Joan Didion, wrote *The Year of Magical Thinking* about her experience of her husband's sudden death, and the emotions and challenges she encountered during her first year as a widow. Didion's daughter's hospitalization for a severe illness coincided with this time. Sadly, Didion's daughter died soon after *The Year of Magical Thinking* was published.

Didion, being a well known and respected author, had no difficulty getting her book published. Didion's style is contemplative. The structure she uses in this book is freer flowing than prescriptive in the literary sense. Didion's writing style in this memoir of her grief does not appear journalistic. She weaves poetry by well known and frequently classical writers into her story. She shares with her reader how the language and content of poetry expresses her feelings and opens the door for her to visit her grief as her feelings emerge and transform. By integrating another person's words and examination of life in the form of poetry into her story, Didion is able to see her situation from other perspectives.

Didion comes to writing her story of bereavement armed with the tools of the writer: tools taught in writing courses, but not in therapy sessions. If the goal of the patient-writer is to have her work published, then she needs to learn to use some of these tools and to understand how they can transform a series of journal entries into a piece of prose.

Throughout time, poetry has been a frequently used form in which to write about grief. Keats' poem "Ode to a Nightingale" is one of the best-known examples in this genre. For a brief overview of the poem and how Keats expresses and explores his grief during an encounter with a nightingale, see http://www.sparknotes.com/poetry/keats/section3.rhtml

It is interesting to note the similarities between what some new student writers believe the purpose of writing to be, and how the person writing toward wellness interprets the purpose of her writing. Observing college students' writing, Nancy Kuhl, warns of the beginning writer's tendency today, particularly when subjected to the barrage of pop-culture, psychobabble, and Oprah-industry of writing, to confuse literary writing with personal therapeutic writing. Kuhl warns of the tendency to see writing as a means of self-expression as opposed to a craft or creative discipline. She advises the teacher to keep in mind the distinction between literary and personal writing. Kuhl suggests that one of the biggest challenges to the creative writing teacher is the belief held by many students that "Honesty about your true emotions is the most important thing in writing." (Leahy. p. 8) I believe that the writer writing her personal story needs to find that balance between writing for self-expression and for a general readership.

There are many forms, or types of structure, a writer of personal essays and fiction can choose. It is worth considering why the personal essay is appealing to the reader and to the writer. The personal essay gives the writer the opportunity to write in the first person, thus engaging the reader in a narrative that can draw the reader into a close "relationship" with the writer. This type of essay expresses a personal truth.

As a student working on my MFA in Creative Writing I studied many of the forms a personal essay can take. While there are several books available on how to write the personal essay, for the purpose of this paper I am recommending *Tell It Slant* by Brenda Miller and Suzanne Paolo. There are two versions of this book. The shorter version is aimed toward the general public and new writers. The longer version is a textbook commonly used in MFA programs. Miller and Paolo teach the writers studying this book specific structures that can be used in writing the personal essay. It is not the purpose of this paper to go into detail about the form and structure of the personal essay, but rather to introduce the concept. Miller and Paolo explore and analyze in depth the origins of various forms of the essay. An anthology in the book is used to demonstrate the literary concepts presented in the text.

Before taking a look at the essay styles put forward by Miller and Paulo, it should be noted that as with all forms of writing, in order to be interesting and approachable, the writer of the personal essay should incorporate the elements of craft, the strong writing techniques that form the backbone of a good story. When telling her story, the writer needs to pay attention to detail, and to be specific about what the story is about. It is easy for us to make assumptions about what the reader knows. The reader doesn't know anything about our story. The reader wants to experience the life event that the story is all about through the eyes of the writer before making it the reader's own story. This means paying attention to detail.

Teachers of writing will tell their students to "show don't tell." I can tell you I felt a heart wrenching grief when Jacqueline died, but you will feel with me when I tell you about how I fell out of my car hearing a terrifying scream somewhere outside of myself, a sound that seemed to come from something not human, a sound amplified by the search lights of the sheriffs vehicle; the scream that sank deep into me when I felt the arms of my own child around me. I can show you my pain when I show you the illuminated mountain scene, the stark while lights, the rescue workers whose faces contorted with pain, the white sheathed body of a child on a stretcher and a mother's wailing in the dark, anise-scented night.

A writer will find herself writing original detail. All the time the writer must remind herself to introduce the characters she wants to talk about to her reader with enough detail so that the reader can feel a connection with the character. I can tell you about one of the police investigators who came to interview me after Jacqueline's death. I can tell you he was looking for evidence of child sexual abuse. I can tell you he was gentle with his questioning, and sympathetic toward me. I can show you how the man in his forties with graying hair that emphasized his maturity validated my hope that he knew and understood pain. I can show you his furrowed brow and teary eyes as he listened to my painful recollection of that night, and other nights with Jacqueline. I can show you how he knelt on the ground in the midst of a sea of toys, of dolls, crayons, and the birthday card Jacqueline made for me just two weeks earlier. I can show you this father who showed me photos of his own children to relax me in his company. You will see him sitting crossed-legged on the ground with me, his suit pants creasing at the knee. You will see him gently handling Jacqueline's toys, looking to me first in a gesture that asks permission.

I cannot tell a story without telling you what someone said. I challenge anyone to leave the details of a conversation out of a story. What we say and how we say it tells a lot about who we are. When a writer tells us word by word, line by line, what a person has said, the writer needs to do it with language that comes naturally, language that is typical of the person who is speaking. Dialogue, therefore, is important. Again, speaking is not the only way we communicate. For every sentence spoken, every emotion unveiled; there will be gestures and looks to accompany speech. Often the gestures, the slight turn of a head, the hand that wipes an eye, the little cough between words, show us far more about the person and what they are experiencing than mere words.

Frequently I find when I am talking to my friends and am struggling to describe something, I naturally use metaphor to communicate indirectly what I am try to say. The use of metaphor and imagery in writing can be very powerful.

When I am teaching and facilitating small, intimate workshops, I like to introduce my students to some of the forms of the essay described by Miller and Paolo. Some forms of the personal essay presented in *Tell it Slant* include the following:

1. Lyric essay
2. Prose poems and flash nonfiction
3. Collage
4. The braided essay
5. The hermit crab essay

For a detailed description of these essay forms, please refer to the text.

I am not suggesting that anyone who wants to tell their personal story needs an MFA in creative writing, what I am suggesting is that attention to and application of some basic elements of craft will make a story more readable.

When writing my story about Jacqueline's death, I did not set out to follow any particular essay style. I did, however, fall into using my adaptation of the Braided Essay structure. Miller and Paolo compare the braided essay to challah bread.

"The Braided strands weave in and out, creating a pattern both beautiful and appetizing." In likening the braided essay to challah bread Miller states, "In this form, you fragment your essay into separate strands that repeat and continue. There's more of a sense of weaving about it, of interruption and continuation, like the braiding of bread, or hair."

Using the braided essay form a writer can weave three stories into one. The reader can experience three stories and see how they relate to each other and come together to form a whole. In *Jacqueline's Swing,* I have used three strands and weaved them in and out of the essay. The strands are not separate stories, but rather expression of various moods, metaphor, and straight narrative.

The close first person narrative tells the reader what happened on the night Jacqueline died. In parts this strand is blunt and shocking. Another strand uses metaphor to reflect and try to make sense of what should have been, and what is. Using this strand the reader engages in the contemplative narrative and emotions working through the tragedy. Another strand reflects catharsis. This strand takes the form of "stream of consciousness." Writers, including Virginia Woolf, used this technique on a number of occasions. In stream of consciousness writing the writer can write in free-flow without punctuation, giving the impression of the spontaneous, unedited rush of feelings or observations frequently experienced during the rawness of the devastation or the anger experienced with a loss.

At this point I will now present excerpts from my essay *Jacqueline's Swing,* and explain a little about some of the techniques I have used. I have chosen these excerpts as samples of the structures I have described. There is a lot more to this essay than will be apparent here. The essay is in the first person close narrative. The first and second sections are contemplative.

As these are excerpts, I have used numbers to indicate different sections of the story. These numbers are not used in the original text.

We start at the beginning of the story. It sets the reader up for the loss the writer is experiencing, for the longing for the time before the event that follows. It is close first person narrative. It introduces the reader to the "characters," the people the writer talks about in the story. Pedro is Jacqueline's father. Maria is her mother.

JACQUELINE'S SWING
By Belinda Shoemaker

Section 1

Today I am supposed to be playing with Jacqueline, but instead I'm sitting on the garden swing on the top of a mountain in Big Sur, mourning her death. She would have arrived about an hour ago. She'd have knocked on my door, and when I opened it she would have stood there smiling. Her shiny white baby teeth, some framed in gold, others crooked and assisted by gravity, were ready to fall out and make space for grown-up teeth. I would have lifted her skinny eight-year-old body into my arms and kissed her. She'd have wrapped her legs around my hips as I climbed the wooden stairs to the apartment over my barn. When I sat her down in the kitchen, Jacqueline would have wiped the sticky remains of sleep from her dark brown eyes. She would have tossed her long black Mexican curls over her shoulder, and then we'd have eaten hot buttered toast and soft scrambled eggs. Her favorite breakfast.

I was Jacqueline's weekend mother. Her parents, my caretakers who lived in the trailer across the dirt road, left Jacqueline with me while they did odd jobs for our neighbors to earn extra money.

Section 2

(Prior to this next section, Jacqueline's father, has agreed to build us a swing set with two swings side by side.) The second section, with a mixture of contemplation and direct narrative, introduces the metaphor of the swing and what it means to the writer.

Swings are made for dreamers. When I was a young girl I'd swing for hours in the back yard on my own. I kicked my legs as high as they would go. I watched the planes scar the sky on their way to unknown destinations, and I longed for wings so I could follow them. I wanted to travel with Dorothy to somewhere over the rainbow.

I loved Jacqueline's enthusiasm about having two swings. I imagined the two of us swinging side by side. I imagined the conversations we would have swinging together as she grew older. I imagined talking with her about her plans for the future, the college she might attend, and the struggles she, like all little girls, would go through as she grew up. I imagined being there for her, listening to her, being her confidante, and occasionally offering her advice.

Section 3

Section 3 abruptly throws the reader out of the sentimental and contemplative paragraphs into the hard facts of the situation. Through the use of repetition the bitterness the writer feels is reinforced. The rhythmic repetition implies pain in the memory and recounting of the event.

The road up from the canyon to my home and the trailer is a steep dirt track, rock ridden and destructive. It deteriorates each winter and is a bone-jarring mile of a ride. Maria lived in fear of the road. She begged Pedro to look for a house at the bottom of the mountain, but Pedro loved the view of the ocean on the climb home, and the ruby grapefruit sunsets he watched from the trailer window.

Jacqueline died at approximately 8:30 pm on July 7th, 2006. The newspaper report said that Pedro's red pickup truck swerved on one of the switchbacks going up the mountain. The truck left the cliff, tumbling over at least five times before coming to a halt. The newspaper reported that Pedro emerged from his truck with only a few bumps and scratches. The newspaper reported that Pedro told a witness to go away, and that there was no one in the truck other than himself. The newspaper reported that Pedro was drunk, that he ran away from the scene, leaving his dead daughter crushed beneath his truck. The newspaper reported that Pedro hid for forty-eight hours until "a couple of sensible residents" convinced him to turn himself in. I was one of those sensible residents. The newspaper didn't report the primordial scream I cannot remember uttering, but my daughter witnessed, when the sheriff stopped me in my car as I returned from dinner to tell me Jacqueline was dead. The newspaper did not report on the state of Maria, Jacqueline's mother as she fell out of her car at the crash site and into my arms screaming, "Belinda! Belinda, Jacqueline, Jacqueline, our Jacqueline."

Section 4

In section 4, we return to the contemplative braid. The sadness and irony of building the swing, and the process involved in doing so is evidenced in the metaphors of digging and swings.

> Some swings, like caskets, are built out of wood.
> The morning after Jacqueline's death I walked to the tree where the swing was supposed to go. Pedro had left a 4x6 wooden post leaning against the oldest tree in the garden. The post was supposed to be the beginning, a starting point for our swing.
> The phone rang. I ran back into the house to answer it. The voice on the phone said, "Sweetie," and "I'm so sorry," and, "Is there anything I can do to help?"
> "Build us a swing," I sobbed. What I really wanted was Jacqueline back, and our swing.
> My friend, Danny, came to my garden to build two swings side by side.
> Danny studied the tree. He hoisted his body up on a branch to test its strength to carry the weight of the swings with people swinging on them. He examined the roots of the tree to check

that they were healthy and not rotting. He shook his head. "This isn't going to work, sweetie," he said. "The tree limbs are not strong enough to hang a swing from."

Pedro was not strong enough to take care of his daughter.

Danny and a helper lifted the top beam for the swing from which to hang ropes. The angry helper said, "Pedro should swing for this. He murdered his daughter."

I left Danny and his helper to sizzle in the garden, while I walked down the summer dried crusty road to the edge of the cliff. Orange dust blew up around me with each whisper of wind. I took flowers and a bottle of water and placed them at the side of the road. I sat down on the edge, my legs swinging into the canyon of loss. I'd sat at the edge of the canyon the day after Jacqueline's death. I'd watched the sheriff hook a rope around his truck's bumper and around himself and descend into the canyon. I'd watched him attach a bag full of clothing to the rope. I'd watched the bag swing from side to side as I reached out to catch it on its way up. I'd fingered the clothes.

"Look closely," he'd said.

"Yes," I'd said, "those are her clothes. I washed those jeans last Sunday."

I'm not good at physics. I don't understand why some swings glide easily side by side without crashing into each other. I don't understand why some swings last forever, and some swings stop suddenly and things fall apart.

Section 5

Section 5 is written as stream of consciousness. It is the cathartic element of the essay. It is raw and painful, and represents the desperateness of loss and death.

A large chunk of the essay prior to section 5 details the celebration we had of Jacqueline's life. I have not used any of it in this paper.

Often Jacqueline and I drove down our mountain, and through the canyon lined with sycamore trees all the way to the village. The road twists and turns. A gnarled ashen tree, scarred for years by long-gone parasitic growths, appears to map the road ahead. It is a rooted sentry. During the day sunlight fingers its way through the moss green branches, dropping silver strands on residents going about their daily business, and on tourists meandering down to the beach at the end of the road.

While we drove, Jacqueline tried to teach me to speak Spanish.

"How do you say my name is Belinda? How do you say I live in Big Sur?"

I kept on forgetting the answers, and Jacqueline had me repeat the phrases after her over and over until I got them right.

I want those lessons back again. I want to drive with Jacqueline in the car, and go to the bakery for hot chocolate and pastries. I want to see Jacqueline's delight as strawberry jam oozes from a doughnut and drips down her chin. I want to see her little pink tongue chase the jam. I want to see her circling her lips to pull back the sugar making its way up her cheeks. I want to take her with me to help prepare for the library book sale, and watch her hide under a table when she's tired of stacking books. I want to sit at the table in the River Inn, waiting for lunch, watching her crayon ice-cream cones, flowers, and hearts all over the paper tablecloth. I want to hear her first attempt at putting her new word, "extinct" into context. That's a big word for a little girl, I said. Jacqueline told me she learned it from the dinosaurs, from our day in Berkeley at the dinosaur exhibit. I want to feel proud of her again as she excitedly acquires new skills. I want to help her wash hands all over again and tease her as we soap up her palms, the backs of her hands and each of her little girl fingers. I want to play Mr. and Mrs. Handy-Pandy again, the names I gave to her hands. I want her to giggle at the silly voices I made for each hand. I want her to ask me for more Mr. and Mrs. Handy-Pandy stories. I want to hear her read and guess at words when I tell her to sound them out. I want her to snuggle up to me after homework as I read her a chapter from *Winnie the Pooh*. I want her to knead the bread dough and laugh out loud when I tell her its stretched out well enough and it's time to stop. I want to watch her watching the dough rise. I want to see her face as she takes a bite out of the still warm baked bread with butter melting into it. I want to help her bake fairy cakes and decorate them with icing and sprinkles. I want to see her play with the kitten I gave her that we named Lilly. I want to see her proud face as she hands her mother some cakes and cookies we made especially for her. I want to hear her tell her smiling mother that she made the cakes all by herself and that I didn't touch them, save for putting them in and taking them out of the hot oven. I want to watch her go home hand in hand with her mother. I want to see her perform again at the school Spring Sing with her father looking on adoringly, watching her as she sings and moves to the music. I want to see her on the ridge with the sun setting behind her as she poses for photos, not dead as the sun sets.

A wooden swing must be sturdy enough to carry the weight of dreamers. Dreamers come in many sizes. Some dreamers sit and dream for a short time and go on their way. Others linger.

Section 6

Section 6 is composed of the final two paragraphs of the essay *Jacqueline's Swing*. It is straight narrative in which the writer tries to verbalize and come to terms with her loss. It is raw and extremely personal. The author speaks to the reader directly. At this point in the essay the appearance is given of a shared understanding between the author and the reader.

Swinging is an act of transition. A swing takes us from one place to another, from one dream to another. A swing moves us through time. A swing has a beginning, middle, and an end. It starts up, it slows down, and it stops. It takes time. Like life. A person pushing and pulling on a swing is a pumping heart. When you stop pushing and pulling back your legs, when you stop pumping, the swing will gradually come to a halt.

Sitting on the swing today, I know I'll keep trying to pump, to move forward without Jacqueline, to try to come to terms with her absence in my life. As I am writing this I am aware that it is early days yet. Jacqueline has only been dead for a little over three months. Perhaps the intensity of this early grief will subside. Perhaps the grief will find a place to settle in me, a calmer place. Perhaps the grief will eventually rise to the surface less frequently. Perhaps I will be able to smile and laugh and talk with less pain about all the wonderful things Jacqueline and I did together. Perhaps in time I will see things with a different sense of clarity. As it gets nearer to Pedro's trial I might feel differently. Who knows how I'll feel during the trial, or when I know the outcome of it. What I do know is that I'll come out and sit on this swing throughout all seasons. I'll swing through winter, spring, summer, and fall. I'll swing on the clear days when the blue cloudless sky dissolves into the ocean. I'll swing through fog and rain and on all the days when I am blinded by the weather, when I can cry in the storm and no one will hear me, when I can sing and swing in the rain. Today I tied a white ribbon to the swing next to mine. I like to imagine her sitting there: Jacqueline sitting on Jacqueline's swing.

In this essay I have acknowledged the value of writing through all sorts of pain. I have demonstrated my personal experience of coping with the death of a child by writing my way through it in the form of a personal essay. I have discussed and suggested the study of one specific text that will help to structure the experiences of people working through pain into a literary form. Understanding and using some techniques will go a long way towards getting work published, and therefore reaching and possibly helping a wider audience experiencing pain and sorrow.

Works Cited

Didion, Joan. *The Year of Magical Thinking.* Knopf, New York 2005.

Keats's Odes. Ode to a Nightingale, http://www.sparknotes.com/poetry/keats/section3.rhtml

Kuhl, Nancy. "Personal Therapeutic Writing vs. Literary Writing": In Anna Leahy (ed.) *Power and Identity in the Creative Writing Classroom; The Authority Project*. MPG Books 2005 (pp. 3-12).

10

The Healing Power of Revision in Therapeutic Writing

Noreen Groover Lape and Kristin N. Taylor

It is a fact of life that most English professors, even those who do not assign topics that instigate painful self-disclosure, have received essays by students who have chosen to reveal their wounds and traumas. In recent years, many composition scholars have begun to investigate the intersection between writing instruction and therapy. Not one of these scholars presumes to have the specialized training of therapists or expresses the desire to turn composition class into therapy. Instead, they value a holistic learning approach — one that acknowledges affective and cognitive processes, expressive and academic voices. For example, Wendy Bishop states, "The analogies between writing instruction and therapy have something to offer me and something I need to offer to the teachers I train" (p. 514). Lad Tobin offers one such analogy when he uses theories of transference and countertransference to understand an interpersonal conflict with three male students in a writing class. Jeffrey Berman, who encourages his students to disclose "dangerous subjects" like sexual abuse and suicide, asserts that "aesthetics and therapeutics can coexist" (p. 27). Similarly, Marian M. MacCurdy acknowledges that writing teachers and therapists have different goals but that the "writing and therapy processes can inform each other" (p. 161). Writing teachers import from psychotherapy, among other things, the concepts of empathy and positive regard, an understanding of transference and countertransference in classroom interpersonal relations, and a theory of trauma and narrative reconstruction.

At the same time, we believe that composition theory has insights to offer therapists, particularly those who routinely use writing as an intervention — an awareness we began to develop in Fall 2006 when Kristin Taylor was a new student in Noreen Lape's American Women's Autobiography course. In an informal essay assigned the first week of class, Kristin disclosed a "romantic" relationship with her former high school teacher. This initial writing assignment prompted Kristin's quest for self-understanding and healing that spanned several subsequent assignments over the course of two years. We will argue in this essay that revision — the process by which a writer re-sees her written thoughts in order to reshape them — has therapeutic benefits; we will also offer suggestions for responding effectively to traumatic writing. As we do so, we will use the collective pronoun "we," and frequently shift to "I." At times, Noreen will speak as "I" in order to explain the rationale behind her feedback on Kristin's writings. At other times, "I" will be Kristin describing the collaborative and revision-centered writing process that enabled her to come to terms with her history of sexual abuse, find her voice, construct her story, and begin to heal her wounds.

Very few in the composition or psychotherapeutic communities have written about how to comment on traumatic writing. Rick Furman and Kathryn Collins write about responding to clients who "spontaneously … introduced poetry into treatment" (p. 573). Their advice reflects the protocol for oral feedback, stressing empathy, positive regard, and nondirective questioning. They suggest asking the person why she wrote the poem and what kind of response she wants, all the while providing positive regard for her willingness to share her writing. They caution against using the poem diagnostically since a poem can be a creation rather than a reflection of the writer. They also advise therapists to ask a writer how often she writes and what prompts her writing in order to decide whether to use writing as a more regular intervention with the client. Ultimately, they approach written disclosure with caution, warning therapists that they may need to normalize the writer's experience and to ask gentle questions about confusing passages, assuring the person that the questions are not a criticism of the writing.

For Furman and Collins, neither revision nor aesthetics (formal/stylistic issues) factor into therapeutic writing. Similarly, Gillie Bolton in her introduction to *Writing Cures* — a collection of essays written by therapists — implies that "aesthetics and therapeutics" cannot coexist:

> The focus on therapeutic writing is upon the *processes* of writing rather than the *products*. A focus upon the products of writing will prevent clients from finding and making use of the particular power of writing. To be therapeutic, the initial stages of writing need to be encouraged to be personal, private, free from criticism, free from the constraints of grammar, syntax and form, free from any notion of the audience other than the writer and possibly the therapist or another reader. Writing as an art form necessitates an awareness of all these things at some stage. Therapeutic writing need never respond to the needs of these forces. (p. 2)

Bolton places therapeutic writing squarely in the *prewriting* stage. In the 1980s the field of composition underwent a major paradigm shift. Whereas composition teachers had been interested in the written product, giving special attention to form and grammatical correctness, researchers like John Hayes and Linda Flower became interested in the cognitive processes writers used and how they were shaped by goal-setting and problem-solving agendas. Since then, composition scholars have identified the main components of the process — *prewriting, writing, revising*, and *editing*. These stages, they find, in the most experienced writers are recursive. One goal of the composition teacher, then, is to model the stages for students and create assignments that provoke them to develop a recursive process. Like Bolton, composition scholars would tend to agree that in the *prewriting* stage, all writers need to shut off the Inner Critic — regardless of topic — and explore their ideas without worrying about grammar and form. Yet in locating the therapeutic benefits of writing solely in the prewriting stage, Bolton disallows the possibility that revision can be therapeutic.

We assert that revision is indeed a therapeutic process for many people because writing is different from speech. In her groundbreaking research on revision, Nancy Sommers defines revision as "the recursive shaping of thought by language." Such shaping of thought is not possible in speech given its "irreversibility"; revision in speech is literally an "afterthought." Drawing on Barthes's assertion that "writing begins at the point where speech becomes *impossible,*" Sommers states: "When we must revise, when the very idea is subject to recursive shaping by language, then speech becomes inadequate" ("Revision" pp. 378-379). Bolton's concept of therapeutic writing with its insistence on the prewriting stage hearkens back to an earlier pedagogy based on speech. For Bolton and others who employ expressive writing therapy, writing is a way for a person to capture her inner speech on paper. As James Pennebaker has shown, this has many beneficial psychological results: the writer achieves catharsis, habituates to the trauma, and processes psychological pain.

Yet many trauma theorists have hinted at the connection between healing and revision. In *Trauma and Recovery* Judith Herman explains how the trauma survivor's need to reconstruct her story is essential to recovery. She even uses the word "prenarrative" to describe survivors' first drafts, which are often "repetitious, stereotyped, and emotionless" (p. 175). Herman describes a process in which survivor and therapist revise the prenarrative, weaving in details, "traumatic imagery," "bodily sensations," and "accompanying emotions" (pp. 176-177). She describes a process much like revision: "Out of the fragmented components of frozen imagery and sensation, patient and therapist slowly reassemble an organized, detailed, verbal account, oriented in time and historical context" (p. 177). For many traumatized people, revision is the means to recovery and survival, as is evidenced by the preponderance of published trauma narratives like Dorothy Allison's *Bastard out of Carolina,* Nancy Venable Raines' *After Silence,* and Alice Sebold's *Lucky: A Memoir,* to name just a few. In fact, a review of each author's acknowledgments page reveals a long list of people whose support and feedback motivated the writers as they revised. Charles M. Anderson and Marian M. MacCurdy in their introduction to *Writing & Healing* — a collection of essays published by the National Council of Teachers of English — make the connection between revision and healing: "As we manipulate the words on the page, as we articulate to ourselves and to others the emotional truth of our pasts, we become agents for our own healing, and if those to whom we write receive what we have to say and respond to it as we write and rewrite, we create a community that can accept, contest, gloss, inform, invent, and help us to discover, deepen, and change who we have become as a consequence of the trauma we have experienced" (p. 7). For Anderson and MacCurdy, like Bolton, therapeutic writing arises from and expresses the self, but is also directed toward an audience — a "community" — whose various responses enable the self to "rewrite," "heal," and even "change."

In Kristin's case, a focus on the writing product via Noreen's feedback not only provoked her revision process but ultimately empowered her as a writer and as a sexual abuse survivor.

When I teach the American Women's Autobiography course, I focus on stories by women from diverse cultures who lived in the American West between the mid-nineteenth and mid-twentieth centuries. A main challenge is to introduce theoretical concepts, among them, that the truth is always a construction and the author's perspective is fraught with blind spots, inconsistencies, silences. Teasing out these theoretical insights is the most difficult challenge with undergraduates. The semester Kristin took the course, I asked the students on the first day of class to think about a significant moment in their lives and write a brief autobiographical essay. I thought that students might grasp the theoretical nuances better having struggled to tell their own truths first. Most students chose safe topics; honestly, I cannot remember the subject of any almost two years later — that is, except for one. One wide-eyed sophomore in the front row, an English major whom I had never met before, confessed in her essay to a recent romantic liaison with her high school teacher — a married man some fifteen years her senior. I was startled by her description of this predator, his enticing her to eat lunch with him everyday, and her tenderly narrated self-disclosure:

> He spoke timidly; "I have something to tell you." "Oh, really?" I flirtatiously replied; "Tell me." "Let me at least enjoy another lunch with you first." I consented, "Okay." We finished eating, and the suspense was killing me; "What did you need to tell me?" Silence. Tears, small but noticeable, formed in his eyes. I slowly leaned forward, softly whispered, "Say it. Say it." "I'm feeling something for you here," he said, placing his hand over his heart, "and it scares me because I know what you've been through before, and I know this is so wrong — I mean, you're only seventeen since you skipped a grade! — but I felt like it would be *wrong* for me *not* to tell you." I sat stunned to hear what I'd known for so long finally verbalized. "Please say some-thing," he pleaded; "Please tell me you feel the same way." I nodded...

Though moved by this painful confession fraught with confusion, I did not know how to reconcile her conflicted self-portrayal. She viewed herself almost as a jilted seductress who "flirtatiously replied," "consented," and ignored several "red lights" along the way. Yet her narration revealed a wounded girl, sexually abused by a former music teacher and prey to a victimizer who even admitted, "I know what you've been through..." How was I to respond?

Thankfully, the essay was technically excellent, so I relied on my basic humanity and an awareness that "composing humane, thoughtful, even inspiring responses is serious business" (Sommers, "Across" p. 248). What's more, as Tobin observes, "To offer no response to a provocative, emotional, confessional essay is to offer a very powerful response, as is the immediate decision to refer the student to someone else for counseling" (p. 48). I also recalled my training as a composition teacher regarding best practices in giving feedback: "offering praise, for instance, is more constructive than criticism; posing questions is better than issuing commands" (Sommers, "Across" p. 249). With much forethought, I expressed my emotional response to Kristin's story, and my admiration for her writing and insight. But I also chose to call attention to the contradictions, as I wrote, "Wow. You really moved me. I felt really angry at HIM and protective of you. Yes, there were red lights in hindsight, but *he* was responsible for obeying those stop signs, not you — a student, a minor. This essay is hard but also beautiful. Your reflections are deep and insightful."

When Noreen gave me feedback on that autobiographical essay, she "encouraged me to be personal," to echo Bolton (p. 2), but she also managed, as Anderson and MacCurdy advocate, to "create a community that c[ould] … contest" my perception of my relationship with Tim in a way that helped me later "discover" the truth of my sexual abuse (p. 7). When I had first disclosed my involvement with Tim to a therapist in July 2005, I adamantly insisted that Tim's relationship with me was a romantic one, but I remember thinking that my therapist perceived the relationship differently. While she never explicitly verbalized her feelings or confronted me, I often found myself struggling to defend Tim — more importantly, his sincerity — as I answered her questions, never feeling like she accepted my version of the relationship. The same feelings I had expressed to my therapist manifested themselves in the autobiographical essay I wrote for the course. In a four-page paper, I spent all but the last paragraph describing the relationship, and while there were many instances of my interjecting self-deprecating remarks about the "red light" moments I missed, I didn't have the insight to consider that perhaps I was misplacing the blame or that he had, in fact, manipulated me. Instead, I chalked the experience up to a case of equally poor judgment on both our parts and a tragically failed romance. In the last paragraph I celebrated my resilience and described the closure I received from sending him an email that said, "'goodbye,' not 'later…' but 'goodbye.'" I then commented in the essay: "How unequivocally final! How lovely!" The closure came so quickly that any astute reader would have sensed it was contrived.

As I read Noreen's feedback on my essay, I gathered that she questioned the sincerity of the closure I claimed in the conclusion and thought differently than I about who was to blame in the relationship. Those sentiments were solidified when she returned my paper to me, asking, "Do you blame yourself?" "Yes, sometimes," I quietly admitted. "Don't," she insisted; "I want to kill him."

Although Noreen's perception of the relationship seemed to align with that of my therapist, Noreen challenged my unwavering trust in Tim's sincerity. Offering positive regard, she was careful not to discourage me from using writing as a medium for wrestling with difficult personal experiences, but she also urged me to reconsider the convictions to which I was so strongly clinging. While her feedback did not prompt revision of the essay, it made me re-see my own story and reconsider, even if only on a subconscious level, the possibility that Tim was a predator. My mind became open to the truths I would later claim about his relationship with me in a second essay I would write in her class.

Besides engaging with instructor feedback, sometimes struggling with form results in therapeutic revision. The final project in the autobiography course gives students an option: a traditional research paper or a "braided essay," otherwise known as autobiographical literary criticism. In the latter, there are three strands to the braid — a critical analysis of a literary text from the course, a synthesis of secondary source research, and a personal narrative with some thematic connection to the literary text. The writer weaves together these strands in order to show how her life experiences affect her reading of the literary text and how the literary text helps her read her life experiences.

Those who choose this assignment often undergo a bibliotherapeutic process as they grapple with the unfamiliar form. Arleen McCarty Hynes and Mary Hynes-Berry outline the steps: recognition, examination, juxtaposition, and application to self. While undergoing the lengthy, recursive process of writing my essay, I was unaware of those steps, but in retrospect, I can observe how I worked through each stage of the bibliotherapeutic process to experience healing.

In the recognition stage there is something in the literary text that "piques interest, opens the imagination, stops wandering thoughts, or in some way arrests attention" (p. 45). In the course, I was introduced to an autobiography, thinly veiled as a work of fiction, entitled *Me: A Book of Remembrance,* published anonymously by Winnifred Eaton in 1915. I recognized myself in Nora Ascough, a seventeen-year-old literary ingénue trying to survive and cultivate her art in the big city of Chicago. Sexually naïve, Nora meets several men who attempt to exploit her, but her affair with the much older Roger Hamilton, who wants to keep her, constitutes the bulk of the story. As I read on, I entered the "examination" phase, "probing feelings until cognitive awareness emerge[d]" (p. 50). Reading *Me,* I felt like a participant-observer, identifying with Nora's role in her relationship with Roger and simultaneously empathizing with her inability to see Roger's true nature.

In the juxtaposition stage, I saw how literature "may correct discrepancies, offer role models, and graphically depict alternatives" (p. 51). I began to unearth uncomfortable parallels between Nora and Roger's relationship and my relationship with Tim, and I came to understand that to view Roger as exploitative meant to view Tim in the same light. At this point, I finally acknowledged the possibility of being a victim. In my efforts to understand both Roger's and Tim's manipulation, I turned to books such as Anna Salter's *Predators: Pedophiles, Rapists, and Other Sex Offenders* that explained the psychology of sexually predatory behavior. Such research led me to conclude that Roger, indeed, fit the profile of a sexual predator. He undertakes a carefully calculated ploy to seduce Nora, taking advantage of the naïveté and vulnerability that result from her prior sexual exploitation by two men whom she introduces earlier in the novel. Writing the braided narrative provided a form in which I could weave my encounter with Eaton's text, the findings of my research, and my personal experiences with Tim, thereby allowing me to integrate the three complex "strands" both verbally and psychologically. That essay became the first forum in which I considered the implications of being sexually abused and, as Anderson and MacCurdy would say, began "to discover, deepen, and change who [I] ha[d] become as a consequence of the trauma [I] ha[d] experienced" (p. 7). Unlike my first essay in which I viewed Tim and myself as equal participants in an egalitarian relationship, in this second essay I came to understand that Tim had used his position of authority to take advantage of me.

As I entered the final stage, application to self, in which I not only became aware of my "new viewpoints" but also used them as a "reference point for response or action" (Hynes and Hynes-Berry, p. 53), I began to consider whether or not I should report my sexual abuse to authorities. I wrote:

> In my journey, I find myself at a crossroads, fully believing I was manipulated and abused by a selfish man who used his hierarchical position to his advantage, yet I live in a state where sixteen is the age of consent. Therefore, my only hope of justice lies in possibly seeing [Tim]'s teacher's certificate revoked for breaching his educational code of ethics. Social responsibility tells me to proceed with accusations anyway, despite the ambiguity of what could ensue, to protect others from his schemes. But why should I feel responsibility to a society who will not even protect me as one who has already been abused? It is November 11, 2006, as I write these words, and I do not know where this path will take me or what decision I will make.

By the time I turned in my final paper, I had already decided that I trusted the truths I had acquired through my writing. On December 6, 2006, I reported my abuser to the police. Contrary to what Bolton claims, I began to see the therapeutic benefits of "grammar, syntax, form." In my interview with a sex-crimes detective, I relied upon my newly acquired "grammar" of predatory behavior to tell my story. Were it not for working through the form of the braided narrative, I would have never come to understand the truth of my sexual abuse, taken the actions to prevent it from happening to someone else, or embarked upon my journey toward healing.

Once the revision process is set in motion, it need not always be prompted by another's feedback. As Sommers explains, revision occurs when writers "recognize and resolve the dissonance" they see in their writing. At times, the mere "anticipation of a reader's judgment" can call attention to "incongruities." Yet writers must develop the ability to spot dissonances; it does not come naturally. Although Sommers does not speak of revision in a healing context, she describes it in a therapeutic way. Writers who revise develop personal agency as they learn "to rely on their own internalized sense of good writing and to see their writing with their 'own' eyes" ("Revision," pp. 385-87). In writing my braided essay, I noticed narrative inconsistencies with "my own eyes." As I moved toward accepting that I was a victim, I struggled with my attempts to "correctly attribut[e] the blame and causality to the predator" — what Heppner and Heppner term "an important realization" and a pivotal part of the healing process (p. 79). In an early draft of the essay, I wrote:

> I have the internal longing to know for certain whether the man I so desperately loved returned my affection, or if I was just another victim of a vicious cycle he repeated with different students every year. After reading of Nora's fate, I believe the latter conclusion to be true, yet accepting that as my truth is only a product of my need for something that excuses me from continuing to blame myself.

Yet in a contradictory passage that appeared a mere three paragraphs later, I wrote: "In my journey, I find myself at a crossroads, fully believing I was abused and manipulated by a selfish man who used the trust of his students to his advantage…" In the former passage, I had trouble accepting the truth of my newfound convictions, and in the latter, I fully embraced them. As I forced myself to consider both the rhetorical and psychological implications of such a contradiction, I learned how dissonance "provokes revision and promises, from itself, new meaning" (Sommers, "Revision," p. 386). Viewing my argument from a writerly standpoint, I recognized that my supporting evidence (in the forms of my psychological research and critical analysis of Eaton's text) validated my argument that Tim, too, was a sexual predator. In subsequent drafts, I worked to eradicate such contradictions. Carefully making those revisions allowed me to write my way into trusting in the truth of my convictions and finding the language to form a narrative of my traumatic experiences.

When I read Kristin's final draft of her braided essay, I was moved to empathize and, more particularly, to offer positive regard as a means to encouraging further "revision" or what I hoped would be her continued re-viewing and reconstruction of her story beyond the course. True, I responded as an English professor to Kristin the literature student, making a few brief "aesthetic" comments about her word choice and documentation style. (I could make so few technical comments because her essay was extremely well written, an exemplary model of the genre.) Struggling with the unfamiliar form of the braided essay, she had deftly connected Tim's seduction of her to Roger's liaison with Nora in *Me*, all the while weaving in her analysis of predatory behavior that she had gleaned from carefully chosen secondary sources.

In planning the endnote, then, I chose to offer positive regard as a means to further her "re-vision." In truth, I marveled at the depth of her insights, her movement from self-blame to self-care in just a few months. For example, commenting on the end of her relationship with Tim, she reflected: "Thus, I spent the next year grieving for the loss of him, too naïve to realize that it was the loss of myself for which I should have been grieving." And in her conclusion, she observed, "Recognizing I am the victim in this situation is indeed an important step, but it cannot be the last. I must somehow create a coherent identity for myself, realizing that identity will now consist of unifying the pieces of my life which have been broken by selfish men and walking toward a positive end of a continuum I will never reach completely." I was taken by the self-understanding she achieved through the reading and writing processes, and, when I automatically offered positive regard, I did not, at the time, even fully understand the power of so human a gesture. As therapists well know, "The experience of being cared about by others helps develop and restore a sense of caring for oneself. It creates energy and encourages a person to respond to the demands of life" (Welfel and Patterson 57). I wrote the following endnote:

> It's been quite a process for you. Who knew this book would change your life so much. [sic] In showing me just how much reading and writing can change a person's life, you renew my faith in literacy…
>
> Let me just say you are a brave woman for risking your own discomfort to prevent this from happening to someone else. I'm honored and humbled by the fact that you let me be your moral support.

My intention behind my feedback was to applaud her bravery, recognize her growth, and support her choice to report Tim's crime. However, I also wanted to let her know that the benefits of the work had been reciprocal; not only had she grown but I had also changed because of my work with her. I had never so keenly observed how reading and writing could heal — an observation that lifted me out of the ivory tower and showed me the power of literacy in the real world. As Kristin recently pointed out, that new "faith in literacy" persists, motivating our collaboration on this essay.

When Noreen gave me her feedback, I was comforted by her validation not only of my processes as a writer but also as a person attempting to heal herself. Throughout the healing that had taken place during Noreen's course, I had worked to overcome feeling shame about my relationship with Tim and telling my story. Her feedback confirmed for me that I had no reason to be shamed, as she praised my braided narrative and my decision to share my story with the police. When she called me a "brave woman," I began to view myself as an autonomous adult who was in control of her own healing process; I no longer felt like a helpless child whose psychological wellbeing was at the mercy of manipulative older men. For the first time, I realized my empowerment came from within myself — that with my own writing, I actually had the potential to heal my own wounds.

As we stated earlier, composition scholars have crossed disciplinary lines, claiming that psychotherapy offers insights that shed light on the dynamics of the writing classroom. In the spirit of reciprocity, we want to suggest some ways psychotherapists who routinely use writing as an intervention in their practice can borrow from composition scholars an understanding of revision and a set of practices for offering feedback. The central work of trauma recovery as survivors reconstruct their stories — the "recursive shaping of thought by language" — may be furthered by a writing intervention that involves revision. A focus on formal aspects of writing could potentially bolster therapeutic gains, as it did for Kristin as she grappled with the braided narrative. What's more, revision could be prompted in the absence of feedback by the sheer presence of an intended reader — the trusted therapist.

However, for a therapist who has created a safe environment in which a client can write therapeutically, nondirective or empathic feedback could be a means to growth. Sommers, a scholar whose work for over three decades has studied teacher responses to student writing, offers several best practices for teachers that might also apply to therapists. On the one hand, Sommers takes into account the affective dimension of feedback. Constructive criticism works because it "pushes [writers] forward" and reveals responders' "investments in their … untapped potential" ("Across," p. 251). Further, "feedback comes, implicitly or explicitly, with messages of hope or despair about who they are or who they might become" ("Across," p. 253). With that in mind, she suggests crafting feedback that is careful not to appropriate the writing but to honor the writer's purpose and intention ("Responding," p. 374). The responder can then concentrate on meaning-making, taking writers "back to the point where they are shaping and restructuring their meaning," perhaps even prompting the "dissonance of discovery" ("Responding," p. 379). Ultimately, effective feedback reveals that the responder has listened deeply/read closely and commented with the implicit belief that the writer can further the work begun in writing — whether that work be continued on the page or in the soul.

* * * * *

Kristin's healing work that began on the page and later resulted in social action culminated in the conviction of her abuser in December 2007 for his involvement with her and another student. Over the course of two years, her writing of three essays carried her from self-blame and self-delusion, to discovering the truth of her abuse and finding the language to tell her story, to seeking justice for herself and other victims. Still, while the narrative we present here is one of tremendous growth, the healing Kristin obtained (and continues to obtain) has been hard-earned. In January 2007, she returned to therapy to grapple with the painful insights she attained through her braided narrative and to have professional support throughout the legal process, when police, lawyers, and former students attempted to silence her and undermine her newfound agency. Further, her abuser's incarceration did not conclude her healing process. Instead, Kristin's pursuit of coherence is ongoing, her healing still something she strives toward daily. That journey continues even now as we pen this essay in which we bear witness to how profound a role writing and revision can play in the healing process.

References

Anderson, Charles M., and Marian M. MacCurdy. "Introduction." *Writing & Healing: Toward an Informed Practice.* Eds. Charles M. Anderson and Marian M. MacCurdy. Urbana, Illinois: NCTE, 2000. 1-22.

Berman, Jeffrey. *Risky Writing: Self-Disclosure and Self-Transformation in the Classroom.* Amherst: U of Massachusetts P, 2001.

Bishop, Wendy. "Writing Is/and Therapy?: Raising Questions about Writing Classrooms and Writing Program Administration." *Journal of Advances Composition* 13.2 (1993): 503-516.

Bolton, Gillie. "Introduction: Writing Cures." *Writing Cures: An Introductory Handbook of Writing in Counseling and Therapy.* Eds. Gillie Bolton, Stephanie Howlett, Colin Lago, and Jeannie K. Wright. New York: Routledge, 2004. 1-3.

Flower, Linda and John R. Hayes. "A Cognitive Process Theory of Writing." *College Composition and Communication* 32.4 (December 1981): 365-387.

Furman, Rick, and Kathryn Collins. "Guidelines for Responding to Clients Spontaneously Presenting Their Poetry in Therapy." *Families in Society. The Journal of Contemporary Social Services* 86.4 (2005): 573-579.

Heppner, P. Paul, and Mary Heppner. "Rape: Counseling the Traumatized Victim." *Personnel and Guidance Journal* (1977): 77-80.

Herman, Judith. *Trauma and Recovery.* New York: Penguin, 1997.

Hynes, Arleen McCarty, and Mary Hynes-Berry. *Biblio/Poetry Therapy: The Interactive Process.* St. Cloud, Minnesota: North Star Press, 1994.

MacCurdy, Marian M. "From Trauma to Writing: A Theoretical Model for Practical Use." *Writing & Healing: Toward an Informed Practice.* Eds. Charles M. Anderson and Marian M. MacCurdy. Urbana, Illinois: NCTE, 2000. 158-200.

Pennebaker, James W. *Opening Up: The Healing Power of Expressing Emotions.* New York: Guilford Press, 1997.

Salter, Anna C. *Predators: Pedophiles, Rapists, and Other Sex Offenders.* New York: Basic Books, 2003.

Sommers, Nancy. "Across the Drafts." *College Composition and Communication* 58.2 (December 2006): 248-257.

Sommers, Nancy. "Responding to Student Writing." 1982. *The St. Martin's Guide to Teaching Writing.* New York: Bedford/ St. Martin's, 2003. 373-381.

Sommers, Nancy. "Revision Strategies of Student Writers and Experienced Adult Writers." *College Composition and Communication* 34.1 (December 1980): 378-388.

Tobin, Lad. *Reading Student Writing: Confessions, Meditations, and Rants.* Portsmouth, New Hampshire: Boynton/Cook, 2004.

Welfel, Elizabeth Reynolds, and Lewis E. Patterson. *The Counseling Process: A Multitheoretical Integrative Approach.* 6th ed. Belmont, California: Thomson, 2005.

11

The Healing Notebook

Diana M. Raab

"The diary is a place where you don't have to worry about being perfect."

—Anaïs Nin

The purpose of this chapter is to focus on the benefits of keeping a notebook as a place to a capture feelings, musings, and sentiments before they vanish. The chapter will be useful for the writer, therapist, or patient. Journal keeping as a healing art will be discussed, as well as the different types of journals that may be kept. Writing exercises and journaling tips will also be shared.

For years, therapists have known about the tremendous healing value of the written word. Dating back to the Lewis and Clark Expedition, writers and non-writers alike have kept notebooks. Readers will benefit from learning how to use journaling to heal and also as a medium in overcoming writer's block.

The Essence of Keeping a Notebook

Whether you call it a notebook, a daybook, or a journal, keeping a notebook means different things to different people. For the therapist, it denotes a tool for a patient's self-analysis. For the writer, it's a place to capture ideas and musings. For others it's a place to heal, to document actions, reactions, and observations during difficult times and turning points.

At some point in all of our lives we will have something that begs to be written about. For instance, when confronted with birth, death, loss, divorce, neglect, illness, abusive relationships, crime, addictions, anger, mental health issues (e.g. depression, anxiety, eating disorders), dysfunctional families, and aging. The notebook can be a powerful outlet for emotions and also be used as a safety net for stress relief.

As Julie Davey says in her book, *Writing for Wellness*, "Just as we know cancer must be removed because of the damage it can do to our bodies, we know we must also rid our minds of the cancers of sadness, anger, and estrangement caused by holding on to negatives in our lives."

James W. Pennebaker, a research psychologist and the author of *Writing to Heal* says that he accidentally discovered the power of writing during an experiment back in the 1980s. After suggesting some people write about a traumatic life experience, he learned that they needed less medical attention in the months following the exercise than they had previously needed. Since then, he's devoted a great deal of time to studying the benefits of emotional writing.

Keeping a notebook is a form of writing that encourages the complete freedom of expression, in addition to recording events as we experience them. It is an effective way to tap into our conscious and unconscious mind.

The History of Notebook-Keeping

The first published diarist was Samuel Pepys who lived in the 17th century. Between 1660 and 1669 he wrote an 11-volume diary that was published after his death in 1825.

Next came the Lewis and Clark expedition in the late 1700s and early 1800s. Sergeant Patrick Glass wrote:

"Captain Lewis and eleven more of us went out immediately, and saw the prairie covered with buffaloe and the Indians on horseback killed them. They killed 30 or 40 and we killed eleven of them." He goes on to say how they killed with bows and arrows.

James Swan, a Native American, wrote extensively in the mid-1800s about whaling practices.

Poet Walt Whitman wrote in his notebook in the mid-1860s and then Ralph Waldo Emerson wrote about friends and activities of special interest to him. As a matter of fact, he wrote about Henry David Thoreau.

In 1885, Susy Clemens (the daughter of Mark Twain), was 13 years old and she began to write a memoir of her celebrated father. She wrote in her journal:

"I shall have no trouble in not knowing what to say about him," she wrote in her first opening paragraph, "as he is a very striking character." For a whole year she recorded her observations of her father, his writing, and his reputation in her journal, which she kept safely tucked beneath her pillow.

The Benefits of Keeping a Healing Notebook

- The notebook is a companion and best friend.
- The notebook is a place to record and remember events.
- The notebook nurtures the creative spirit.
- The notebook is a place to work through an illness.
- The notebook witnesses the healing process.
- The notebook increases awareness.
- The notebook is empowering.
- The notebook clears the mind.
- The notebook builds self-confidence.
- The notebook allows self-expression.
- The notebook improves communication skills.
- The notebook improves mental health.
- The notebook is a safe place to vent bottled up emotions.
- The notebook is a vehicle for letting go of cloudy thoughts.

- The notebook connects us with our inner voices.
- The notebook encourages reflection.
- The notebook invites imagination.
- The notebook is an emotional release

In her book, *You Can Heal Yourself*, Louise Hay says, "It's so important for each of us to take a journey and discover what attitudes and beliefs we hold within ourselves and the healing notebook helps with this endeavor."

My thought is, "think it, ink it."

Notebook Tools

A notebook or journal. The notebook should resonate with the writer's personality, mood, and taste. It should lay flat to ease the writing process and be of a convenient size for the writer's lifestyle. Men might prefer smaller notebooks to fit into their shirt pocket for jotting down quick notes while on the run. Others may lean towards a larger format that fits easily into a briefcase.

Some prefer plain books, and those with scientific inclinations might be inclined to write on graph paper, while others might prefer narrow or wide-ruled pages. Artists might find lined notebooks too restrictive and be compelled to use books without lines or even those more expensive notebooks made with parchment paper. Unlined notebooks can also be very liberating for those writers experiencing writer's block.

A pen. The pen should feel comfortable in the hand and it should also be fast-moving because our thoughts are often quicker than our hands. Some people have a favorite pen; most writers do. Others might want to carry around a selection of pens depending upon their needs or moods on a particular day. For those with a more creative slant, a selection of colored gel pens may be suggested.

The place. Choosing a comfortable and safe place to write is critical in keeping a notebook, whether it's in the backyard, at the kitchen table, or curled up in an oversized chair. Some people like journaling in bookstores or at train stations, malls, or parks. Sometimes it's fun to sit in a public place to people-watch while documenting observations and impressions. Public arenas such as airports, bars, restaurants, and doctors' offices can also be inspiring. Writing about other people's lives brings us deeper into our own.

The writing place, whether real or imaginary, should be in a healing environment, and be a place of relaxation and calm.

Exercise: How to create an imaginary room

- Get comfortable.
- Close your eyes, uncross your legs, and take some deep breaths. Listen to your breath and concentrate on it.
- Imagine visiting a room of great importance in your life. It might be a real or imagined place or somewhere you've spent time reflecting.
- Use your third eye (space between your eyes) as a movie camera, and try to visualize the room. Stay in that room for the next few exercises.
- Now try to describe the room. What do you see and how do you feel right now in your room? Stay in the moment.

Cathartic Writing — In this type of writing, the person writes when they are under the pressure of intense emotions and they have a need for an immediate release. It's much easier to direct the rage to the page than to other people. If there is repetition of the same type of pain, anger, or sorrow in the notebook, it may indicate the enormousness of the internal pain. Documenting the pain is a way of acknowledging it and it also helps create distance from it.

According to Tristine Rainer in her classic book, *The New Diary*, "Psychological pain sometimes needs to be expressed again and again because it may come…like the intermittent waves of labor. Repetition of the same pain or the same anger or the same sorrow in the diary indicates only that the pain is great. It must come out until it is all out."

Depression is another reason to write. Some proponents of writing during depression say it helps to formulate an image that may be expressed in the journal. Rainer says that when you are anxious or depressed, so much energy goes into resisting conscious awareness of your emotions, and so you feel depleted and listless. Rainer suggests an exercise to help move forward. She calls the exercise, "Speeding up into the future." She suggests making a list of all the things you have been putting off because of depression and then picking one to accomplish immediately. Often doing one of the things on the list can push you out of the slump.

> **Exercise: Write about a trauma or personal incident that caused you pain.**

Free (Intuitive) Writing — This type of writing releases the voice of the subconscious and oftentimes can help explain what is going on deep inside of us. For many people this is a liberating type of writing because it provides clues to their existence and importance.

This type of writing is done fairly quickly so that one thought leads to another thought and then another thought, some of which may not necessarily be connected. The purpose of this type of writing is to get to the core of the feeling and to see where your mind takes you. Like most journaling, this type of writing may be done in a beautiful environment, such as on a park bench or in a garden. Sometimes it's easy to start writing by glancing at something beautiful and the pen just glides across the page.

> ### Exercise: Free writing
>
> - Write for 10-15 minutes non-stop. Do not lift pen off the page.
> - Write about an experience that had a huge impact on your life — happy or sad. Include your emotions and reflections and how you feel now. Remain in the moment.
> - Write about what you should pay attention to in your life and what is holding you back.

Reflective writing — This type of writing is sometimes called musing or self-reflection and often follows a cathartic entry. It involves standing back to make observations about our lives in order to make connections and find the significance. According to Tristine Rainer, it also allows the inner voice to speak in free/intuitive writing and concludes and summarizes many of the other diary methods. This technique comes quite naturally to journal keepers and writers who spend a lot of time musing about this and that.

Letter Writing — The notebook is a safe place to write a letter to someone alive or deceased. This can be a very cathartic and healing exercise, whether it is sent or unsent. If angry with someone, it's much easier to speak in a letter than to their face. If the person is deceased, it's a good opportunity to tell them whatever you were unable to tell them and to reflect on the good times spent together.

In all her journal volumes, diarist Anaïs Nin wrote to her deranged father who he left Nin and her family when she was ten years old. Many writers use the letter form in their journal if they are having difficulty with a particular person. It is much easier to blow up on the page than in person. If you want to confront someone, it's easier to gather your thoughts on the page first, and then deal with them personally.

There are also many other benefits to writing unsent letters. For example, it is an easy way to begin writing a novel or memoir. Novelist John Steinbeck said,

"Your audience is one single reader. I have found that sometimes it helps to pick out one person — a real person you know, or an imagined person and write to that one."

Exercise: Letter Writing

- Write a letter to someone who is gone and who you miss.
- Think of two or three people who you've not communicated with for some time. Write a letter to one of them.
- Write a letter to someone who you've had a disagreement with or someone you had difficulty expressing yourself to.

Gratitude Writing — Instead of focusing on the negative sentiments, the positive side of life is highlighted. The person writes down all those things they are thankful for. Some people enjoy doing this exercise at the end of the day in order to identify all the wonderful things to be thankful for.

Exercise: Gratitude

- On the top of your page write, "The Things I Love."
- Take a deep breath and write for five minutes about what you love and what makes you happy.
- Paste the list in the front of your notebook for those melancholic days.

The Writing Process

It is usually suggested to a person who is new at keeping a notebook that they create a regular writing pattern. The best time to do this is in the morning when thoughts are the most clear. However, if this is not possible because of morning tasks, then a more convenient time should be arranged. The important thing is to keep to the routine of writing for 20 to 30 minutes a day. After a routine is established, then additional writing can be done on an "as needed basis."

The best advice is to keep writing, but when it starts hurting or too much sadness seeps in, then it is time to stop.

There are many ways to begin. Diarist Anaïs Nin, for example, would sit quietly for a few moments with her eyes closed. Before writing, she would allow the most important feeling or incident to drift into her head and that became her first sentence. This is a good way to record what is important at any given moment.

Tips: How to Start a Healing Notebook

- Date entries.
- Grammar and spelling do not matter. Never judge, censor or correct your journaling.

- Brag, exaggerate, be happy or sad.
- Be as honest as possible. Allow gut reactions and intuitions to come forth.
- Write quickly. Keep the hand moving — write through the negative thoughts and beliefs and layers of stored emotional and psychological perceptions.
- Don't erase or cross out. It's best to use a pen to avoid the temptation to erase.
- Write deeply. How much is put into the writing is how much you will get out of it.
- Remember to write for your eyes only. Allow yourself to play and have fun.
- After a journal entry, take a walk or go for a drink. Some people like coming back to what they write and then reflecting and writing thoughts about it. Others just leave it and might return to it at a later date.

Other Issues

Sometimes people seem easy going, happy, and strong on the outside, but inside they are fighting demons, as a result of something that happened in the past or something currently happening in their lives. This is often pertinent for the family of a loved one who is ill. They want to be strong for their loved one, but they are hurting inside. Often times it's good for them to put their words on paper.

Exercise: Hidden Pains

- If you're putting on a happy face, but are really hurting inside, write about how you are feeling. Write about how you really feel. What are you afraid of? What frustrates you?

Notebook-Keeping for Writers

Robert Frost said that often the most important gifts we receive as writers are gifts we're unaware of at the time. Therefore, the notebook comes in handy for those unexpected moments, and then it becomes a potpourri of ideas and a plethora of things to write about.

Whether you are crafting a memoir, fiction, or poetry, your journal can be mined for all sorts of writing topics. The notebook is an extension of our memories. It's a source of inspiration. It's a place to store odd facts, cool facts, lines, lists, images, and ideas for future writing projects. I often dive into my notebooks if I am stuck in writer's block.

Anne Lamott, in her timeless book, *Bird By Bird,* says that when she is blocked she simply lives as if she is dying because that gives real presence. Instead of staring at her computer screen, she asks herself if it were her last day on earth what should she do? Whether it's to read a book or go to the beach, she does these things which fill her back up with observations, flavors, ideas, visions, and memories — all the things which get her writing again. She goes on to say, "Do your three hundred words and then go for a walk. Otherwise, you'll want to sit there and try to contribute, and this will only get in the way. Your unconscious," she says, "can't work when you're breathing down its neck."

Some writers believe that writer's block is merely the loss of concentration. This may have to do with other issues or situations in our lives that must be fixed or healed. Sometimes it is due to a lack of confidence in writing because of a slowdown in acceptances, fear of failure, stress, or depression. This results in writers feeling a sense of paralysis in their words. The best thing to do is to either get up and do something else, or simply pull out the journal and get to work!

References

Davey, Julie. *Writing for Wellness: A Prescription for Healing.* WA: Idyll Arbor, Inc., 2007.

Gustavoson, Cynthia Blomquist. In-*Versing Your Life.* New York: Blooming Twig Books. 1995.

Lamott, Anne. *Bird by Bird.* New York: Anchor Books. 1995.

Pennebaker, James. W. *Opening Up: The Healing Power of Expressing Emotions.* New York: Guilford Press. 1990.

Pennebaker, James. W. *Writing to Heal.* Oakland, CA: New Harbinger Publications. 2004.

Rainer, Tristine. *The New Diary.* New York: Jeremy P. Tarcher. 2004.

Part Three:
Workshops and Programs

12

Writing for Wellness

Julie Davey

Atlanta Writing & Wellness Connections Conference, October 2008

When I learned I would be speaking with my fellow writers, I couldn't decide where to start. The plot in this story I am going to tell you is unique, its characters evoke a vast array of emotions, and its messages are compelling and inspirational.

Should I begin with Lindsey, the 10-year-old girl who wrote about her mother's cancer? Should I read her poems, tributes to her mother's incredible strength, which she compares to that of a lion? Lindsey writes about cancer robbing her and two sisters and leaving them with only memories of their 35-year-old mom.

Or how about Violet, at the other end of the spectrum at 96, who came to my class to write her life story and got it published two weeks before she went to "sit on a cloud?" I didn't actually believe she had known both Sergei Rachmaninoff and Amelia Earhart. Turns out, she was friends with both and brought in the photos to prove it to me, to show me.

Show me, indeed.

Robert had pancreatic cancer and had never written poetry. He said his biggest fear was not dying but reading aloud. He not only enthralled the Writing for Wellness class with his creativity, he became our town's poet laureate and addressed hundreds of people over the next two years. He beat cancer. He overcame his fears, all through learning to express himself in writing.

Then, there's Joy, blind with breast cancer, who found herself a single mother of teenagers, yet she had humor enough to write "The Tale of Two Titties" a hilarious explanation of how one of her "twins" went missing.

Bill and Carole and Christine and Doug and Steve all survived bone-marrow transplants. This makes some of the things we all complain about daily seem pretty insignificant. Their stories make me laugh, cry, get frustrated and inspired all at once.

Or how about Elizabeth who met every other week for four years with Princess Diana? Then, following Princess Diana's death, Elizabeth was diagnosed with an especially aggressive form of cancer. Did she retreat into a shell? Hardly. She began a very different form of writing that she found healing. She came to Writing for Wellness class to learn how to write about *herself*, something she had consciously avoided for the 20 years she had been a journalist for such publications as *People Magazine, O, In Style,* and *Vogue.*

You can appreciate why I felt I had to write a book, which contains contributions from 60 participants in my classes.

How can I fully describe to you the class I have taught for more than seven years? By telling this story one word at a time. That's the instruction I always give my students when they stare at a blank sheet of paper.

"One word at a time," I say. "Trust that your story will write itself."

It works for them. It will work for me.

I'll start with the title.

Writing for Wellness: A Prescription for Healing

Writing for Wellness

Cancer and other life-threatening illnesses and
no matter our age, our position in life or our ?
someone in our family or among our friends
suffered. And sometimes, for millions of us, we hav~
personally.

According to statistics, one out of three people will be diagnos~
with some form of cancer during their lifetime. For those who have not
experienced it directly, there is the unspoken but nagging concern that
cancer might pay us an unexpected visit one day. This is an unwelcome
but common bond we all share.

Even if you don't have personal experience with cancer, you may
have suffered a tragedy or loss in your life — as a victim of child abuse,
crime, abandonment, or neglect, or perhaps by losing someone close to
you through illness or accident or divorce.

In seven years of teaching expressive writing techniques to cancer
patients and those who have experienced a vast array of tragedies, what I
have learned is simple: words can help you heal. A doctor can help heal
your body and a psychiatrist or a good friend with a soft shoulder can
help heal your spirit. But, focused and directed writing about what you
are going through in the depths of your soul provides a unique and
sometimes immediate sense of relief. That experience can also be the
beginning of a special kind of healing.

I have written a book about my experiences for many reasons, first to
chronicle a unique and continuing class called Writing for Wellness, and
next to provide guidelines for the reader to also experience the healing
process.

It is my hope to inspire others to start Writing for Wellness classes in
small towns and large cities everywhere. Already some cancer centers,
wellness communities, libraries, and churches are using the book and our
class format.

Today, as I look out at this group, where some might see an audience,
I see potential teachers. Make my day, become one.

My personal journey with cancer connects me with those who are going through diagnosis or treatment. Since both my parents and my brother died from cancer and many of my friends have as well, I can identify with the caregivers, children, and friends of those going through traumas.

It is a been-there, done-that sort of relationship.

Each chapter in the book begins with some of my personal experiences. I concentrate on the facts and feelings of those events, a writing technique I use and teach to those attending my classes. It is simple. It works. It is effective.

Under *Healing Words* my students' writings appear in the middle of each chapter, and the quotations that begin chapters are also student-written. *It's Your Turn* ends each chapter and contains writing prompts, ideas, and suggestions for the reader to use to begin writing his or her own story. There is also a *Jump Start* section with a sentence or two to complete if readers need ideas to help them begin to write.

Throughout the book, I use what we in teaching call the "tell-one, show-one, do-one" method of writing instruction. First, I *tell* you, the reader, my experiences through my own writings, next I *show* written examples of how others (my students) have expressed themselves on the same topic, and finally, I ask you, the reader, to *do* your own writing on that same theme.

As in my classes, each person writes on the same topic from their own perspective. An example would be, "Write about a day you'll never forget."

Time is given for in-class writing just as time is suggested in the book for quiet, individual writing. The class participant or the reader of the book is directed to that particular topic.

This is not journaling.

Each chapter has a specific topic, each chapter has writing samples from class participants, and each chapter ends with writing prompts to help the writer begin to address that subject.

This process can be used effectively in conjunction with journal writing, but it is quite different in its approach and outcome. The two are not mutually exclusive. I find my method to be easy to follow for so-called non-writers, as well as professional writers. I have had both types in class.

Students in my classes who say they used to have trouble getting started, begin writing almost immediately and are eager for the next lesson.

As readers proceed through the writing exercises, I tell them to listen to their own feelings and to guard them. Once they have completed a lesson, there is no need to rush to share their writing. They may want to wait until they feel very secure with another person. Or they may choose never to share some of the things they have written.

I have also found that asking someone at home to read what you have written is, in effect, asking for the person to "love" what you have written, not merely to read it. This can cause all kinds of residual and negative effects. Love me, love my writing. I advise my students to avoid showing their "significant others" anything for a while. Never works for some people.

On the other hand, I encourage them to share their writing with participants in class, people who they are not married to, have children with, or are in a relationship with. So far, this advice has proven to be useful.

I follow it myself.

It has been my experience after having taught writing for 33 years, that it is the writing *process* alone that is healing. The sharing of that writing is secondary.

When I tell others that I work with cancer patients, caregivers, medical staff members and friends and family members of those going through chemotherapy, bone-marrow or stem-cell transplants or sometimes radical surgeries, I am often greeted with basset-hound eyes as people comment in sympathetic tones, "Oh, gee, how depressing!"

I quickly respond that it is anything but.

"We laugh as much as we cry. Maybe more," I respond.

Granted, there have been and will continue to be sad times. Not everyone survives.

But, having said that, I have seen this form of writing free the souls of participants in my classes and provide them with opportunities to express in words many emotions that would have otherwise never been shared with friends, family, or colleagues.

Participants report feeling relief, joy, and happiness. Real physical changes occur, the participants tell me. They can face their medical appointments with new outlooks and perspectives. Writing for wellness works.

Perhaps Edna Teller, one of my students in Writing for Wellness class says it best in her words that begin my book:

> *You are not your disease.*
> *Cancer does not define you; you define you.*
> *It can never steal your identity or essence.*
> *You are not cancer and cancer is not you.*
>
> — Edna Teller

Since 2001, I have been teaching writing to cancer patients, their family members, caregivers, nurses, and others who may have suffered tragedies in their lives. I continue to do this as a volunteer.

Writing for Wellness classes are held at the City of Hope National Medical Center in Duarte, California, the site Lance Armstrong selected to start his 2004 cross-country bicycle tour to increase cancer awareness. Symbolically, I have always felt that was the perfect choice of locations. City of Hope is where many clinical trials have saved those who would otherwise have been lost. City of Hope has pioneered new treatments and procedures that have become standard for other cancer centers and hospitals throughout the world. The center routinely and successfully performs bone-marrow transplants.

Here is how Writing for Wellness classes became a reality: My experience began a few days following 9/11 when I was walking on the

City of Hope grounds to an appointment at my oncologist's office. (Did I mention that I am a two-time breast-cancer survivor?)

I witnessed a group of very young children, some only five or six years old, dressed in slippers and hospital pajamas. On that clear, warm fall day they were in single file led by a young man in his 20s, who wore a volunteer's identification badge on his workout suit. He looked like a P.E. teacher from a local public school. He had a whistle hanging from a chain around his neck.

As they walked around the medical center grounds outside the pediatric oncology building, they skipped, clapped their hands, and waved their arms. Each tiny child had a bald head from chemotherapy and wore a surgical mask for protection against germs. They were obviously young leukemia patients on an exercise field trip from their hospital beds.

While their leader blew the whistle or counted out, "One! Two!" the children kept time. Some marched in military style; others bobbed their heads to imaginary music. All of them seemed to be enjoying their outing. None of them looked sad or as if they were seeking sympathy from the outside world. This was their life as they knew it and understood it.

As the children passed by, I felt a tug at my heartstrings. They were so young to have a major disease, yet they seemed to be coping with what life had dealt them. I watched and suddenly realized that the volunteer was doing something significant, something selfless.

At that defining moment, I vowed to take action myself to help other people. I had never consistently volunteered anywhere before. From time to time I had helped with various civic projects and education causes when my husband served on the city council and was later mayor of our small town, but this time I knew I wanted to try to make a continuing and significant difference in people's lives.

Following that young volunteer's example, I was determined to give something back.

Less than a week earlier, two hours after the World Trade Center towers collapsed, I had faced my class of 30 journalism students at Fullerton College as we all tried to make sense of what had just happened. I told them we should promise to devote ourselves, in any way we could, to ridding the world of evil.

With tears in my own eyes, I stared at their tear-stained faces barely able to speak.

"We all have skills," I told them. "Use yours; help somebody. Make a difference." Students ranging from 19 to more than 60 years old nodded in agreement. I told them I was convinced that volunteering could help us begin to heal from the tragedy. I was their teacher; my students looked to me for answers.

Over the years my parents, who were both very generous with their time and money, told me that when bad things happened not to feel sorry for myself but to take action because, "There's always someone worse off than you." Recalling their words, I asked myself what I could do immediately.

That day during my appointment, I revealed to Dr. Lucille Leong my deep desire to volunteer. She encouraged me and gave me some names and numbers for contacts at City of Hope.

I had seen volunteers driving cancer patients around in golf carts from building to building on the 112-acre campus to assist those who had trouble walking to their doctors' appointments. I could do that.

Or, perhaps I should offer my assistance to the public relations office since I knew how to write news releases. Maybe I could publicize new cancer treatments to get the word out to those who needed help. My mind was searching to find a place for me.

Driving home I continued to think about what I had to offer. Then suddenly, it came to me. I realized I could teach writing to my fellow cancer patients/survivors and their caregivers to help them express what they were going through.

As soon as I got home, I called the Patient Resource Office and outlined my plan. I explained I was a two-time survivor, having had breast cancer in 1984 and again in 1996, telling them that I was also a full-time college writing professor. I said I had discovered first-hand that when people write about tragedies in their lives, they seem to feel better.

I told the people involved in patient education classes and support groups at City of Hope that I wanted the class to be open to the public, not just to cancer patients. Then, with the assistance of Linda Baginski, herself a breast cancer survivor, and another cancer survivor, Jeanne Lawrence, both part of the Patient Services team, we agreed to offer the class and named it "Writing for Wellness." Sessions were scheduled almost immediately.

The time and place were set and flyers posted. As we had outlined, the class would be open to cancer patients, their family members and caregivers, as well as all staff members at City of Hope. The flyer also said the class would be open to anyone who had experienced a major illness or tragedy. We stressed that no previous writing experience was necessary.

I became excited about the prospect of the class, but I wasn't sure if anyone would actually show up.

The room I was assigned to for the class instantly created a positive atmosphere. Named the "Hope Village Comedy Theatre," it is a small room with all its walls colorfully painted with life-sized caricatures of comedians, actors, and cartoon characters. Lucy and Desi, Laurel and Hardy, Bart Simpson, Garfield, and many others smile at all who enter. I could not help smiling back.

The room had tables, two pianos, a small stage, and lots of comfortable chairs.

Strongly believing in the power of effective group dynamics, I immediately moved some tables and chairs into a horseshoe shape with the opening facing my chair. That way, everyone would be able to write and to see everyone else. I did not want to lecture or stand at a podium. I wanted no barriers between my "students" and me. I wanted to be on the same level as them. After all, we were all in this cancer thing together.

I later learned that there were weekly Bingo games held there for the pediatric patients and their family members, and it was also the site of many adult support-group meetings. The room exuded an aura of positive energy.

My first class was in the evening. I set the time from 6:30 to 8:00, realizing that many cancer patients still had jobs, as did their family members and caregivers. I also wanted people from the general public to be able to attend after work. I brought coffee, soft drinks, and desserts.

As I left my house with the food, plus a coffee maker, cups, plates, plastic utensils, and a table cloth, my husband, Bob, teased, "What are you teaching anyway, cooking?"

Throughout my years of teaching high school and college, I have been known as a "feeder," bringing snacks to most of my classes, especially when overseeing the late-night production of campus newspapers. Bob had seen this all before.

My journalism students, notoriously hungry and frequently broke, always ran to help me as I negotiated my way to class with shopping bags stuffed with food they would soon be devouring.

But, that night at City of Hope I felt odd, unsure of myself.

Over the years, I had taught thousands of students ranging from high school sophomores to senior citizens taking college courses, but this class would be like none other.

Then, suddenly, as I was setting up the room and refreshments, I became very nervous. My palms started to sweat; I had a feeling of dread.

What had I gotten myself into? What if the cancer patients or their family members broke into tears and sobbed? What if someone who had suffered a great tragedy felt worse after coming to my class? I wasn't a trained psychologist. How arrogant of me to think I could actually help someone in such a simple manner, "Writing for Wellness" indeed.

As I saw the clock indicating 6:25, I wanted to run out of the door. Then, a short Hispanic man in his late 60s who spoke with a slight accent walked in. He was smiling and shook hands enthusiastically. He picked up some refreshments, sat down, and opened a notebook. He had his pen ready. He talked very rapidly.

"I'm Bob. I had pancreatic cancer. I should be dead, but I beat it! Plus, I'm a diabetic, too!" he told me proudly. "Now, I want to write poetry."

I sighed and immediately felt at ease. Then, as eight more people showed up, carried desserts and drinks to the tables, and sat down facing me, I realized I might be able to handle it after all. They all looked eager and friendly.

As soon as everyone was seated, I asked the participants to introduce themselves and tell about their experiences with cancer or other diseases or tragedies. I wondered if people would be hesitant to share that information with total strangers. They were not. I had to choose from among several raised hands as we started to meet one another.

Joan, late 60s, who had almost no hair, talked about battling breast cancer. Marilyn, 50s, a registered nurse with daily and often stressful interactions at City of Hope with cancer patients, revealed how her job affected her. Milynne, 30s, who had a slight jaundiced look and very little energy despite the sweet smile on her face, told us she had liver cancer but she was determined to write about what she was going through. Ramona, 60s, fighting cancer for 12 years said she wanted to thank her daughter for helping her. Tony, late 40s, was not a cancer patient. He had come to the class because he had lost his only child, a 27-year-old son in an accident. Tony said he wanted to see if writing about the tragedy would help him find some peace.

On it went. Some were patients, some were family members, and some were health-care professionals. Others merely had seen the flyer and thought the class might help them deal with some catastrophe in their lives.

One thread tied us all together — the desire to write about our experiences.

As each person spoke, I began to see what a great need there was for such a class, an outlet for those holding in the stress that dealing with cancer or any other serious medical situation or tragedy can create. People needed to talk, to write, and to interact with others going through similar experiences. I became aware of how intently the students were listening to one another's stories and I completely forgot about my nervousness.

Following their introductions, I gave mine. I told them I had been a college writing professor for more than 15 years and had written many newspaper and magazine articles, one published novel and, like everyone else who lives near Hollywood, a couple of unsold screenplays. But, when I said I was also a two-time breast cancer survivor, I could see visible changes in their faces. They knew we had a lot in common.

I wasn't just another teacher.

And, from my experiences in that room, I continue to realize that it isn't just another class.

In a hands-on workshop format, Julie Davey also demonstrated her techniques used in Writing for Wellness classes and in her book Writing for Wellness: A Prescription for Healing. *She asked conference attendees to use several writing prompts, gave time for participants to write, and then asked for volunteers to read what they had written. As a follow-up, participants also were asked to report on how using the writing techniques made them feel physically and emotionally.*

13

Tell it Slant: History, Memory and Imagination in the Healing Writing Workshop

Sara Baker

Tell all the Truth but tell it slant —
Success in Cirrcuit lies
Too bright for our infirm Delight
The Truth's superb surprise
As Lightening to the Children eased
With explanation kind
The Truth must dazzle gradually
Or every man be blind
— Emily Dickinson

Practice Seeking Theory

In my work teaching creative writing to cancer patients, I have come across a pattern that has puzzled me. Despite the literature supporting the healing efficacy of writing directly about trauma — of naming, containing, and re-externalizing the traumatic event in order to integrate it (1), I have often found that having my patients write explicitly about a trauma — whether it is a cancer diagnosis or an earlier trauma that surfaces at the time of diagnosis — can inhibit their writing. Many times, as patient writers edge closer to their own histories, they shut down. This paper explores why this can be so, and is written from the point of view of practice seeking theory, rather than practice implementing theory.

In my previous experience as a teacher of writing for college students, I discovered that requiring writing in which the students were the authorities, writing from their experiences, produced powerful texts with force, inherent structure, voice, and telling detail.

However, when I began working with cancer patients, I naively assumed that, as with my students, traumatic material would come up rather quickly and transparently. I also assumed that, as I had read in the work of Pennebaker, Herman, and others, that it would be good for my patients to confront their feelings, feel them, and deal with them in their writings. I was prepared for this. What I wasn't prepared for was the ways in which patients, many of whom had worked enthusiastically with image, fairy tales, and poetry, often retreated from the task of writing directly about their own experiences of illness.

This left me with many questions. How do we avoid retraumatization when facilitating a writing experience for patients? How does expressive writing — writing which asks the patient to confront a trauma by expressing both the cognitive and emotional aspects of the trauma — compare with imaginative or creative writing in effectively allowing for the three stages of recovery from trauma: safety, remembrance and mourning, and reconnection? (2)

Trauma and the Cancer Patient

In exploring why writing from their own experiences might be difficult for some patients, and why it seemed to be a distinctly different experience from my student writers, I began to examine the factors that might influence inhibition. Cancer patients have a spectrum of forces bearing on them, as well as coming into the workshop with various predisposing attributes and histories. In contrast to my student writers, patients for the most part are older and may have less resiliency than students. Students, even those with traumatic histories, tend to be oriented towards the future in a positive way. For cancer patients, whether their prognosis is good or poor, the diagnosis of cancer changes one's sense of the future. Secondly, while not all patients are traumatized by their diagnosis, others exhibit symptoms typical of trauma, including feelings of detachment or estrangement from others: restricted range of affect, difficulty falling asleep or concentrating, hyper-vigilance, irritability, and exaggerated startle response. According to the National Cancer Institute, a division of the National Institutes of Health, a diagnosis of, and treatment for, cancer can in itself be considered traumatic.

In addition to how they respond to a cancer diagnosis, patients are in various stages of diagnoses and recovery, and each stage has its own psychological task. (3) Also, patients have various pre-existing psychological attributes that may make them more or less amenable to writing directly about their experiences. Research indicates that disclosure produces decreased stress for women low in avoidance, but not for high avoidant women, for whom it can increase stress (4). Patients have different types of emotional awareness, understanding, and expression. Those with repressive personalities may be harmed or at least not benefit from written disclosure (5). Studies also show that disclosure was found to have no effect on a large sample of bereaved older adults (6) and to have deleterious effects in a small sample of people with PTSD (7).

Other findings involving journaling suggest that "dwelling on emotions alone may be counterproductive in terms of health outcomes. ...writers may be able to relive the physiological and emotional activation of the trauma during its recall, but because they are focused on the affective experience, they may not be able to work through the trauma to reach a state of resolution from which they have a different perspective (8)." However, writing that avoids emotional content and goes directly to abstraction does not provide a healing opportunity, as it perpetuates disassociation from sensory and emotional experience. (9).

Given these variables, how does one structure a writing experience for cancer patients that allows for the maximum healing opportunities while avoiding both inhibition and retraumatization?

As a practitioner, my experiences did not seem to be fitting the theory of expressive writing nor my own previous experience in the classroom. Expressive writing takes as its premise that healing comes from writing directly about trauma. James W. Pennebaker, a research psychologist, is perhaps the best-known advocate of expressive writing. His research has measured the biological benefits on the immune system, as well as mood and behavioral changes that can result from spending as little as twenty minutes a day writing about an emotional upheaval (10). However, in working on memoir, I was not finding the responses I had found in earlier work with more imaginative writing. Charles M. Anderson and Marian M. MacCurdy, in the introduction to their book, *Writing and Healing: Toward an Informed Practice*, assert

> failure to complete the normal process of grieving perpetu-
> ates the traumatic reaction. Grieving, and the healing that accom-
> panies it, allow the survivor to reclaim the self and its agency. As
> we manipulate the words on the page, as we articulate to our-
> selves and to others the emotional truth of our pasts, we become
> agents of our own healing.

For me, the key phrase here is *the emotional truths of our past*. That the work of mourning is essential to the healing process for traumatized individuals has been well established (11).

The work of recovering our selves, of mourning our losses is, it seems, is tricky business. The question is not whether it must be done, but *how*. How do we uncover the *emotional truths* of our past if our history is a loaded minefield? What if the ego is not yet strong enough to face into the "reality" of a person's history? What if recounting such history results in retraumatization?

These questions bring up issues of history, memory, and imagination — how we understand these terms, how these processes interact, and how they can be useful in understanding the place of creative writing in a setting in which we have healing objectives. Can emotional truths only be accessed through a recounting of actual events, or can the emotional truths that need to be externalized and shared also be accessed just as powerfully through the obliqueness of poetry, or the alternate realities that fiction constructs?

History, Memory, and Imagination

Hilary Mantel, a British novelist, after writing eight novels, wrote her autobiography, *Giving Up the Ghost*. In it, Mantel reveals how hamstrung she feels by the constriction of the memoir form. "I hardly know how to write about myself," she says early in the book and we witness her self-admonition that she will put "plain words on plain paper." Yet, like the messy little girl she describes herself to have been, she finds herself scribbling outside the lines: "I stray away from the beaten path of plain words into the meadow of extravagant simile." (12)

Ironically, the novel she wrote on the heels of *Giving Up the Ghost*, *Beyond Black*, takes up the story of a woman facing into her past. As Terrence Rafferty observes in his *New York Times* review of *Beyond Black*, describing the premise of the book, "The process undergone in the pages of *Beyond Black* by its fat, middle-aged English heroine, Alison Hart, is self-analysis and memory recovery of almost unimaginable psychic violence... Alison is a professional medium and clairvoyant — in her preferred terminology, a 'Sensitive' and depends for her peculiar living on the services of a 'spirit guide' named Morris who is ... an exceptionally nasty piece of work. He is also a constant reminder of the unspeakable childhood that Alison, for all her extrasensory powers, *can recall only dimly*." (13)

In this novel, Terrence Rafferty goes on to say, Mantel "allows herself to gorge on simile and metaphor and wild comic invention — the treats she had tried and, guiltily failed, to deny herself while following the hard-fact regimen of *Giving up the Ghost*. *Beyond Black* feels like a great, gleeful binge, a wallow in the not-good-for-you riches of this writer's extraordinarily vivid, violent imagination." (14)

What is it about simile and metaphor and "wild comic invention" — the province of the imagination — that seemed to free Mantel to address the *emotional truths* of her past in a way her memoir did not?

Ms. Mantel is a particularly apt writer for this question. Her own life, as revealed in her memoir, has been a series of emotional and physical upheavals, not the least of which is chronic illness. Like many cancer patients, she is negotiating not only a traumatic past, but a difficult present.

In an article entitled "Memory and the Inner Life; Fiction, Between Inner Life and Collective Memory" (15), Lavenne, et al. posit: "In the writing of their fictional works, novelists often have to reflect on the functioning of memory, for memory lies at the heart both of inner life and of human experience in general ... literature provides more than a means of reflecting on memory: it is also the site of the rebirth and construction of individual and collective memories, which can serve as a foundation for the writing of fictional works. Creative writing has a meiotic function and is as such a powerful tool capable of rescuing memories from oblivion and bringing them to life, thus reconciling the past with the present."

Here, then, we encounter the triad of memory, history, and imagination. Donald Winnicott, the leading object-relations theorist, posited that between the outer world of objective reality and the inner, subjective world is a "transitional space," which is where we play and imagine. In this case, there is the psychic reality of memory, the objective reality of history, and the third space, which is neither but partakes of both, literature, the work of the imagination.

Indeed, the authors assert that fiction is able to "convey something about past events and experiences that could not be expressed otherwise." They cite Vincent Engel's claim that literature can also help overcome the three major obstacles potentially obstructing the recollection of a traumatic event: "a traumatic event can seem *unimaginable, incommunicable, and unspeakable.* However, it is essential, when confronted with these three impediments, to imagine, communicate, and speak, which can be achieved in fiction, as Elie Wiesel's novels have shown" (16). Here we come back to the necessary work of mourning as described by Anderson and McCurdy, but work which is done obliquely. It is not an eschewing of history or memory, but a way of getting at "buried truths," or, as Gabriele Schwab describes in *Writing Against Memory and Forgetting*, truths which have been consigned to the psychic crypt (17). Fiction, the authors assert, "does not have the obligation to tell the truth and can thus express things that would otherwise remain unsaid. *Paradoxically, fiction is able to say essential things about reality precisely because it does not have to tell the truth about this reality"* (18).

Writing Well and Being Well

Marian MacCurdy, in her essay, "From Trauma to Writing: A Theoretical Model for Practical Use," discusses how traumatic memories differ from other memories. "Traumatic memories are sensory, that is, the body reacts to them even when the conscious mind is not aware of the cause of such reactions ... while these images are non-cognitive, they have deep emotional presence" (19). According to an article cited by MacCurdy, researchers John H. Krystal, Steven M. Southwick, and Dennis S. Charney assert that traumatic events are encoded via "emotional, pictorial, auditory and other sensory-based memory systems ... traumatic memories may not be encoded or retrieved linguistically unless that retrieval encourages the survivor to integrate the emotional memory with the description" (20).

The difficulty in linguistically retrieving traumatic memories is borne out in the experience of healing practitioners from many fields. Belleruth Naparstek, who has done extensive work with trauma victims, including Viet Nam veterans and survivors of both the Oklahoma City bombing and 9/11, makes this observation in her book, *Invisible Heroes*: "If a person is deeply impacted by trauma, it is more than likely that he first needs to find an oblique route through the imaginal realm, using metaphor and symbolic language, to help him manage his symptoms, find a sense of safety, recontact his most whole self and make language a viable avenue again" (21). I take her use of the word *language* here to mean *discursive* language. The *Random House Unabridged Dictionary's* second definition for discursive is "proceeding by reasoning and argument rather than intuition."

In teaching creative writing to traumatized individuals, then, the oblique route may, in the end, for some individuals, be as effective or more effective than the direct route. Trauma disrupts one's sense of identity, and those traumatized often lack a coherent self and therefore cannot regard their history from a safe place. Often, those traumatized find their perceptions biased, according to Naparstek, "towards what is worrisome or frightening at the expense of registering what is pleasurable, beautiful and nourishing" (22). So for a person who has experienced trauma, memory can include negatively biased habits of perception. The way one sees one's story, the story one tells oneself about the memory as well as the memory itself, can be defeating. To simply trigger a defeating story does not necessarily lead to healing. You can say, "Well, maybe the way you see it isn't the whole truth," but it may be a *felt* truth. It may be a stubbornly worn rut in the person, not only in her mind, but in her body — her reactions, her flight-or-fight response, her ability to feel her feelings, her ability to live safely and fully in a sensate world.

Craft and Catharsis

A healing writing experience, then, is not so much about genre — memoir, fiction, or poetry — but about clarity, emotional tone, concreteness, etc. I think it is also about form, and finding the form suitable for one's voice.

Writing, by its very nature, contains chaos (23). It is an ordering of chaos, even as it is an exploration of chaos (24). Often, it is first exploration and then an ordering. The goal, then, in using an oblique approach, in inviting the imagination to come out and play, is neither to deny history nor to suppress memory. Instead, the goal is, through the creative act, to allow the person to experience the vast resources she has within her. As participants are able to create texts to be shared, and as they experience "the joyous self-love that comes from accomplishment" (25), they become more able to face and integrate traumatic material. Writing something as small as a fable or a short poem may seem insignificant compared to the overwhelming task of fighting cancer, but that small text represents an act of self-agency, a defiant rejection of hopelessness. To create out of the self, when the sense of self and its symbolic order has been fragmented, is often an opportunity not to be restored to a former wholeness, but to find a different wholeness, one which acknowledges loss, but is not devastated by it.

Crafting that text, that artifact, seems to be an inherently important part of the process of healing. Mark Robinson, in his research, found that:

> To sum up, there were strong indications that writers of all kinds felt they gained psychological benefits from their writing practice. Only in a few cases was this separate from the normal literary writing and redrafting process necessary for good writing of any genre, form or school. An interest in quality, in producing a text which was more than instant or an outpouring but in some way crafted, was clearly integral to the process of writing enhancing wellbeing (26).

The Better Story

In Yann Martel's novel, *Life of Pi,* several characters refer to the *better story.* At the end of the book, when Pi is being questioned about the veracity of his story of surviving on the life raft with a tiger, he answers with "So tell me, since it makes no factual difference to you and you can't prove the question either way, which story do you prefer? Which is the better story, the story with the animals or the story without the animals?" (27) For some people, the better story may not adhere to the historical facts, but may be more true to the emotional truths of their experience. In his author's note, Martel claims that "fiction is the selective transforming of reality, the twisting of it to bring out its essence." It is essence that concerns the writers of fiction and poetry, the writers of memoir and the practitioners of healing writing. In the writing of memoir, the selection and emphasis of certain details, the selection of point of view, the feeling tone, all structure the memory of an experience — there is no absolute memory without the shaping powers of the imagination (unless you have Dumbledore's pensieve!). The tools of fiction are used to create "true" narratives of memories, often to the point of blurring the distinctions between the two.

Patients who have "encrypted" trauma, may, as a default position, escape into abstract language, superficial language, or silence to avoid feelings when asked to write directly about traumatic events (28). Offering them an oblique route may allow them to dismantle habitual defenses, and offering a transitional space in which to play may allow them to locate resources within themselves that were previously unknown to them. Furthermore, the possibilities of leaving the literal facts of one's history can give rise, paradoxically, to more freedom to connect with emotional and often buried truths.

As a practitioner, I do not eschew the efficacy of writing directly about trauma. However, I wish to expand the palette, as it were, of the facilitator, and to respect the complex and circuitous ways people are able to integrate such memories into their life stories. It is important to follow a patient writer's own intuition about the route they need to take, rather than forcing on them a template of how they should proceed. Ultimately, there is a mystery at the heart of writing which resists formulation into a schema. "The job of the artist is always to deepen mystery," wrote Francis Bacon. Similarly, there is in the process of facilitating others' writing an element of the unknown.

Notes

1. See Pennebaker, *Telling Stories: The Health Benefits of Narrative,* which reprises his research from 1990 to 2000. His paradigm of having participants write for short periods of time — 15-20 minutes — over several days about their deepest thoughts and feelings about a traumatic experience yielded measurable improvements in health. One broad explanation for this is that "converting emotions and images into words changes the way a person organizes and thinks about the trauma... By integrating thoughts and feelings, then, the person can more easily construct a coherent narrative of the experience." Judith Herman, in her seminal *Trauma and Recovery,* asserts much the same thing: "After many repetitions, the moment comes when the telling of the trauma story no longer arouses quite such intense feelings. It has become a part of the survivor's experience — but only one part of it."(p. 95)
2. See Herman, stages of recovery.
3. Dreifuss-Kattan, Esther, *Cancer Stories: Creativity and Self-Repair.*
4. Stanton, Annette L. and Danoff-Burg, Sharon, "Emotional Expression, Expressive Writing, and Cancer," In *The Writing Cure,* Lepore, Stephen J. and Smyth, Joshua M., p. 43.
5. Lumlye, Mark A., Tojek, Tina M., & Caclem, Debra J., "Effects of Written Disclosure among Repressive and Alexithymic People," Ch. 5, *The Writing Cure.*
6. *Ibid.*
7. *Ibid.*
8. Lutgendorf, Susan K. and Ullrich, Philip, "Cognitive Processing, Disclosure and Health: Psychological and Physiological Mechanisms," Ch. 10, *The Writing Cure,* p 182.
9. See Wilma Bucci quoted in "From Trauma to Writing," by Marian M. MacCurdy, in *Writing and Healing,* pp. 168-171.
10. Pennebaker, *Opening Up,* pp. 35-37
11. See Judith Herman's *Trauma and Recovery,* specifically the section on Remembrance and Mourning.
12. Mantel, *Giving Up the Ghost,* p. 4
13. Rafferty, Terrance. "Demons Revealed.
14. *Ibid.*
15. Lavenne, et al, *New Arcadia Review,* p. 7
16. *Ibid.,* p. 4
17. Schwab, "Writing Against Memory and Forgetting," *Literature and Medicine,* p. 99.
18. Lavenne, et al., p. 7.
19. MacCurdy, p. 162
20. *Ibid.,* p. 163
21. Naperstek, Belleruth, *Invisible Heroes: Survivors of Trauma and How they Heal,* p. 13
22. *Ibid.,* p. 40.
23. Schwab, p. 116
24. Rico, Ch. 2, "Spirals, Chaos and Clustering: Discovering the Hidden Patterns in Feelings," *Pain and Possibility,* p. 26.
25. Naparstek, *Invisible Heroes,* p. 40.
26. Robinson, Mark. "Writing Well: Health and the Power to Make Images," p. 80
27. Martel, *The Life of Pi,* p. 317
28. See Schwab, p. 108, on haunted language

References

Anderson, Charles M. and MacCurdy, Marian M. *Writing and Healing: Towards an Informed Practice.* National Council of Teachers. 1999.

Doctorow, E.L., and David L. Ulin. "The Writing Life: An American Tale." *Los Angeles Times*, September 24, 2006

Dreifuss-Kattan, Esther. *Cancer Stories: Creativity and Self-Repair.* Hillsdale, NJ and London, The Analytic Press, 1990

Herman, Judith Lewis, *Trauma and Recovery*, Rivers Oram Press/Pandora List, New Edition, 2001.

Lavenne, Francois-Xavier; Renard, Virginie; Tollet, Francois. "Fiction, Between Inner Life and Collective Memory: A Methodological Reflection." *The New Arcadia Review,* Volume 3.

Lepore, Stephen J. and Smyth, Joshua M., *The Writing Cure: How Expressive Writing Promotes Health and Emotional Well-Being.* Washington, DC: American Psychological Association, 2003

Levine, Stephen K. *Poiesis.* Philadelphia: Jessica Kingsley Publishers. 1997

Martel, Yann. *Life of Pi.* New York: Harvest Books/Harcourt Inc. 2001

Mantel, Hilary. *Beyond Black.* New York: Henry Holt. 2005.

Mantel, Hilary. *Giving Up the Ghost.* New York: Picador. 2003

Naparstek, Belleruth. *Invisible Heroes: Survivors of Trauma and How they Heal.* New York: Bantam. 2005

Pennebaker, J. W., and S.K. Beall. "Confronting a Traumatic Event: Toward an Understanding of Inhibition and Disease." *Journal of Abnormal Psychology 95:*

Pennebaker, James W. *Opening Up: The Healing Power of Expressing Emotions.* New York: Guilford Press. 1990

Pennebaker, James W. "Telling Stories: The Health Benefits of Narrative," *Literature and Medicine*, 19.1, 2000, Johns Hopkins University Press.

Rafferty, Terrance. "Demons Revealed." *New York Times.* May 15, 2005.

Rico, Gabriele Lusser. *Pain and Possibility.* New York: Jeremy P. Tarcher/Perigee Books. 1991

Robinson, Mark. "Writing Well: Health and the Power to Make Images." *Journal of Medical Ethics: Medical Humanities*, Durham, England, BMJ Publishing Group. Ltd. 2000.

Schwab, Gabriele. "Writing Against Memory and Forgetting." *Literature and Medicine,* Volume 25.1, 2006. Johns Hopkins University Press

Winnicott, Donald. *Playing and Reality,* 2nd Edition. London. Routledge 2005

14

Writing for Recovery: Working with Cancer Patients, Survivors, and their Loved Ones

Angela Buttimer

Writing saved my life. I began writing around the age of six. Tucked away in the sanctuary of my childhood bedroom, I found both the solace and the power of pen and paper. I learned to authentically express my emotions, without editing, and to explore my views of the world with curiosity, knowing I could change my mind at any time, and slowly gain clarity. I could be as angry or as melancholy as I wanted without anyone's opinion on the matter. I could write poetry without a critic. I could write fiction endings to real-life situations, teaching me about possibility, empowering me to seek options outside of the dictates of society around me.

As I evolved into a young adult, I continued to write, along with practicing yoga and meditation. These practices kept me out of seductive realms of "trouble." They were an ally in my search to find balance and stability within, key components to my own healing process. And so, becoming a psychotherapist and yoga and meditation teacher, I have encouraged my clients to explore writing as a path for healing and transformation.

I encourage writing as a tool in my private practice for individuals, couples, and families. I facilitate writing sessions in workshops and retreats, finding the energy of a group to be especially beneficial. I am always amazed and humbled at what people express. They, too, are often surprised at what they have to say and how much they have to say. Many of us have learned, as adults, to self-contain and compartmentalize our honest and authentic thoughts and emotions, and, when given permission, the process of opening and expressing oneself can be like a flood bursting through a dam when pen hits paper (or fingers hit keyboard). Because writing has been such a reliable ally in my life, I am delighted to help others access their own inner writer and watch the questions emerge, the light bulbs come on, and, at times, catharsis take place.

As I've expanded the scope of my professional practice, I was fortunate enough to meet Carolyn Helmer, the manager of Cancer Wellness at Piedmont Hospital. I began facilitating various programs under her leadership including mindfulness meditation, gentle yoga, and writing for recovery groups and workshops. The participants in this program include cancer patients, cancer survivors, and their loved ones. We offer our services free of charge to anyone affected by cancer in the metro Atlanta area, at any phase of his/her journey. Cancer Wellness is a non-profit program funded solely by the philanthropy of our generous donors. Focusing on integrative medicine, we offer a broad scope of programming based on psychoneuroimmunology (how thoughts and emotions affect and intersect with physical health), including the above-mentioned programs and also services such as nutrition, education, counseling and coaching, support groups, humor, massage, guided imagery, art therapy, and specialty workshops.

Various research findings have been compiled on the benefits of the writing modality as a healing force. In his book, *Opening Up*, James Pennebaker, PhD, the father of journal writing, explains that inhibition of thoughts and feelings gradually undermine the body's immune system and can place people at risk for disease.[1] In Dr. Pennebaker's keynote at the 2007 Wellness and Writing Conference, he stated that the benefits of verbally expressing what is written can increase benefits of well-being to the writer.[2] In addition, research at Dana-Farber Cancer Institute and Harvard Medical School found that expressive writing boosts both mental and physical health in patients suffering from cancer.[3] Many other benefits have been reported from participants of expressive writing including stress relief, lowered blood pressure and heart rate, resistance to illnesses, and generally improved sense of physical and psychological well-being.

I have been facilitating "Writing for Recovery" at Cancer Wellness for a few years now. My goal is to offer participants a safe place to explore and express issues that they are facing both related directly to the cancer experience as well as the issues that life presents. Below is a review of my model, some ideas for structuring such a group that I have found to work well, and some suggestions to consider.

Population and Model

The participants in this group include cancer patients, survivors, and caregivers. The age range is wide, between 25 and 75 years, both male and female.

This is an open group, with core members who attend most classes. The class is held every other week for two hours. Each participant receives a journal. Group size averages between two and ten people.

This is a creative journal-writing group, so we work in many different modalities to get pen to paper including:

- Stream of consciousness — writing down whatever comes across your mind, may be disjointed and random or may be deep and connected, keep the pen moving until time is up.
- Sentence stems — beginning sentences with I statements or other types of statements such as "I feel…" or "I trust…" or "My body is saying yes to…"
- Mind-mapping — a visual technique that begins with one subject in the center, like "cancer" and the writer creates stems off of

that center like "treatment options," "feelings I'm having," "support systems," etc.

- List making — a great tool when you don't feel like writing a lot of words, simply making a list of the topic given or a topic of your choice.
- Questioning — using the Socratic method to guide writers into deeper inquiry and exploration about their internal process.
- Free writing — write about whatever is on the mind: the struggles being faced, the stresses and/or the joys, the issues that the writer wants to explore.
- Art therapy — using color to depict what you would like to express or to go deeper in expressing what you have written, can be representational or abstract.
- Conversations or dialogue — may be a conversation between writer's voices/different selves, the writer and his/her body, etc.
- Letter writing — generally, this is "unsent letters" — letters to self, others (things I would like to say, didn't have a chance to say), God, cancer, etc.
- Fiction — exploring various topics by writing fiction or lending a fictional ending to a real situation.
- Memoir writing — writing about the memories of any aspect of one's life, particular moments, days, or events and exploring the thoughts/feeling and impact of those times.
- Poetry — using the poetic form to express one's experiences, requiring fewer words and sometimes allowing a writer to be more direct or symbolic.
- Third person — writing about one's situation from a third party's perspective, for example, how a third party may observe the struggles one is experiencing.
- Song lyrics — exploring words and lines and melodies from a song and how it may relate to the writer's experiences, thoughts, feelings.

I use a theme for each class. The themes are chosen to help give participants a focus for their writing and a consistent stream of exploration. There are times when I don't use a particular theme, and, instead, focus on working with various essays or poems and songs. When I do work with themes, I have found that because I leave them open enough, participants are able to get to whatever they need to express. All of the themes I have used have been extremely rich in the group. I do feel that it's important for the facilitator to read the emotional energy in the room and to discern from what is being expressed, how to present the next writing exercise in order to be of most benefit. There are times, given what is being expressed, that I may change course mid-stream. And as I mentioned, all participants are reminded at the beginning of class that they are free to use the time to write outside the given theme. Regarding "themes" I would also like to add that my themes are created from my work as a psychotherapist and meditation teacher. There are common universal themes that all of humanity faces that consistently surface in individual, couples, and group sessions. It is from these experiences that I create themes, as well as being mindful of the needs in the group.

A few examples of the themes I use include:

- My Healing Journey
- My Various Selves/Voices
- My Inner and Outer Selves
- Challenges We Face
- Acceptance and Letting Go
- My Phenomenal-ness (based on Maya Angelou's work)
- The Past, Present, and Future
- Exploring and Expressing Emotions

Note: There are times that participants veer off in a different direction than the theme given, which is always welcome in class.

Writing for Recovery

Structure

We open by introducing ourselves briefly if there are new participants in the room. I give a brief handout and overview of the research
around writing for healing, discuss ways in which we can get pen to
paper, and discuss the process of sharing in group. I always let people
know that they can share process or content (be it discussing or reading)
or not share at all. We honor and respect the need and desire to be quiet
with your writing.

I tend to structure my group in this way, each piece related to theme
for that day:

- Stream of consciousness
- Opportunity to process
- Relaxation exercise (breathwork, guided meditation, progressive
  muscle relaxation)
- Warm-up (may be sentence stems, mind-mapping, lists,
  questioning)
- 1st writing
- Opportunity to process with group — dialogue
- 2nd writing
- Opportunity to process with group — dialogue
- 3rd writing — (usually art journaling)
- Opportunity to process with group — dialogue (Note: At times,
  depending on the theme, I wait to process with group until this
  point. If I do wait, I ask them to look back over their writing and
  art and note any observations they have about what they've
  done.)
- 4th Writing — (usually poetry)
- Opportunity to process with group — dialogue

I often give them some homework they can choose to work with
between classes. I overwhelmingly hear from participants that the blank

page is so daunting that it often paralyzes them, so having a springboard between classes helps them get pen to paper.

I offer other events for this community including poetry readings, retreats, and specialty workshops.

Suggestions

1. Schedule the group on a consistent basis as this creates a sense of safety for the participants.
2. Cancer patients and survivors may or may not want to write about cancer. Allow a broad enough theme so that they may work where they would like. At times, they may want to write on another theme altogether, which should be welcomed.
3. Allow time for people to share their experience between writing segments.
4. Allow participants to share in the way they feel comfortable (sharing process, sharing content either by reading their writing aloud or simply talking about it, or not sharing at all). It's important that each participant feel safe wherever they are in their process and not be pushed to share.
5. Help to create a sense of quiet in the room. This is a time for reflection. Participants may be thinking as much as writing during this time and sidebars between participants can create a distraction.
6. As a clinician, focus on what is being expressed rather than the craft of writing.
7. As a clinician, it is essential to be strong in clinical skills and experience in group dynamics when leading this type of group.
8. My approach is to refrain from my own writing while in the role of clinician as it may contaminate the therapeutic process for the participants.
9. I often bring in the writing of others on the theme we're working on to share what others have done. I get an overwhelmingly positive response to this addition.

10. Be flexible. Have a back up plan. Be able to prioritize which writing may be most helpful if time runs out.

Many participants come to this group ready to write. Others come with curiosity. And still others come reticent. I have found that creating a safe space is the crucial component. Giving them lots of prompts and options to guide them to getting pen to paper is also helpful as I often hear that the hardest part is just getting started.

I would like to share a few comments from participants about their experience in our "Writing for Recovery" group:

"The magic or the grace of the class seems to be in creating a safe space where one can share their humanity (to whatever depth is feels right) and thereby in the sharing with others, to heal. This is how it works for me." — PT

"I make myself laugh and cry, but I clear out cobwebs and emotions that need to be dealt with. Listening to others' writings inspires me and helps me feel better about my own. The structured yet free form format of the class is phenomenal." — FH

"I am less than a year out from breast cancer surgery and taking proper care of myself is crucial to recovery. This course has pointed me in the direction I need to go to be my best physically, mentally, and spiritually." — BB

I am delighted to be able to share a poem with you written in class from the third-person perspective:

She Let Them Love Her

She let them love her.
It had been far too long since she did that.
She let them comfort her.
It was time to share the burden.

After all she had been through,
she welcomed the community of those
whose hearts were open to her weakness
and her needs.

Not her strength and coping skills
but to her very admission of need.

Rose petals fell from a mysterious source.
The goddess mourned with her.
The spirits wept with her.
And music was heard as shape notes of love.

Hope had the last word.
It said, "Only good can come of this."

— Vicki Woodyard

Written in the Writing for Recovery group after sharing the loss of my daughter and husband to cancer.

To close, I am very grateful and honored to be doing this work. I thank each of the courageous participants and clients for trusting me, allowing me in, and allowing me to witness and share in their process. My heart and soul have been deeply nourished.

References

[1] Pennebaker, James W. *Opening Up: the Healing Power of Expressing Emotions* (1990). New York: Guilford Press.

[2] Pennebaker, James W. Keynote Address. Wellness and Writing Conference 2007. Atlanta, Georgia.

[3] Norris, RL, Bauer-Wu, S. Being mindful, easing suffering. *J Palliat Med. 2007 Feb; 10*(1): 261-2. Dana Farber Cancer Institute, Boston, MA.

15

Entering Your Life: Lessons from the Patient Voice Project and the Challenges of Teaching Expressive Writing to the Chronically Ill

Austin Bunn

In November of 2004, in a dim conference room on the third floor of the student center at the University of Iowa, I sat across from a sweet and disarming school librarian named Stephanie, with a spray of pages between us. Stephanie had a stage-four brain tumor that had been discovered, and she wore a flashy, tropical scarf over her head, her hair wispy from chemotherapy. She'd driven up from Hills, a small town about twenty miles to the south of Iowa City, and even though she spent her days around books, sometimes she had trouble reading words on the page. I had decided, improbably, to light a candle, for the ceremony of it all, though I was nervous the flame would trigger the fire alarm and we'd end up drenched. I'd had this idea, to start an expressive writing program for people struggling with chronic illness a few weeks before, in my first weeks as a graduate student. Suddenly, here I was, in a room, acting on my good intentions and I realized I had no idea what I was doing.

I asked Stephanie to describe her childhood bedroom. This was, and remains, a classic Patient Voice Project (PVP) exercise, because the assignment has a big front door. Everybody had a childhood bedroom. And the memories of the place invoke immediate feelings and precise observations, with a whole range of responses — we all spent a lot of time in our childhood bedrooms: staring at our pet rocks, our posters, or in my case a Space Shuttle model hanging from a sewing thread. As a rule, I do my own assignments (when I'm not distracted, as a college professor, by attendance and prep!), and I think this is an important principle of civic-minded writing instruction: no prompt should be flung at students like homework. When teachers hand down assignments like edicts, it's easy to ignore your own vagaries or the subtle stumbling blocks. This assignment gets complicated by one constraint: the writers are not allowed to use "to be" as a verb. It's flat, it's easy, I told Stephanie, and it's a "state-of-being" verb and we're looking for vibrant life here.

I started writing and this assignment, for a reason I only half understand, entered me anew. I suppose the stakes seemed higher with Stephanie in the room, and her bravery and willingness — and trust in me — made me risk a new honesty. I found myself returning to the loft in my father's house, a spare bedroom built by my father and, oddly, branching off *another* guest bedroom. Inside, two twin beds tucked against the eaves, covered by my father's scratchy, thin army blankets. These beds served as the sleeping arrangement for my twin brother and me. An air-conditioner hung in the window, where the cicadas wiggled in and scared the bejesus out of us. The beds folded up, and the mattresses, for compensation, seemed made of super springs, so on boring afternoons, they turned into makeshift trampolines. This was not exactly my childhood bedroom. We occupied this bedroom on alternating weekends and on nights like this specific one, when, at ten years old, I wept and whispered my last wishes into the ear of my brother's stuffed animal, terrified of what would happen to me the next morning.

My surgery was scheduled for seven A.M., a time that seemed to me the hour of doom. The hospital was an hour away, in Philadelphia at the Children's Hospital, and my father's house was closer than my mother's, hence this impromptu sleepover mid-week. I was fairly certain I would not come back. Convalescence didn't occur to me. It was not in the realm of my understanding. My trip to CHoP (as it was known, terrifyingly) was for a minor surgery, but when you're ten, no surgery is minor. The question that typically and understandably follows is, *what for?* Answering that question, without awkwardness and shame, took me years and led, in no small way, to the Patient Voice Project, the program that, at that moment in Iowa Memorial Union with Stephanie and the spell of our scribbling, I claimed to be launching.

It is now five years later, and the Patient Voice Project, through the generosity of the University of Iowa and the commitment my fellow graduate students at the Writers' Workshop, has taught over a hundred students in the Iowa City area, funded by an array of university, state, and national grants. The premise: The Patient Voice Project offers free expressive writing classes for people struggling with chronic illness — cancer and mental illness, primarily — taught by Writers' Workshop graduate students. Through a grant from Johnson and Johnson/The Society for Arts in Healthcare, the PVP is now beginning its first real expansion beyond Eastern Iowa. Stephanie's tumor is in remission, she continues to run her library in Hills, and her daughter is beginning to discover Stephen King (another reader is born).

The Iowa Writers' Workshop is the oldest graduate program in creative writing in the country, and I couldn't begin to encapsulate the instruction I received there. My own writing feels like it has gone through boot camp, and certainly the Patient Voice benefits from the intense culture of young poets and fiction writers there. But I know that the hours I spent with Stephanie, over the course of ten weeks that stretched for a year, taught me at least as much — about humility, resilience, the way stories make experience (not the other way around), and, most important, how our personal narratives tell us equally about what will come next as what has come before.

* * * * *

Teaching expressive writing to those coping with illness is, no doubt, a privileged and rewarding experience. If you believe writing matters, there may be no stronger proof than reading or listening to the writing of those unable to describe to their doctors, friends, or family the inner experience of pain. As instructor, you may see writers begin to emerge from what sociologist Arthur Franks calls the "narrative wreckage" of illness, and, as a teacher, it doesn't get much better. But I also believe that, if you're reading this anthology, you're already convinced of this. In my experience, too much of the conversation about art therapy and expressive writing seems occupied with warm self-congratulation and vague uplift.

After a handful of years developing the PVP and talking with other teachers, I feel there's a critical conversation that needs to happen among those passionate about expressive writing and wellness. As the medical community wrestles increasingly with the challenges of long-term chronic care — from diabetes to cancer to Parkinson's disease to mental illness — we have, as social workers and teachers, a special opportunity to participate in the changes. I see a place for the PVP and programs like it at clinics, support-groups, and community centers across the country. But an honest assessment of the vulnerabilities of expressive writing as art therapy needs to take place before that becomes possible.

Foremost, I believe expressive writing programs, in their current iteration, lack pedagogy, an instructional method that emphasizes *ideas* instead of *off-loading* onto the page. This isn't surprising, since the tradition of art therapy centers on distractionary techniques — music or painting that happen *in situ* and strive to help patients get their minds off their condition. These therapeutic models try to foster creative positive experiences and soften the clinical atmosphere. They are, by and large, one-offs: a guitarist visits a hospital for an afternoon or a visual artist teaches a watercolor class for a rotating and irregular audience of in-patients. Most often, these *in situ* offerings emphasize play and escape and socialization. I'm all for them. But they are not enough.

Similarly, many expressive writing classes operate on the principle that any writing is good writing. Writing itself — journaling, letter writing, intentional reflection of any sort — may be rare enough (both for the ill and the rest of us) that it is worth cultivating and celebrating. And the health benefits, we know, are real. The Patient Voice trains its instructors to tell students, at the first class, about Pennebaker's findings that regular writing four times a week for fifteen minutes each time can strength the immune system by raising T-cell counts. And further research, by Howard Butcher at the University of Iowa, shows that writing by caregivers, on any subject, can lower cortisol levels, the stress hormone. Based on these, it's understandable that writing and wellness programs may simply emphasize writing anything, or what I call first-draft "off-loading" — the impulsive expressiveness of mental journalism. It is a ticker of daily frustrations, mysteries, and wishes we all wade through.

But I believe that patients are idea poor. They may be eager to write but also to perceive anew. In my experience, the students in writing classes tailored for the ill want new techniques for experiencing their own condition. They have come as far as they can on their own. They are aware that their own stories seem elusive and shapeless. They see their listeners grow bored or lost, but the effort to repair that narrative wreckage exhausts them. If they do have stories to tell, then they seem almost rigid and overly ordered. The performance artist Anna Deveare Smith deemed this burden the "track" (as in a train rail) of a personal story, which can limit the range of detail, emotion, and even power of the telling. Smith, a MacArthur Grant winner and author of *Fires in the Mirror* and *Twilight*, interviews people and then performs the transcript as the characters themselves. In her work, she has discovered that people often don't tell stories — they re-tell them. They hone the story to the point of absolute control over them. So, in her work, she seeks to "interrupt the grammar" of these stories to drive people to new depths in their experience, to see their stories with fresh eyes. She does this by asking three questions: Have you ever been close to death? What were the circumstances of your birth? and Have you ever been accused of something you did not do? (These questions are likely too pointed or too abstract for work with the ill.)

So we have work to do as writing teachers in this field, but we need to think about *outcomes* instead of soft objectives like "expressiveness." We have stories to excavate, delineate, and shape. We have perceptions to refine and make accessible. And this repair of patient stories is not simply an inner act. These stories will be told to friends, family, and doctors (foremost), and helping the teller develop and strengthen these narratives benefits not only them but their audiences. My mother has Parkinson's disease, and I have personally experienced how her scattered narrative of her condition can confuse and ultimately frustrate her caretakers (including me). The looming social danger of chronic illness is compassion fatigue.

Furthermore, as the health care industry seeks a greater understanding of chronic illness itself — how to implement care, how to listen better, and what to listen for — we have an opportunity for these stories to provide invaluable perspectives. It might be my bias as a formal journalist and college writing instructor, but I can't help but consider how these stories leave the classroom and where they will go next. We need to consider the broader *reception* of these stories as much as their production. In the Patient Voice, we have produced an anthology, held a public reading by the students at the public library, printed table tents of poems and essays for distribution on hospital cafeteria tables, and printed broadsides for distribution. (We'd dreamed of recording our students reading their own work for radio broadcast, but there's only so much you can pull off with volunteers.) All of these, I feel, were attempts to open the door of the classroom, to bring writing into the world.

* * * * *

Currently, the field could use more research to tell us which curricula work (and which don't) for specific conditions. It's obvious in a classroom that you can't duplicate the pedagogy with the depressed and those struggling with breast cancer. At the same time, PVP classes tend to circle two common themes — an increased attention to state of mind and a focus on narrative agency — and I'll explain more about them in a moment.

What is a Patient Voice class and how does it work? Typically, each class begins with an in-class writing exercise, tethered to an idea — working with images, say, or stretching empathy. No student has to share their work publicly, but we invite them to. We have created a binder of selections of poetry and non-fiction (fiction seems to be the least compelling for our students), and we aim for a short discussion of some reading. The writers include Anatole Broyard, Jane Kenyon, Anne Lamott — all accessible masters of the form. Many students, as eager to write as they may be, don't read, and the central dynamic of writing instruction is that writing practice only improves when reading increases. We have built this model from literacy and ESL instruction, which uses a wheel of modeling/social interaction/individual performance to help students master language skills. Class concludes with another writing prompt — again, aiming for fifteen minutes of writing time per class, following Pennebaker's research showing that is the threshold for health benefits.

We spent a lot of time thinking: what are we teaching exactly and why? I think the PVP distinguishes itself on intentions of its pedagogy. The Iowa Writers' Workshop emphasizes uncommon aspects of writing that have, not surprisingly, found their way into our teaching philosophy and practice. I don't have the space here to outline them in great detail, but as an overview, Patient Voice classes (one hour a week, for between six and ten weeks) are split into two distinct fields of emphasis: state of mind and narrative agency. The first asks students to consider how their mood and attitude influences what and how they perceive, how language reflects those attitudes, and how that process might be reversed: how language might influence perception itself. The second seeks to develop a stronger sense of "choice" in their stories, to eradicate passivity and focus on moments of personal control and resilience. As these two build on each other, we ask each class to build to something — a poem, a single essay, a lyric — that can act as the culmination of the class. This final project goes through one revision, in an attempt to teach the basic principle that all effective writing is in revision.

An attention to state of mind, or "consciousness," works almost like biofeedback. It asks writers and readers to move the question of writerly attitude or tone to the foreground and to relegate the matters of subject matter and narrative force to the back. In doing so, these writers gain more control over the tone of their self-expression, which, typically for the ill, has become dominated with melancholy, disappointment, and despair. Sickness is a melancholy experience, certainly (hence the Greek root of the word: "black bile"). But if we can agree that a variation in tone is critical for effective self-expression, then students have to first become aware of it and then experiment with changing it.

Here's how. One early Patient Voice exercise asks participants to consider the prior week of their life. For fifteen minutes, they will write three separate short paragraphs on different episodes: a moment of conflict, a moment of confusion, and a moment of grace or beauty. This is a multi-part exercise, of which I'm a great fan. (It seems to me that far too many prompts treat writing like strip-mining: get in and out fast. But multi-part exercises encourage depth, complexity, and commitment.) As has been the case in every class I have taught, students immediately come up with one or two of the episodes but struggle with the third. In Iowa, for example, many students had trouble with a moment of "conflict," largely (I believe) because Iowans are deeply conflict-avoidant. Invariably, they would smile in agreement when I said this, a former New Yorker. I propose this exercise as a sort of litmus test, a core sample of the writer's psychology. As the poet Allen Ginsberg taught, "notice what you notice." If you can't come up with a moment of beauty or grace your irritation may be keeping you from appreciation of the outer world. Likewise, a writer who doesn't remember a moment of conflict — with friends, with a door lock, with the Internet — is probably in denial. In most cases, from my experience, students with a chronic illness have trouble noticing beauty and grace. Their illness, their scattered and self-involved consciousness, keeps them from seeing it positively.

After a series of exercises on observation and description, we move to questions of personal agency, a special weakness in patient stories. It's apparent from any conversation with those dealing with chronic care that they feel like pinballs in an arcade. Shuffled from doctor to doctor, facing a flurry of scans and prescriptions, patients experience their treatment often happening *to them.* They are made passive. And passivity, as any non-fiction or fiction writer knows, is a narrative problem. We wondered if there might be a way to increase the sense of control, of decisiveness, in the narrators of these stories.

So these essays grow out of a simple structure — a scene, a character, a choice. The scene description asks the writer to conjure up a specific scenario with the strongest, most vivid language possible. The character can be themselves or their doctor or a friend — some way to locate us in the scene itself and perhaps to deploy dialogue. The choice refers specifically to a moment when the writer decided something of consequence.

We have several techniques to approach this sense of impact and intention. One prompt has the writer describe the "moment when you knew something was wrong. The first symptom, the first diagnosis..." The challenge here is that the writer must only describe the room or situation *without mentioning the news itself.* Can they convey it through description alone, through the register of words and adjectives? (Perhaps the most important element here is slowness — creating a context for information.) Once this scene is established, then the writer is asked to describe the "news" and then what they *chose* to do next. To get specific, I taught a diabetes support group this exercise and asked them to describe what they had for dinner the day they were diagnosed: what kind of meal

do you make when you know you will not eat the same for the rest of
your life? Almost everyone had a story.

We want to give students in a Patient Voice class an opportunity to
wrestle with the big issues of their care, but we don't want them to
remain over-focused on their identities *as patients*. To that end, around
the third Patient Voice class, we ask the participant to draw up what we
call "The Two Benchmarks." This looks like two chronologies — one of
their peak experiences in their life, in seven-year intervals, and one of
their major experiences as a patient. With these two chronologies, the
patient has thrown a lot of clay onto the table and given the instructor a
lot of material to work from. Together, they look for linkages,
unexpected connections, patterns of response. As the poet Louise Glück
says, "Everything that happens to us, happens to us in our childhood and
from then on it is repeat, repeat, repeat." Stephanie, for example, wrote
about getting lost at a Fireman's fair when she was a girl and feeling
abandoned. This connected to the experience of getting lost at the giant
Houston hospital. From these two related experiences, Stephanie wrote a
short piece about how she coped with being lost.

Most time, students know what choices they have had to make. They
simply need to allow it emerge more vividly in the way they tell their
stories. They breeze over them as if they are unimportant. Once, I asked
Stephanie to write about what she did to get herself strong when she felt
weak. I wanted her to story her resilience. She wrote about her long-
distance travels to Texas for her experimental trial. Each trip back from
Houston to Iowa meant hours of nausea from the treatment in the family
minivan.

Here's is the opening of her first draft:

> We were early for the MRI scan. We've been early for
> almost all of my scans. You begin to understand the system no
> matter where they take place. At this point, I've had a total of
> six: three in Iowa, my hometown hospital, and three in Texas.
> The Texas variety, like everything in Texas are bigger. The scans

down south, which are a part of my clinical trial, are "dynamic" MRIs.

This is a terrific start — it creates a sense of incident and tension. What will she find in this new scan? Plus, Stephanie looked at her life a little anthropologically, from the outside in, explaining the patterns and routines of her radiation and check-ups as a cancer patient. (We encourage this "anthropological" view, especially for readers or listeners who might not know much about the disease.)

In the spirit of revision, I gave her some edits to help polish and smooth out the opening. I asked her to make the verb tenses agree and to set up a theme she would be exploring over the piece: the loss of appetite and desire for sustaining food. I also wanted her to think even *more* anthropologically, to make sure to explain just what these dynamic MRIs had to do with the non-dynamic kind. Here are my edits:

> We're [CUT "were" The rest of the piece is in present tense, so I think we should stay in it!] early for the MRI scan. We've been early for almost all of my scans. [Why have you been early so much? Also: DID YOU EAT ANYTHING that morning? Are you not allowed to? I mention this because then we could INTRO the motif of food and eating and pleasure early so that it gets woven into the piece.] You begin to understand the system no matter where they take place. At this point, I've had a total of six: three in Iowa CITY, my hometown hospital? and three in DALLAS, Texas. [Is this where we should explain WHY you've gone to Texas? Your status as a patient and something about the clinical trial to fight the tumor? Else, won't readers wonder why you switched location? To me I think this would be the spot.] The Texas variety, like everything in Texas are bigger. [NICE] The scans down south, which are a part of my clinical trial, are "dynamic" MRIs. [Does this mean they are physically BIGGER? Or do you just mean longer/more time-consuming/two dyes? I want to connect it to the "bigger" punch line before.]

Here is the final draft:

We are early for the MRI scan, so early that my husband Jay
and I have skipped breakfast. We've been early for almost all of
my scans. You begin to understand the system no matter where
they take place: if you get there ahead of schedule, there's a
small chance you'll get scanned ahead of schedule. At this point,
I've had a total of six: three at the University of Iowa hospital in
my hometown of Iowa City, Iowa, and three in Houston, Texas,
at the renowned MD Anderson Cancer Center. In August of
2004, just five months ago, I was diagnosed with an inoperable
brain tumor and am now seeking treatment there. Every six
weeks I'm back in Houston for another scan and to see my
oncologist. Well, the Texas variety MRI, which stands for magnetic resonance imaging, like everything else in Texas is bigger.
The scans down south, a component of a clinical trial in which I
am taking part, are "dynamic" MRIs. They involve using a contrast dye twice during the procedure as opposed to only once,
and last about 45 minutes each instead of the usual 15-20; these
are used to track the status of my tumor.

Stephanie did a great job incorporating the edits into her own voice
— flinty, sweet, and strong.

Later in the piece, she explained how she decided to have a three-
course meal with her husband *before* the treatment in Texas — when she
could actually experience her own hunger. In her first draft, this was a
throwaway sentence. In revision, I asked her to expand the moment of
her decision so that her readers (and she) could experience a greater
sense of choice and power. Eventually, that meal she had — and the
comedically mountainous dessert she struggled to eat — grew into three
paragraphs. She called her essay "Celebration Dinner."

The frustrations of writing instruction with the chronically ill are
predictable. The Patient Voice works with, almost exclusively,
outpatients, and they can make irregular students. Their health gets in the

way. And an uneven attendance makes any pedagogy almost pointless. They can be lonely and needy — a part of our training now includes policies on "over-talking" (instead of writing) and preparing patients for termination of the class.

Perhaps most frustrating is the sense that the class only reaches those who are already converts to the benefits of writing. Without question, the vast majority of participants in the Patient Voice (it is voluntary after all) are women. They journal, they like to read, and expressive writing makes sense to them. Men, in my experience, treat writing exercises as though they were chores they want to finish as quickly possible. They drop their pens noisily to the table when they are done, inevitably before everyone else, punctuating their work.

I remember visiting a prostate cancer support group to do a short expressive writing session on the Patient Voice Project. Many of the men attended with their wives (and, I suspect, at the insistence of their wives). I made sure to mention the specific health benefits of writing *first* — my instinct said that these men wanted to know about the results before they dealt with their self-expression. I brought with me an excerpt from Anatole Broyard's *Intoxicated by My Illness*, in which he describes his doctor. I asked them to do the same, with the intention of (later) having them describe *themselves* from their doctor's point of view. When they finished writing, few of the men were willing to read their pieces aloud — a common issue in a first-time class for a new instructor. Of the one piece that was read, it had what I call the "All Points Bulletin" style: an almost police-style physical breakdown, starting with height, hair color, and size. The wives, interestingly, supplied far more vivid and interactionally based descriptions — partly because they were the keepers of the doctor "diaries," and recorded the sessions. (This was Iowa, and a traditional and older population.) The second part of the exercise was far easier for the wives than the husbands, understandably, as they already view them from the outside.

This struggle taught me some valuable lessons. First, I think one-off-style writing instruction, at the hospital or elsewhere, will always have serious limits — much of the time is spent simply building trust. To truly develop a writing habit, you need multiple exposures. Secondly, the writing modality itself might be incorporated in smaller ways by social workers dealing with men to help establish it earlier, with short writing exercises each meeting, so that a visit by a writing instructor would not seem so uncommon. And lastly, I might have miscalculated my model; it may be that men (and women, too) have diminished interest writing about their illness *first*; a stronger opening exercise might have met them at their passion — for ice fishing or car repair or baseball. I wondered, afterwards, if that audience wanted an opportunity to *not* think about their sickness. We want to tell the stories that inspire us. Ultimately, how many people want to describe their doctor except to complain? This exercise now appears mid-way through the PVP curriculum.

This gender bias won't be overcome easily. It is a heuristic in the publishing industry that men read non-fiction and women everything else; if memoir and personal essays disinterest men, I don't think a PVP class will help them overcome it. Perhaps, like homeopathy, we need to admit to ourselves that only a certain portion of the population will be interested in expressive writing for wellness. But for programs like the Patient Voice Project to thrive, they need to identify new audiences and new communities of writers. This work is tiring and demands strong marketing sensibilities, another vulnerability of small non-profit programs. The hospital itself has proven to be a difficult site for promoting our work; support groups turn out to be excellent resources along with local, independent clinics and agencies. In recent months, the PVP has turned to local Gilda's Clubs and hospices to offer their services — places that already do the work of inviting populations in so that we can do what we do well.

* * * * *

The problems of the body can seem unspeakable, as common as they might be. One third of all people will get treated for cancer at some point in their lifetimes. One percent of all boy babies are born with *cryptorchidism* ("missing flower"), or undescended testicles, as I was. Most are operated on within the first two years of their life. I was diagnosed in the spring of fifth grade, at the threshold of puberty, when the risks for life-long impact (infertility, testosterone imbalance, maturation delays) are highest.

I missed school for a week for the surgery. I suspect that that would have been the sum total of the experience — some bruising, some shame, nothing exceptional for a teenager — except the first surgery failed, and the story of my illness took on greater proportions. I returned to the Children's Hospital a second time, more terrified than ever. Would I grow up? Would I become a man? On the drive there, I was inconsolable, stuck in the cone of silence around my body's failure. This time at the hospital, though, I looked around me. Kids with catheters, IV trees, sutures, and shaved heads passed me in the halls, on the elevator. I knew I had gotten off easy. I awoke in the post-op room in a welter of screaming with no nurses or parents present. I remember propping myself up on my elbows and calling out, "It's OK, we're OK, we're going to be fine." I thought that if we could just talk, maybe we'd be rescued. We could rescue each other.

Later, as I recovered, I would never get any therapy for the surgery, nor did I ever speak to a social worker. Even my mom — a good Catholic ashamed of explicit anatomy — told me to tell everyone I had had a "hernia" operation. When friends asked what that was, I had no idea. It was a terrible lie but I told it. It would be an overreach to say this was the origin of the Patient Voice Project, but it would not be wrong either.

After that evening with Stephanie, I kept writing. The story would not leave me alone. I continued to tell the story of what happened, how, years later, I went back for follow-up tests. Standing in the giant atrium of CHoP, I felt the bellows of the years crunch together and I was a boy again, my body wrong. It was strange to have come to class expecting to teach writing and, improbably, turn into the student, but perhaps this is why we all show up in the classroom. (Not surprisingly, many of the PVP instructors have personal experiences with illness.) To speak in our PVP story form, my "choice" became the decision to create the PVP.

Oliver Sacks, in his terrific memoir of recuperation, *A Leg to Stand On*, quotes the 18th century German writer Novalis: "Every sickness is a musical problem, every cure a musical solution." For Sacks, this meant learning to walk again after knee surgery to the rhythmic phrasings in classical recordings. But in light of Franks and Pennebaker, every sickness is a problem of narrative, and every cure is partly a story. For me, the plot of my illness did not exist for me until the fall of 2004, when I found myself beginning a conscious effort to put it into form with Stephanie, in a conference room, our single, ridiculous candle winning against a cold November night.

16

The Voices of Innocence

Lara Naughton

I. Exoneree Is Not a Word

November, 2007. The second floor library of the Innocence Project/New Orleans. Mismatched chairs — some with ripped vinyl seats, others with battered legs — are scattered around a large wooden desk. Thick, leather-bound books line the floor-to-ceiling shelves, crates of papers form chaotic stacks high in corners and low against walls, a tattered couch rests in a cozy alcove. I'm a writer, my role is to look beyond the visible, so I survey the room and imagine a complex system of organization hidden within all the stacks.

I am there to meet four men: JT, Gregory, Ryan, and Dan. They are exonerees, which I'm told is not a real word. I'm told this by one of the legal assistants who is volunteering from Ireland. There are few American lawyers who work in the office. Most are from England. This seems odd to me; it makes me wonder if the job of defending the wrongfully convicted is somehow not sexy enough or high paying enough for American lawyers, and suddenly I feel deflated. If American prisoners rely largely on the volunteer efforts of foreign lawyers and law students to help prove their innocence, how will the criminal justice system ever be truly reformed? I decide to use the word "exoneree" anyway and the legal assistant from Ireland agrees it's a word that should be a word.

JT, Gregory, Ryan, and Dan are exonerees from Angola Prison in Louisiana. JT, Ryan, and Dan each lived on death row in 6' x 9' cells, in solitary confinement 23 hours a day, for a combined 35 years while the State of Louisiana prepared to execute them. JT survived seven execution dates. When he tells me this I know I should ask him another question, but I am momentarily speechless. Gregory spent 27½ years of his life incarcerated in Angola Prison, a dangerous, violent home. As Gregory says, "Everything about the place was intimidating. From the long snake ride leading up to the front gate, to the Mississippi River surrounding the prison on three sides, to the endless cycle of human deterioration. Only a short time after I arrived, on the way to chow a young convict jumped out of line and stabbed another convict in his neck. Everybody kept walking as if nothing had happened. Oh, yeah, something had happened. Someone's son was lying on the walk bleeding while dying an agonizing death. As I walked by I asked God to forgive him for his sins. I also asked God to forgive me for mine."

None of the four men I am there to meet committed the murder for which he was convicted. None of the men knew the victim, and none of the men knew about the murder before he was arrested. Gregory never even owned a gun. To this day he has never owned a gun.

I am there to help them tell their stories, which we choose not to call stories because that makes them seem less true, and what they lived through is already hard enough to believe, even for a writer like myself who is trained to imagine. The four men agree to honestly share their life experiences, and I agree to help each of them shape his life experiences into a narrative that he can use for public presentations. They are beginning to book speaking engagements, mostly in churches and college classrooms, and they readily acknowledge that their talks are currently disjointed and rambling. JT and Greg are born talkers who have decades of injustice to express — so many thoughts, so many tangents, so many details, so much information it is overwhelming, it is hard to follow, even in its disjointedness it is heart-wrenching to hear, it is horrifying, it is hard to catch my breath.

Ryan and Dan are more reserved, and tend to speak in partial sentences, leaving gaps of information that dilute the strength of their chronologies. All of the men want guidance and they are sincere in their desire to improve their skills. They genuinely want to be effective in front of audiences; they feel a deep sense of responsibility to present the issue — the reality — of wrongful conviction to the general public. They want the criminal justice system to change. They want their lives to change. They want to help change the lives of other innocent people in prisons across the country. They want to change the fact that when they walk out of prison in Louisiana, exonerees are given a $10 check and a bag with their belongings. They want apologies. They want compensation for the years they lost. They want jobs. They want homes. They want health care and opportunities for education and job training. They want jobs. They want employers to stop turning them away. They want to be financially stable. They want to own cars and cell phones and to be able to pay their electric bills. They want jobs. They want to resist the temptation of easy money on the streets. They want to stop being harassed by police. They want peace of mind. They want to be of service. They want to be heard. They want jobs. They want to heal.

II. Unleashing the Words

Gregory is the writer of the writing group. The others are talkers and I record their words, which I assure them is valid. There is no right way to have a writers group, the right way is the way that works, that fits the needs of the particular people within the group. JT, Ryan, and Dan freeze when they put a pen to paper. The flow of their words comes to a screeching stop. I tell them words don't only belong on the page. Sometimes words belong lingering in the air, with someone to catch them. I offer to be the catcher, if they will unleash what they want to say.

Gregory prefers to write for himself, which I find poetic since he is also the one who could not read or write when he went to jail. Gregory wrote:

> When I got to prison I couldn't read. I was getting a lot of mail from home and the letters was piling up. One of my cellmates was this old timer called Pop. Pop kept a Bible in his hand so I figured Pop must know how to read. I'll offer him some cigarettes to read my mail to me. Turns out Pop couldn't read either. Why do you keep that Bible if you don't know how to read, I asked him. He said that he only kept it to read the little that he knew by heart, like the Lord's Prayer. His words didn't make sense, yet it started me thinking. I didn't have a Bible so I found an old *Watchtower* magazine and began underlining the words that I recognized... and that's how it all began. Later I found half of a dictionary tore at the letter P and kept it as part of my studies. Soon I was able to read a letter from home. I was very proud of this accomplishment.

Then Gregory "went to the books" and taught himself the law. Without the help of a lawyer, Gregory submitted appeals all the way to the State Supreme Court before the Innocence Project learned of his case and helped him secure freedom. So while I'm writing with the speakers, Gregory puts pen to paper. I've given him prompts.

Why is it important to share your experiences?

> A legal, moral, social and spiritual obligation has been placed on the shoulders of those who have walked in a valley low and seen the lightning strike, to not simply explain their journey but to do so with the utmost clarity so that all who hear know that these experiences have no value if untold.

> For those listening, it is equally important to understand that going through much in life prepares us for what is to come ahead. And that the knowledge and wisdom born from these

experiences shows us which way to go. These truths are the first steps in the right direction.

How can writing be healing?

Only by understanding the many complexities facing the judicial system can we begin the healing process. We are never 100% certain as to the guilt of one convicted, which is reason enough for our judicial system to have some provisions in law for compassion. A failure to take responsibility for one's crime has long been the battle cry of many DA's across the country. The irony of this cry is that of the many cases of exonerations, not many DA's have spoken out against the crimes committed against innocent men and women who have been wrongly convicted.

Writing has allowed me the chance to look at my situation from two perspectives: as both victim and as narrator. As victim, the question is what has been done. As narrator, the question becomes what can be done. When innocent people are convicted of crimes they did not commit, society loses. Only by understanding our judicial flaws can we begin the healing process. I truly hope that by sharing these experiences an urge to intervene is the feeling of those who are listening.

III. In Their Own Words

JT

My name is John Thompson. On January 17, 1985, while most people in the city were celebrating Martin Luther King's birthday, I was being arrested and indicted for first-degree murder. My picture appeared in the newspaper and on the news the next day. A week later I was booked separately on five counts of armed robbery, which I did not commit. In April 1985 I was found guilty of attempted armed robbery and sentenced to 49½ years in prison. Two weeks later the murder trial ended in a guilty verdict and I was sentenced to death. Eighteen years, three months, twenty-two days later I was exonerated of all charges in both cases.

Ryan

Hello, my name is Ryan Matthews. When I was 17, I was wrongly convicted for the crime of first-degree murder and armed robbery. I spent 7½ years incarcerated — 2½ in the Parish Prison and when I was 19, I went to Louisiana's Death Row for the next five years. I was exonerated in August of 2004 when I was 24. I'm 27 now.

Gregory

Hello, my name is Gregory Bright. I have served 27½ years in prison for a crime that I did not commit. On November 15, 1975, two months after my 20th birthday, I was arrested with a co-defendant — we did not know each other at the time — and charged in violation of R.S. 14.30.1 (second-degree murder). On July 29, 1976, after 13 minutes of deliberations an Orleans Parish jury found both of us guilty as charged based solely upon the unsubstantiated and uncorroborated testimony of one witness who did not see the actual shooting. Subsequently, we were both sentenced to serve the balance of our natural life at hard labor, in custody of the Louisiana State Penitentiary at Angola, Louisiana, without benefit of parole, probation, or suspension of sentence.

Dan

My name is Dan Bright. I spent 10 years in Angola Prison on death row. The Criminal Justice System doesn't work for society as a whole. It failed me. It is failing everybody.

I was thrown in a cage and I had to adapt to a bunch of madness. I used to live in my six by nine cell, the size of an average bathroom, 23 hours a day, seven days a week. I lived there for 10 years. I can't find words to explain living in that bathroom. How can you? But now my bathroom is much larger.

JT

The Criminal Justice System doesn't recognize poor people are human, too. The prisons are full of the poor. Families — who can't afford $80,000 to $100,000 for a capital attorney with experience — become victims of a powerful criminal justice system that survives off convictions. My family couldn't afford that kind of money. Does that mean I lose my rights as a citizen to be protected under the laws that govern our state? Who is the victim here? Me? My family? The jury? Society? The deceased's family? They were all deceived. Better yet, who are the real criminals here? The DA, my trial attorney, the judge, the police department?

My wrongful convictions didn't just happen to John Thompson, it happened to my whole family; everybody felt the effects of destruction. This experience goes deep. My grandmother died thinking I might be executed. My father died and left this earth with me on death row. My two sons walked around wondering if their father was a killer.

Dan

I haven't received an apology for living ten years on death row for a murder I didn't commit. No one has taken responsibility for the nightmare I lived. My wrongful conviction destroyed my family. I lost a grandmother. I nearly lost my mother due to heart attacks she had while I was on death row. I was gone so long my children stopped looking at me as a father.

Gregory

While the judge sentenced me to life in prison, I looked at my family and friends in the courtroom. They were all in tears. I wondered when, or if, I'll ever see them again. I glanced across the courtroom. There was a lot of hand shaking going on by the DAs. These people orchestrated a case and WON…the rest of my life in prison. I am not comfortable knowing that the 27½ years that I spent in prison for a crime that I did not commit is more time than I've spent out here in society. I am not comfortable with this because it may appear that all that I have lost over those years outweighs all that I have gained. Yes, indeed, I have been down through there. I have walked in the valley of darkness where evil rose to the next level, where my worst nightmare became my harshest reality.

Ryan

My life was disrupted at such a young age. When most people were thinking about what college they'll go to, who they'll take to the prom...I'm thinking about whether I'd get a life or death sentence. I didn't say I was thinking about if I'd be found guilty or innocent. I didn't have money for a paid lawyer. The odds were against me. I didn't have anyone fighting for me. I knew to expect a conviction.

But I always knew after I was convicted I'd be free one day. The evidence was overwhelming in my favor. I had DNA in my case and it didn't match me. My issue was black and white. There was no physical evidence linking me to the crime.

While I was on death row, I had a lot of patience. You need patience being in a cell 23 hours a day. I just had to be calm. The average appeals process is 10 years. I decided I was just going to do what I could to advance myself. So I started teaching myself. I studied my GED book; I read philosophy, psychology, novels. To tell the truth, my patience ran out while I was in prison. Now, I want to finish school and live comfortably. I want an equal opportunity. I'm working extra hard but the results are slow.

JT

I believe everything has a reason and a purpose. My experience living on death row has to have purpose in order for me to continue to live. I arrived on death row September 1, 1987. That year was the most deadly year death row has ever experienced in Louisiana. Seven men were executed. Why did I survive? Yes, I am innocent. But who's to say the other guys who were executed weren't innocent? Why did the light shine on me? I believe God put me here to reveal my experience with the criminal justice system. When we are placed in a position to make decisions about people's lives, we need to be very very careful.

Gregory

People often ask me am I angry, and I answer them, "yes I was." I was angry, bitter, and mad, just to name a few. Over time I learned how self-destructive any of these emotions can be. Eventually I was able to let them all go, but not until I allowed myself to stand in the next man's shoes. Only then was I able to walk in my own.

I am not here because I woke up one morning and decided this course of action. This course of action had been decided for me. I am not sharing this experience with hatred or vengeance in my heart. I share this experience because I know that forgiveness is a powerful tool. Any way you use it, it works.

If all things are done according to God's will, then all bad things happen for the overall good. In this light, this experience is not about me, it's about the next man. And I am humbled and thankful to be able to share this experience with you on this side of the gate.

Ryan

My ultimate goal is for you to have a better understanding of who I am and what I've been through so that there's more awareness about wrongfully convicted people in this country.

Dan

I want my words to open your hearts. I want my words to make you stop prejudging people. I want my words to make you have compassion. I want you to listen.

JT

I want my words to linger in your heart and mind. Let us take you on this trip. We are not looking for sympathy. We are home and safe. We don't want you just to think we're telling you a remarkable story, this is far more important to us than another story. I hope you walk away with a better understanding of our experience. And ask what you can do to help. Thank you for hearing us today and be blessed.

IV. Healing Power

As a group, the exonerees and I meditate before we write in order to help us focus, and to create a calm energy in the room. But before we meditate, there is often disorder. The exonerees are easily distracted. If our group is scheduled to meet at 11 A.M., they might all arrive by noon. Then there's conversation, then smoke breaks, then someone makes coffee or goes to the office kitchen to make a peanut butter sandwich, someone's phone rings. When we finally sit down as a group, when I've reminded everyone to turn their phones to vibrate, when we've completed our 10 minutes of meditation, when I look the men in the eyes and ask them if they're ready, the answer is always a resounding yes. Yes, they want to talk. None of them has had professional counseling and while I cannot serve in that capacity, I know the healing power of releasing the thoughts that cycle through our minds. Of being respectfully heard. Of discovering our own wisdom as we speak.

There are other exonerees who want to join the project, but they live outside of New Orleans. Gregory and I drove four hours to Lake Charles, Louisiana, to meet with Allen, who was in excruciating pain and dying of cancer at his sister's home just months after being released from prison. Still, though he could barely sit up, though he was unable to eat even a spoonful of soup, he wanted to share his experiences, wanted to have his life recorded, wanted there to be witnesses to his journey. Allen passed away a month later, but before he died he gave a copy of his narrative to his family — a powerful, reflective record of his experience with the justice system. It was important to him to set his words on paper, to be able to hold in his hands a copy of his own memories. There is a sense of relief when some of the pain is trapped in ink.

V. Voices of Innocence

In February 2008, JT, Gregory, Ryan, and Dan presented their narratives, *Voices of Innocence*, to an audience of more than 200 people at the New Orleans Center for Creative Arts. They rehearsed for several weeks. They grappled with choosing just the right words. They faced their fears of public speaking. *Voices of Innocence* is a full-length stage presentation that runs over an hour. The men presented a powerful, profound, riveting performance and the audience gave them a standing ovation that lasted nearly five minutes. So many people in the audience had questions we had to cut off the question and answer session after almost an hour and a half. It was an extraordinary event. Because of the circumstances forced upon them, by the choices they are now making in their lives, and through their writing, JT, Gregory, Ryan, and Dan have become activists for criminal justice reform.

Audience member Michel Varisco said, "The powerful thing for me after listening to the presentation was that I felt the urgency of the issues and felt compelled to share this news with other people right away. And I *have* shared this right away because it *is* urgent and it's scary and needs to be corrected. It's human rights abuse within our midst. And we're all part of it. We get caught in the trap of wanting someone convicted of a crime, forgetting so many innocent lives can be broken down by a wrongful conviction to suit a quota or serve an illusion of a society under control."

There are three layers within their writing. One layer is the arc of the factual drama, told in five parts: life before arrest; details of the arrest and conviction; life in Angola Prison; details of exoneration; and life after exoneration. These personal accounts reveal the complexity of the exonerees' experiences, their character, actions, reactions, thoughts, and emotions as they relate to wrongful conviction.

The second layer of their writing is the political/social story, which widens the lens on their personal accounts in order to reveal systemic failures of the criminal justice system. This layer exposes the racial and economic factors that played into their arrest and conviction; the eyewitness misidentification, inadequate defense representation, and prosecutorial and judicial misconduct that is rampant within Louisiana's judicial system; the social and cultural realities of life in Angola Prison; and the challenges of reintegration, exacerbated by the complete lack of available social services and financial compensation.

Louisiana has one of the highest per capita exoneration rates in the country; twenty-one men have been exonerated since 1990. The high number of exonerees points to Louisiana's staggering incarceration rates, as well as to the system of public election for prosecutors and judges who run on conviction records, and the lack of judicial oversight that creates an environment ripe for political corruption and prosecutorial abuse. Louisiana's alarming rate of poverty, its woeful school system, and persistent racism and classism are further at the root of the criminal justice system's wild inequities and renegade practices.

The exonerees' experiences are indicative of the system failures that lead to wrongful convictions: a system marked by overzealous prosecution and prosecutorial misconduct; inadequate defense strategies; eyewitness misidentification; fear-inspired juries convinced they are fighting a war against crime; maximum sentencing practices; and lack of accountability, reintegration services, and compensation.

The third layer of their writing tells a spiritual story of hope, faith, and forgiveness. Exonerees are often asked how they survived incarceration without giving up. What did they think about? How did they keep themselves going? Were they angry? Are they angry now? How did they make sense of the violence around them? What did they dream about? What gave them hope? What did they gain? What did they lose? Each of the exonerees has a remarkable capacity for self-reflection and self-expression, and is able and willing to relive the emotional and spiritual journey of their incarceration and release. They continue to see their writing as having meaning and value because of the ways it can help "the next man."

Gregory wrote: "Through this experience it had to be faith that got me through. Faith is the belief in sights unseen. You can't see it, or touch it, but you know it's there. When I saw good things happen for others, faith said it could happen for me. It happens when God puts his people in place. When God does that, MOUNTAINS SHALL BE MOVED. I don't share this experience with hatred or bitterness in my heart. I share this experience with forgiveness because I know that forgiveness is a powerful tool — any way you use it, it works. I came face to face with forgiveness while in prison, and I came face to face with forgiveness when I got out. When I moved back to New Orleans, I moved to a place right across from the lady who testified against me. I didn't know she lived in the area. When we finally met, she approached me with tears in her eyes. She asked me to forgive her. I hugged her. The forces that worked against me and my family had also worked against her and her family, as well as the victim and his family. It's not by chance that the police came knocking on my door charging me with a brutal murder I had nothing to do with, but this was not my fight. This battle had already been won. Man may have decided this course of action, but he did not have final say. "Victory is mine," said the Lord."

Part Four:
Bibliography for Further Study

17

Expressive Writing: Selected Bibliography of Recent Literature, January 2008-June 2009

Cheryl Stiles

Baikie, Karen A. "Who Does Expressive Writing Work For? Examination of Alexithymia, Splitting, and Repressive Coping Style as Moderators of the Expressive Writing Paradigm." *British Journal of Health Psychology* 13 (2008): 61-66.

Barclay, Laurie J. and Daniel P. Skarlicki. "Healing the Wounds of Organizational Injustice: Examining the Benefits of Expressive Writing." *Journal of Applied Psychology* 94.2 (2009): 511-523.

Boswell, Stefanie Suzon. "Increasing Narrative Coherence in the Bereaved: The Effect of Narrative Review on Grief Reaction." Diss. U of Southern Mississippi, 2008.

Bruera, Eduardo, et al. "Expressive Writing in Patients Receiving Palliative Care: A Feasibility Study." *Journal of Palliative Medicine* 11.1 (2008): 15-19.

Chung, Cindy and James W. Pennebaker. "Variations in the Spacing of Expressive Writing Sessions." *British Journal of Health Psychology* 13 (2008): 15-21.

Corter, Arden L. and Keith J. Petrie. "Expressive Writing in Context: The Effects of a Confessional Setting and Delivery of Instructions on

Participant Experience and Language in Writing." *British Journal of Health Psychology* 13 (2008): 27-30.

Daniels, Jennifer B. "Writing as a Coping Mediator Between Psychological and Physical Health." Diss. Auburn U, 2008.

Davidson, Janice Unruh and Barbara Robison. "Scrapbooking and Journaling Interventions for Chronic Illness: A Triangulated Investigation of Approaches in the Treatment of PTSD." *The Kansas Nurse* 83.3 (2008): 6-11.

De Moor, Janet, et al. "Expressive Writing as a Presurgical Stress Management Intervention for Breast Cancer Patients." *Journal of the Society for Integrative Oncology* 6.2 (Spring 2008): 59-66.

Fernandez, Itziar, Dario Paez, and James W. Pennebaker. "Comparison of Expressive Writing after the Terrorist Attack of September 11th and March 11th." *International Journal of Clinical and Health* Psychology 9.1 (2009): 9.1 (2009): 89-103.

Fonteyn, Marsha E., et al. "Developing a Codebook to Guide Content Analysis of Expressive Writing." *Applied Nursing Research* 21.3 (Aug. 2008): 165-168.

Fraas, Michael and Magdalen A. Balz. "Expressive Electronic Journal Writing: Freedom of Communication for Survivors of Acquired Brain Injury." *Journal of Psycholinguistic Research* 37 (2008): 115-124.

Garden, Rebecca. "Expanding Clinical Empathy: An Activist Perspective." *Journal of General Internal Medicine* 24.1 (2009): 122+.

Graf, Maria C., Brandon A. Gaudiano, and Pamela A. Geller. "Writing Emotional Disclosure: A Controlled Study of the Benefits of Expressive Writing Homework in Outpatient Psychotherapy." *Psychotherapy Research* 18.4 (2008): 389-399.

Harber, Kent D. "Can the Love Ranger, Molly Bloom, and Emile Durkheim Be Friends." *Emotion Review* 1.1 (Jan 2009): 90-91.

Hiltunen, Lynnette. "The Psychological and Physical Effects of Expressive Writing in Individuals with Binge Eating Disorder Tendencies." Diss. Alliant International U, 2008.

Horowitz, Sala. "Evidence-Based Health Outcomes of Expressive Writing." *Alternative and Complimentary Therapies* 14.4 (2008): 194+.

Kallay, Eva, et al. "The Benefits of Classic and Enhanced Tasks of Expressive Writing for the Emotional Life of Female Freshman Students." *Cognition, Brain, Behavior* 12.3 (2008): 251-264.

Kim, Youngsuk. "Effects of Expressive Writing among Bilinguals: Exploring Psychological Well-Being and Social Behaviour." *British Journal of Health Psychology* 12 (2008):43-47.

Klvisalu Hickey, Bethany. "The End of Idyllic Summers: A Narrative of Life, Loss and Transformation: An Autoethnography and Analysis." Diss. State U of New York, Empire State College, 2008.

Kuiken, Don, Shelagh Dunn, and Tatiana LoVerso. "Expressive Writing about Dreams that Follow Loss and Trauma." *Dreaming* 18.2 (2008): 77-93.

Longo, Perie J. "Tearing the Darkness Down: Poetry as Therapy." *Introduction to Alternative and Complementary Therapies*. Ed. Anne L. Strozier and Joyce Carpenter. New York: Haworth Press, 2008.

Marshall, Amy and Sandy Harper-Jacques. "Depression and Family Relationships: Ideas for Healing." *Journal of Family Nursing* 14.1 (2008): 56+.

Mackenzie, Corey S., et al. "Seeing the Glass Half Full: Optimistic Expressive Writing Improves Mental Health Care among Chronically Stressed Caregivers." *British Journal of Health Psychology* 13 (2008): 73-76.

Murray, Michael. "Health Psychology and Writing." *Journal of Health Psychology* 14.2 (2009): 158-160.

Nicholls, Sophie. "Beyond Expressive Writing: Evolving Models of Developmental Creative Writing." *Journal of Health Psychology* 14.2 (Mar. 2009): 171-180.

Nitkin-Kaner, Yael. "Relationships between Expressive Writing about Traumatic Events and Reduction in Depressive Symptomatology." Diss. U of Connecticut, 2008.

Oppenheim, D. "A Writing Workshop for Children with Cancer." *Archives of Disease in Childhood* 93.8 (2008): 708+.

Pinhasi-Vittoria, L. "Poetry and Prose in the Self-perception of One Man Who Lives with Brain Injury and Aphasia." *Topics in Stroke Rehabilitation* 15.3 (May 2008): 288-294.

Robbins, Joy M. and Dale-Elizabeth Pehrsson. "Anorexia Nervosa: A Synthesis of Poetic and Narrative Therapies in Outpatient Treatment of Young Adult Women." *Journal of Creativity in Mental Health* 4.1 (2009): 42+.

Romero, Catherine. "Writing Wrongs: Promoting Forgiveness through Expressive Writing." *Journal of Social and Personal Relationships* 25.2 (Aug. 2008): 625-642.

Sagan, Olivia. "The Loneliness of the Long-Anxious Learner: Mental Illness, Narrative Biography and Learning to Write. *Psychodynamic Practice* 14.1 (Feb. 2008): 43-58.

Sloan, Denise M., Brian P. Marx, Eva M. Epstein, and Jennifer L. Dobbs. "Expressive Writing Buffers Against Maladaptive Rumination." *Emotion* 8.2 (2008): 302-306.

Smyth, Joshua M., Jill R. Hockemeyer, and Heather Tulloch. "Expressive Writing and Post-traumatic Stress Disorder: Effects on Trauma Symptoms, Mood States, and Cortisol Reactivity." *British Journal of Health Psychology* 13 (2008): 85-93.

Smyth, Joshua M. and James W. Pennebaker. "Exploring the Boundary Conditions of Expressive Writing: In Search of the Right Recipe." *British Journal of Health Psychology* 13 (2008): 1-7.

Stepakoff, Shanee. "From Destruction to Creation, from Silence to Speech: Poetry Therapy Principles and Practices for Working with Suicide and Grief." *The Arts in Psychotherapy* 36.2 (Apr. 2009): 105-113.

Stratton, Stephen, et al. "Forgiveness Interventions as Spiritual Development Strategies: Comparing Forgiveness Workshop Training, Expressive Writing about Forgiveness, and Retested Controls." *Journal of Psychology and Christianity* 27.4 (2008): 347-357.

Tan, Leon. "Psychotherapy 2.0: MySpace Blogging as Self-therapy." *American Journal of Psychotherapy* 62.2 (2008): 143-163.

Tomczyk, Daniel A. "An Exercise in Story Repair: A Guided Written Disclosure Protocol for Fostering Narrative Completeness of Traumatic Memories." Diss. U of North Texas, 2008.

Vannatta, J., et al, "Definition of Narrative Medicine." *Journal of the Oklahoma State Medical Association* 3.3 (2009): 94+.

Willig, Carla. "'Unlike a rock, a tree, a horse or an angel…': Reflections on the Struggle for Meaning Through Writing During the Process of Cancer Diagnosis ." *Journal of Health Psychology* 2.3 (2009): 181.

Wong, Y. Joel. "Potential Benefits of Expressive Writing for Male College Students with Varying Degrees of Restrictive Emotionality." *Psychology of Men & Masculinity* 10.2 (2009): 149-159.

Yogo, Masao and Shuji Fujihara. "Working Memory Capacity Can Be Improved by Expressive Writing: A Randomized Experiment in a Japanese Sample." *British Journal of Health Psychology* 13 (2008): 77-80.

Contributors

Sara Baker, MA, is a published fiction writer and poet. Baker studied English Literature from Boston College, and has taught at The Georgia Institute of Technology, the University of Georgia, and Piedmont College. She has been an Artist-in-Residence for the State of Georgia. She created the Healing Writing Workshop at the Loran Smith Center for Cancer Support at Athens Regional Medical Center in Athens, Georgia. She has poems forthcoming in *The Journal of Poetry Therapy*, and has been published in the *Healing Muse*, the *Yale Journal for Humanities in Medicine*, and in *ARS MEDICA*, as well as other venues.

Austin Bunn, MFA, is the Axton Fellow in fiction writing at the University of Louisville, and a 2007 graduate of the Iowa Writers' Workshop (in both fiction and playwriting). In the fall, Bunn will begin a tenure-track assistant professorship at Grand Valley State University, part of the Michigan State system. He is the creator of the Patient Voice Project, and has written for variety of major magazines, including *The New York Times Magazine*, *Wired*, *The Village Voice*, *The Advocate,* and others.

Angela Buttimer, MS, LPC, is a licensed psychotherapist in private practice in Atlanta. She also works with cancer patients and survivors at Cancer Wellness at Piedmont Hospital, facilitating groups including Writing for Recovery, Mindfulness, and Gynecological Support Groups. Her focus with clients emphasizes the mind, body, spirit connection. She also enjoys facilitating personal growth and healing workshops and retreats for the public. She has worked in various settings including corporations, universities, employee assistance programs, hospitals, non-profits, and private practice.

Julie Davey, MA, combined her background as a full-time college writing and journalism professor with her two-time breast-cancer survival to create a unique and successful Writing for Wellness program at City of Hope National Cancer Center in California. Davey teaches patients, medical staff, caregivers, and family members how to write effectively to relieve stress and frustrations. Her book, *Writing for Wellness: A Prescription for Healing* is being used in several wellness centers and medical facilities.

Fran Dorf, MS, MSW (2009), Dorf's acclaimed, internationally published novels include *A Reasonable Madness* (Birch Lane, Signet, 1990/91), *Flight* (Dutton/Signet, 1992/93), and *Saving Elijah* (Putnam, 2000), which was inspired by the tragic death of her son, Michael, and which a starred *Publisher's Weekly* review called, "a stunning tale that crackles with suspense, dark humor, and provocative questions." Dorf holds a BS in journalism from Boston University, and an MA in psychology from New York University, where she is currently finishing her MSW. Dorf writes poetry, essays, and articles; and conducts "Write-to-Heal" workshops to help people cope with grief, illness, and loss. Dorf is also an active philanthropist, and blogs on grief, life, and everything in between at www.bruisedmuse.com.

John F. Evans, EdD, served several universities in various roles including English professor, department chair, and associate dean of general education before he retired from full time academic work in September 2008. In 2007 he founded Wellness & Writing Connections, a nonprofit corporation. He is executive director of the international Wellness & Writing Connections Conference and Institute, providing an interdisciplinary forum for writers and health care professionals interested in the wellness benefits of writing.

Leatha Kendrick, MA, English; MFA Creative Writing; Teaching experience at the college level since 1971; Currently teaching memoir and poetry writing, plus writing to heal at the Carnegie Center for Literacy and Learning in Lexington, Kentucky; has taught creative writing at the University of Kentucky and in Morehead State University's graduate program as well as at regional writing conferences; has been a presenter at the Associated Writers and Writing Programs' national meetings, 1999, 2006.

Luciano L'Abate, PhD, is Professor Emeritus in the Psychology Department at Georgia State University in Atlanta; Diplomate and former Examiner of the American Board of Professional Psychology; Approved Supervisor of the American Association for Marriage and Family Therapy; published (authored, co-authored, edited, and co-edited) 41 books with two additional ones in press, published over 300 papers, chapters, and book reviews in scientific and professional books and journals. His books have been translated for Argentina, China, Finland, Italy, Japan, Korea, Germany, and Poland.

Noreen Lape, PhD, is Associate Professor of English and Director of the Writing Center at Columbus State University where she teaches writing, composition pedagogy, writing tutor training, and literature. She has published two academic books and several articles in scholarly journals. She also keeps a journal and writes poetry as a means to her own personal growth. Her recent interests have moved her to explore ways to bring the writing and wellness/healing connection into the academic learning community. This fall she will be collaborating with a psychotherapist to offer a writing workshop for returning Iraq War veterans.

Debbie McCulliss, RN, MSN, CJI, CAPF, a nurse for 30 years, became passionate about writing ten years ago when she began to take journal-writing classes. A lifelong learner, she earned a certificate in Creative Writing and is a Certified Journal Instructor and Certified

Applied Poetry Facilitator. She is passionate about inspiring others to write and facilitates women's writing/poetry groups and retreats.

Lara Naughton, MPW, has published poetry, fiction, and non-fiction, and her stage plays have been produced in Los Angeles theatres. She was formerly Director of Creative Arts at a K-12 public charter school in South Central Los Angeles and is currently Chair of the Creative Writing Department at New Orleans Center for Creative Arts. She has taught creative writing and multi-disciplinary workshops to all ages, and has led documentary programs with groups including international torture victims, children affected by HIV, southern African writers, and Louisiana death row exonerees.

James Pennebaker, PhD, has earned honors for his research from the American Psychological Association and research grants from the National Science Foundation and the National Institute of Mental Health. An internationally recognized leader in this field, he is the author of several books, including *Opening Up: The Healing Power of Expressing Emotions* and *Writing to Heal: A Guided Journal for Recovering from Trauma & Emotional Upheaval.* Since 1980, he has published over 150 journal articles and research studies on the connections between writing and health.

Diana Raab, BS, RN, MFA, is a two-time cancer survivor, memoir-ist, poet, and essayist whose award-winning work has appeared in national publications. Her memoir, *Regina's Closet: Finding My Grandmother's Secret Journal* won the 2008 National Indie Excellence Award for Memoir, the proceeds of which she donates to the American Foundation for Suicide Prevention. She teaches in the UCLA Writers' Program and the Santa Barbara Writers' Conference. She's editor of *Writers and Their Notebooks* (foreword by Phillip Lopate) forthcoming by the University of South Carolina Press (Summer 2009). Her book, *Getting Pregnant and Staying Pregnant* won the Benjamin Franklin

Book Award for Best Health and Wellness Book in 1992, and she is currently working on its update, due out in 2009. She has two poetry collections, *My Muse Undresses Me* and *Dear Anaïs: My Life in Poems for You*. Raab has been keeping a notebook since the age of ten, which has been her lifeline during difficult times and has also nurtured her passion for writing. http://www.dianaraab.com.

Gail Radley, MA, is the author of twenty-one books for young people as well as articles and short stories for adults. An English instructor at Stetson University, her courses have included expository and creative writing and literature on themes of spiritual quest and the ordinary hero. She has lead workshops in both creative and memoir writing. Disciplined and schooled by fibromyalgia for nearly 35 years (and, more recently, degenerative disk disease), she has discovered firsthand the benefits of journaling and writing poetry. Monthly poetry readings in her home offer a venue for participants to share their writing.

Belinda Shoemaker, MFA, in Creative Writing, Fiction, and Creative Nonfiction, from Antioch University Los Angeles. She also has an MSc Degree in Human Communication from The City University, London. Currently Shoemaker is an assistant teacher in the Creative Writing Program at San Francisco State University, and also in the MFA program at Antioch University, Los Angeles. Prior to her writing career, Shoemaker was a speech and language pathologist with an additional specialization in counseling families of mentally and physically handicapped children, and adult patients with cancer of the larynx. She lives in Big Sur and in the San Francisco Bay Area.

Emily Simerly, PhD, is a licensed clinical psychologist who is clinical director of a 550-bed mental health unit at a maximum-security prison south of Atlanta. She has written essays for *Voices: The Art and Science of Psychotherapy* that include comparing borderline personality to desert flora and fauna, why working in the prison system is a privilege, and why she became a psychotherapist, among others. She is a therapist for the severe and persistently mentally ill in prison, including inmates on Georgia's Death Row. She also maintains a small private practice office.

Cheryl Stiles has published numerous poems, essays, and reviews in journals such as *Poet Lore*, *The Atlanta Review*, *Storysouth*, *SLANT*, *Plainsongs*, *Red River Review*, *POEM*, *Heliotrope*, *Ink Pot*, and *The Healing Muse*. Her work has also been included in several anthologies including *Sincerely Elvis*, a collection of original poems about Elvis Presley. She has given readings and workshops throughout the Southeast. For the past twenty-five years she has worked as a librarian and she recently completed her fourth year of doctoral studies at Georgia State University. She can be contacted at castiles@gmail.com.